BEHIND THE WHITE PICKET FENCE

SARAH MAYORGA-GALLO

BEHIND THE
WHITE PICKET FENCE

Power and Privilege in a
Multiethnic Neighborhood

The University of North Carolina Press *Chapel Hill*

This book was published with the assistance of the Z. Smith Reynolds Fund
of the University of North Carolina Press.

Designed and set in Quadraat, Quadraat Sans, and Aller types by Rebecca Evans
Manufactured in the United States of America

The University of North Carolina Press has been a member of the Green Press
Initiative since 2003.

Cover illustration ©iStockphoto.com/ImagineGolf

Library of Congress Cataloging-in-Publication Data
Mayorga-Gallo, Sarah.
Behind the white picket fence : power and privilege in a multiethnic
neighborhood / Sarah Mayorga-Gallo.
pages cm
Includes bibliographical references and index.
ISBN 978-1-4696-1863-0 (pbk   )—ISBN 978-1-4696-1864-7 (ebook)
1. Durham (N.C.)—Ethnic relations. 2. Durham (N.C.)—Social conditions.
3. Community life—North Carolina—Durham. 4. Community power—
North Carolina—Durham. 5. Segregation—North Carolina—Durham.
6. Neighborhoods—North Carolina—Durham. I. Title.
F264.D9M39 2014
305.8009756′563—dc23
2014017585

18 17 16 15 14   5 4 3 2 1

This book was digitally printed.

FOR THE CITY OF DURHAM | PARA LA CIUDAD DE DURHAM

Contents

Tables and Maps

Acknowledgments

The writing of this book has benefited from the kindness, time, and backing of so many individuals. Thank you to Charlotte O'Kelly for your mentorship over the years. Thank you to Rebecca Bach for being a great source of support and wisdom. I thank Kim Blankenship, Linda Burton, Phil Morgan, and Emilio Parrado for your encouragement and helpful skepticism. This project was a large undertaking, and because of your expert feedback and tough questions my research was as successful as it was. And a special thank you to Eduardo Bonilla-Silva. Saying thanks for all of the meetings and emails over the years doesn't seem like enough, but please know I am deeply grateful for your time, insight, and investment in me.

Thank you to the Sociology Department's Race Workshop at Duke University and its vibrant, supportive group of coordinators. I'm proud and grateful to have been a part of the community. I would also like to thank Paula McClain, Kerry Haynie, and the Center for the Study of Race, Ethnicity and Gender in the Social Sciences at Duke for including me as a REGSS Graduate Fellow. Thank you to Michelle Christian and Serena Sebring for helping me with my book proposal and to Rose Buckelew for your valuable chapter notes. Thank you to Elizabeth Hordge-Freeman for your support and always insightful annotations. Thank you to Candis Watts Smith (CITB) for your perceptive comments and advice. And to the many people whose friendships sustain me: thank you for the laughs, heart-to-hearts, and companionship.

Thank you to my colleagues at the University of Cincinnati who played an extremely important role in my rewriting and finishing of this book. To my writing group—Danielle Bessett, Erynn Masi de Casanova, and Rina Williams—thank you for your thoughtful and invaluable feedback. Thank you to Jennifer Malat for your astute comments and being a source of support from day one. And a big thanks to my wonderfully encouraging colleagues in the Sociology Department at UC.

Thank you to everyone who worked on this book at the University of North Carolina Press, especially my editor, Joseph Parsons. Thank you for believing in this book and your tireless efforts in getting it published. It was a true pleasure working with you. Thank you as well to the anonymous reviewers for your thorough and insightful feedback. This book has greatly benefited from your time and expertise. I would also like to thank George Mayorga for his patience and work on the featured tables and maps, and thank you to artist Edith Vaca for helping bring Creekridge Park to life.

The study presented in this book was funded by a generous grant from the National Science Foundation. Thank you to the NSF, the proposal reviewers, and the program officers for your support and helpful notes. Thank you to the Charles Phelps Taft Research Center and the Kunz Center for Social Research at the University of Cincinnati for the research support. I would also like to thank Duke University's Sociology Department (particularly Ed and Josefina Tiryakian), the Graduate School, and the Latino Studies program (especially Jenny Snead-Williams) for their financial backing. I would also like to thank the Society for the Study of Social Problems and their Racial/Ethnic Minority Graduate Scholarship program. Your support not only helped fund me but gave me a much-needed vote of confidence.

To my Gallo half: thank you Dad, Mom, Amanda, AJ, and everyone for your love and confidence in me. To the *Mayorgada*—Dad, Mom, Oscar, Jill, Carla, Roger, Luis, and George—you taught me the importance of social justice and hard work. Thank you for all of the life lessons, love, and championing. And to my most steadfast supporter, Jonathan-thank you for reading, listening, strategizing, and celebrating with me. I am unendingly grateful for you.

Finally, thank you to all of the Creekridge Park residents who took the time to speak with me. I appreciate your candidness during our interviews and your trust in my ability to share your stories. This book, thanks to you, will hopefully facilitate an important conversation locally and nationwide on diversity, inequity, and whiteness.

BEHIND THE **WHITE PICKET FENCE**

CHAPTER 1 Inside Creekridge Park

Creekridge Park is an urban, multiethnic, and mixed-income neighborhood in Durham, North Carolina (see map 1).[1] During the fall of 2010, the Creekridge Park Neighborhood Association (CPNA) once again held its annual picnic at the home of Burt, a White homeowner and established resident, on Harris Street.[2] Temperatures in the low seventies and clear skies made it a perfect day for a picnic. The main purpose of this gathering was holding the CPNA board elections. Burt has a covered garage with a long, wide driveway that served as the party area. The property seems uncharacteristically new and large for the neighborhood. I heard on several occasions from Creekridge Park residents that these happenings are "really well-attended." In fact, Cynthia, an established resident and White homeowner in her sixties, stated, "We get amazing turnouts. . . . It's just been phenomenal." The attendance at the annual picnic was highlighted by some respondents and attributed to a location change from a neighborhood-adjacent park to Burt's house. "It just felt friendly to have it there [at Burt's]," said Stephanie, a thirty-something White homeowner and established resident.

Residents ranged in their familiarity with the neighborhood association and its events. For example, White longtime resident Matt told me that "these uh, [neighborhood events] are times of extremely, uh, valuable and informal conversations that do make you feel part of something that works in our country." White established resident and homeowner Rhonda said that while she was familiar with the association and its events, she never attended. "Um, just 'cause I don't have that many frien—you know what I mean? Like, true friends, we haven't gone [to any neighborhood events]. And I also, like, we don't have kids, I feel like if we had kids we might [attend]." Martín, a newcomer and Latino renter in his forties, also did not attend the annual picnic. During his interview he stated that he was familiar with neither the association nor its events: "Como viene todo en inglés, vemos, y como no nos importa, no sabemos qué es lo que dice, lo tiro." (Since everything comes in English, we look at it, and since it doesn't matter to us, we don't know what it says,

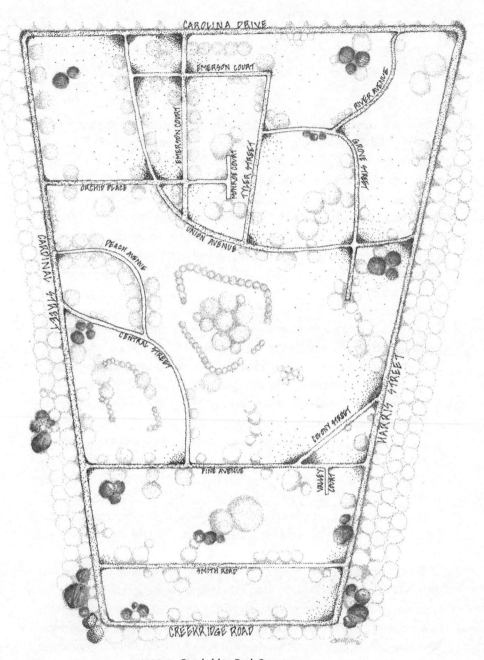

MAP 1 Creekridge Park Streets

I toss it.)[3] I specifically asked Martín during his interview whether he had seen any of the bilingual advertisements for the annual picnic; "No," he responded.

As I chat with a few residents at the annual picnic (all White and most of whom I have met through neighborhood association events and interview referrals), Roberta walks up. Roberta is a short Black woman whom nobody seems to know; her arrival is met with silence. As she signs in, I see that she is carrying a plastic grocery bag. I think it includes a food item she has brought to share, as the picnic advertisements requested. She asks Tammy, who is running the registration table, how much a CPNA shirt costs. Roberta buys one, although she comments that the $12 price is "steep." Another woman in attendance agrees, although she does not make eye contact with Roberta. Roberta proceeds to buy a $1 raffle ticket and is told by Tammy not to write on top of the book they are raffling off. I notice Tammy's tone, which seems cold, but Roberta appears unfazed. Roberta then heads to the food table nearby, cuts herself a piece of cake, grabs a drink, and sits down in a chair away from the sun. Most other attendees are standing around, chatting. Although many of the other participants already know each other, some residents are being introduced to neighborhood folks they have not yet met. When Roberta sits down, I wrap up my conversation with Scott, a White homeowner and established resident; say hello to Deborah, a longtime Creekridge Park resident and a White homeowner; and then say hello to Roberta. She comes across as friendly and open, although she also seems content to be sitting down in the shade. She tells me that she is a North Carolina native who lives in an apartment off Cardinal Street and that she walked to the party. She said that she learned about the picnic from a flier and decided to step outside her "comfort zone" and attend.

Over the course of the next hour, I greet other residents that I know and introduce myself to some new faces, hoping to schedule a few more interviews. I also, however, keep track of Roberta throughout the evening. She never leaves her chair, and the other residents generally ignore her as they continue to chat and enjoy hotdogs, snacks, and iced tea. Deborah and Beth, both White CPNA board members, and Connie, a Black homeowner, are the only individuals I see speak to Roberta. Toward the end of the picnic, I go back and ask Roberta if she is having a good time and if she would like to speak with me about my project at a later date. She agrees without hesitation and gives me her phone number. She also tells me where she works as a medical records clerk. As we are chatting, we get called over to start the elections process. They need twenty neighbor-hood association members for a quorum, and they have twenty-one. Before I leave the picnic, I say goodbye to a few people, mostly board members, but also Roberta and Robin (a White homeowner), who agreed to be interviewed.

I share this story about the annual picnic because it exemplifies what this book is about: the interactions between Black, Latino/a,[4] and White residents and how they shape the character of this multiethnic neighborhood. Using the events I observed, the interviews I conducted, and the analysis of survey data, I deconstruct the activities, codes of conduct, and ideologies of White, Black, and Latino/a residents in Creekridge Park. For example, how does a predominantly White neighborhood organization understand and justify their representation of a neighborhood that is almost 60 percent non-White? What does it mean when organizers of neighborhood association events characterize the annual picnic as well-attended when about 40 of 1,570 residents participate, most of whom are White homeowners? This book unpacks the meanings White and non-White residents attach to this multiethnic space and their experiences within it.

A central concern of this book is reorienting the conversation around residential segregation and integration. Over the last few decades, segregation research has focused on quantitative measurement. Indices of segregation, such as the dissimilarity index, dictate our national academic and policy conversations on segregation. The dissimilarity index is a number between 0 and 1 that indicates how evenly a racial group is represented across subregions in comparison to a larger, encompassing area. The dissimilarity index is commonly understood to represent the percentage of people from one racial-ethnic group that would have to move from one subarea to another to create 100 percent evenness within the larger area. Zero represents complete "integration" or evenness, and 1 represents complete "segregation" or unevenness. For example, a dissimilarity index of .3 would indicate that 30 percent of White residents in Creekridge Park would have to move to another block within Creekridge Park to create perfect neighborhood evenness—a 0 on the dissimilarity index. According to recent news publications, some analysts are even heralding a new era of reduced segregation based on city-level dissimilarity indices.[5] In this book, I challenge the premise of these conversations. Rather than assume that segregation indices speak to the day-to-day interracial experiences of Americans, as many social scientists and policy makers do, I examine the social relationships, neighborhood norms, and ideological elements of life in multiethnic America.

Although Creekridge Park qualifies as "integrated" under the traditional statistical definitions, I argue that integration must be understood beyond spatial concerns. The measurement of residential integration should include the quality and the quantity of interracial interactions in a neighborhood. Instead of defining integration as the opposite of segregation or using proportionality and minority representation as markers of neighborhood integration, I use qualitative data to capture life in Creekridge Park. I argue that spatial proximity among Blacks, Latino/as, and Whites is not a guarantee of interracial interactions or relationships, let alone positive ones.[6]

In the following sections of this chapter, I discuss relevant research on segregation, integration, and multiethnic settings and specifically address the importance of Durham as a new Latino/a destination city. I also present background information on Creekridge Park, including demographic and historical data. Lastly, I reflect on my role in the field, discuss why I focus on White residents in Chapters 2 and 3, and outline the direction of the book.

WHY STUDY A MULTIETHNIC NEIGHBORHOOD IN DURHAM?

Clarifying Concepts

In the social science literature, integration has generally been measured using racial-ethnic population percentages and proportions, which I call statistical integration. The two dominant conceptualizations of statistical integration are not mutually exclusive but represent two distinct theoretical approaches to integration research. The first definition is the "proportional representation of all groups," which concerns proportionality between neighborhood-level and city-level racial group percentages.[7] Using this definition, one can argue that integration exists in Creekridge Park because the county and neighborhood percentages of Blacks, Latino/as, and Whites are comparable (see table 1.1). The other definition, used by those who argue for the importance of "sharing spaces on relatively equal grounds," designates integrated neighborhoods as those with a Black population that comprises 10 to 50 percent of the total population.[8] Creekridge Park also qualifies as integrated under this criterion, since according to 2010 census data, Black residents comprise 39 percent

TABLE 1.1 *2010 census estimates for Creekridge Park and Durham County*

	Creekridge Park 2010 (%)	Durham County 2010 (%)
Male	816 (52)	127,656 (48)
Female	754 (48)	139,931 (52)
Under 18	377 (24)	61,321 (23)
18+	1,193 (76)	206,266 (78)
White, non-Hispanic	533 (34)	112,697 (42)
Black, non-Hispanic	612 (39)	100, 260 (38)
Hispanic	408 (26)	36,077 (14)
N	1,570	267,587

of the neighborhood population. Thankfully, social scientists have begun to challenge the flawed theoretical foundations of these numbers-based definitions.[9] For instance, why is a predominantly White neighborhood with a 10 percent Black population designated as integrated, while a predominantly Black neighborhood with a 10, 20, or even 40 percent White population is not? These definitions of integration fail to challenge the normativity of whiteness and predominantly White neighborhoods as well as the tyranny of proportionality. If integration is intended to speak to issues of equity, then its definition must include measures of power, resource sharing, and reciprocity in relationships.[10] Proportionality between neighborhood and city racial-ethnic percentages should not be the sole determining factor in naming a neighborhood as integrated. As I showcase throughout the following chapters, zeroing in on statistical integration lets social scientists and policy makers make arguments that are not reflected in sociological data but based on statistical assumptions.

Throughout the book I generally use "multiethnic" to describe Creekridge Park, a more exact label than "integrated" or even "statistically integrated." The term "multiethnic" highlights that there are more than two distinct racial-ethnic communities in Creekridge Park, moving the analysis beyond the traditional Black-White binary, a limitation of previous research. In addition, by using "multiethnic" rather than "integrated," I do not presume that the experiences and interpretations of residents in this neighborhood are explained by proportions and percentages.

My analysis brings people to the forefront in order to understand how a community that is statistically integrated may still experience norms of high social distance between Black, White, and Latino/a residents.[11] To collect these data I conducted in-depth interviews with 63 residents, participant observation over an eighteen-month period around the neighborhood, and a household survey (N = 114 total, 85 from Creekridge Park). Each of these methods complements the others, facilitating a complex and nuanced analysis. I observed, documented, and questioned (1) the types of neighbor-to-neighbor relationships residents engage in; (2) the factors that influence how residents approach and characterize their relationships with their neighbors; (3) the types of events that structure neighbor-to-neighbor relationships, including block parties, neighborhood association meetings, and conflicts; (4) the types of social roles residents assume within the neighborhood; and (5) the racial attitudes of neighborhood residents. For a more in-depth discussion of data and methods, please see Appendix A.

Durham's Racial History

Durham County was established in 1881 when it separated from adjacent Orange County as a result of the area's population growth and the tobacco industry's size and import. Tobacco in Durham was dominated by two firms: the Blackwell Durham Tobacco Company (producer of the famous Bull Durham tobacco) and W. Duke and Sons Tobacco Company (founded by Washington Duke, Duke University's eponym). The cotton industry also became an important part of Durham's economy in the 1880s and into the twentieth century. The labor for these industries was furnished by Black workers, many of whom lived in Hayti, a nearby unincorporated settlement. Durham's development in the late nineteenth century was largely directed by wealthy White men, including William T. Blackwell, Julian Carr, Washington Duke, and Duke's three sons, Benjamin N. Duke, Brodie L. Duke, and James B. Duke.[12]

At the turn of the twentieth century, Durham experienced a population growth spurt. Between 1900 and 1910, its population rose 173 percent to 18,241. This swell was due to the broadening of Durham's city limits as well as improvements in transportation, including new roads and an electric trolley service.[13] For the White elite, plentiful social and civic clubs were important facets of life in Durham in the early 1900s. Durhamites of the late nineteenth and early twentieth centuries also lived through a period of Black prosperity. W. E. B. Du Bois cited the city as an example of Black entrepreneurship and middle-class success, achievements that are attributed to the "hands off" approach of the White elite.[14] Prosperity, however, was not experienced across the board. In *The Souls of Black Folk* Du Bois specifically addresses the distinction between the realities of Durham's Black middle and lower classes.[15] As in other former Confederate cities, the division between Black and White was also very clear: "It is usually possible to draw in nearly every Southern community a physical color-line on the map, on the one side of which Whites dwell and on the other Negroes."[16]

While Durham remained highly segregated, Black residents continued fighting for advancements in higher education, political representation, and housing, among other arenas of inequality. The Negro Business League, the Durham Committee on Negro Affairs, and the Independent Voters League all played roles in demanding "equal opportunity to share and enjoy rights and privileges of citizenship."[17] Despite some successful campaigns, inequality was still a many-sided obstacle after the Great Depression. For example, while the funding for North Carolina College for Negroes (now North Carolina Central University) was expanded due to a Supreme Court decision in 1938, a housing survey conducted by the city identified that 80 percent of the Black population in Durham was living in substandard housing. During the late 1940s and 1950s, while the first Black councilman was elected to the city council (voted in by a biracial labor alliance), white flight to the suburbs by middle-class and upper middle-class Whites and increased enrollment in the Ku Klux Klan by poor Whites characterized the period. This exodus of White residents gave Black Durhamites more political power within city limits, although as Durham County historian Jean Bradley Anderson cites, "sit-ins, boycotts, threats of violence, litigation, and the intervention of the federal government" would be required to create social change.[18] These bifurcated patterns of prosperity and racial inequality continue today.

The recent arrival of Latin American migrants in Durham provides an opportunity to see how an area with an existing racial order adjusts to the introduction of a new group.[19] Studies on multigroup segregation have focused on traditional sites of immigration, such as Los Angeles, New York, and Chicago.[20] Over the past two decades, immigrants have begun to settle in nontraditional sites, such as small cities in the Midwest and South.[21] Like all other new immigrant destinations, Durham can be characterized by the absence of any historic Latino/a population in the area. In 1990 Durham's Latino/a population was estimated at 2,054. This number grew to 17,039 in 2000. As of 2010, Durham's Hispanic population was estimated to be 36,077, 13.5 percent of the total population of Durham County—a 111 percent increase since 2000.[22] Durham's population shift reflects changes across the nation, and, arguably, its dynamics are more comparable to those of burgeoning American cities than to New York, Los Angeles, or Chicago. Studying Durham complements research on other major southern locales experiencing a recent growth in their Latino/a population, including Atlanta, Charlotte, and Nashville.[23]

My analysis unfolds the multifaceted power relationships between established and new racial-ethnic communities. It also facilitates a nuanced exploration of the complexities of living in Durham as a Latino/a migrant. One cannot ignore the clear differences in power between native Whites and Latino/a migrants, particularly those who are undocumented.[24] For example, a heightened sense of vulnerability in North Carolina is created by stories of White officials targeting Latino/as.[25] At the same time, institutions such as El Centro Hispano, a nonprofit organization in Durham, are emerging to provide resources, community support, and a unified public face for the city's Latino/a communities. I address these varying contexts through the voices of Latino and Latina residents, particularly in Chapter 4.

PLACING CREEKRIDGE PARK

Who Lives Here?

Creekridge Park spans more than ten census blocks and was home to 1,570 total residents and 589 households in 2010.[26] Renters occupied 389 (66 percent) of these housing units, while owners occupied 200 units (34 percent). Most non-Whites live in rental housing; 17 percent of Blacks in Creekridge Park are homeowners, while 13 percent of Latino/as in Creekridge Park own their home. Whites are equally as likely to be renters and owners. The 2010 estimates indicate that the White, non-Hispanic population has decreased in both numbers and as a percentage of the population to 533 residents. The Black population has remained stable, estimated at 612 in 2010, while the number of Latino/a Creekridge Park residents grew to 408 by the decennial census. Only about 5 percent of the 2010 population in Creekridge Park did not identify as either Black, Latino/a, or White. For a full comparison of the 2010 block-level and county-level data across race, gender, and age, please see table 1.1.

Census data on occupations and incomes are not available at the block

TABLE 1.2 Creekridge Park racial attitudes based on survey data

Responses to racial attitudes questions in household survey questions	Percentage of Creekridge Park residents
On the average, Blacks/African Americans have worse jobs, income, and housing than White people. Do you think these differences are mainly due to	
Discrimination	25
Lack of opportunity	57
Lack of willpower	18
How important is the issue of race relations to you?	
Extremely important/important	73
Somewhat important	17
Somewhat unimportant	4
Extremely unimportant/unimportant	6

level. My research, however, indicates that residents hold a variety of occupations and participate in several industries, including agriculture, real estate, educational services, and arts, entertainment, and recreation. The neighborhood is described by the neighborhood association as mixed income, with most respondents agreeing the "mix" includes working- and middle-class households. Housing values also vary. For example, two homeowners I spoke with who live on Pine Avenue have tax values of about $69,000 and $201,000, respectively. Based on my research of county tax data, the range on Pine Avenue reflects the variation across Creekridge Park.

What is the political context of Creekridge Park? Although electoral data are not available at the block level, state and county data give some insight into the neighborhood. On the one hand, historically speaking, North Carolina is a conservative state. Its electoral votes were won by Romney/Ryan in 2012 (50.39 percent of the popular vote). Although the state went blue in 2008 (52.87 percent of the popular vote), it was only the second time in contemporary elections that a Democratic nominee won the state (Jimmy Carter was the first in 1976). On the other hand, Durham is a consistently Democratic county. In 2008 and 2012, respectively, 75.6 percent and 75.8 percent of Durham voters cast their ballot for President Obama and Vice President Biden.[27] Based on household survey data, Creekridge Park residents rate more liberally than the national average on racial attitudes. As you see in table 1.2, when asked why, on average, Black

TABLE 1.3 *Comparison of national and regional racial attitudes*

Some people say undocumented or illegal immigrants help the economy by providing low-cost labor. Others say they hurt the economy by driving wages down. Which is closer to your view?

Respondents	Help the economy	Hurt the economy
Creekridge Park	66%	34%
NYT/CBS Poll 2010	17%	74%

Americans are worse off economically than Whites, 57 percent of my respondents said it was because of lack of opportunity, while 47 percent of the national sample acknowledged lack of opportunity as an issue. None of my respondents said it was because of less in-born ability, while 10 percent of the 2010 national sample did.[28] As table 1.2 also indicates, 72 percent of my respondents said the issue of race relations was either important or extremely important to them. Lastly, table 1.3 shows that over 66 percent of my respondents believe that undocumented migrants help rather than hurt the economy, while a NYT/CBS News poll from the same period shows that over 74 percent of Americans believe undocumented migrants are detrimental to the economy.[29] Based on these numbers and that residents chose to live in this multiethnic neighborhood, Creekridge Park is an excellent location to study interracial interactions.

Neighborhood History

Although Creekridge Park has experienced significant change over the last few decades, it is not a traditionally gentrified neighborhood. Scholars define conventionally gentrified neighborhoods as neighborhoods where middle- and upper middle-class residents, who are often White, migrate into poor/lower income areas, which are often non-White.[30] In contrast, Creekridge Park was a predominantly White working- and middle-class neighborhood in the early twentieth century. In fact, redlining data from the 1930s indicate that the Creekridge Park area had less than 10 percent Black and "foreign" residents at the time.[31] As the housing stock aged and original owners passed away, Creekridge Park began a transition from an almost exclusively White neighborhood to a multiethnic space in the late 1980s. According to the 1990 block group census estimates,[32] which include a few blocks in addition to Creekridge Park, the White population was 75 percent, the Black population was 20 percent, and the Latino/a population was less than 1 percent. After the growth in the Latino/a population during the 1990s and 2000s, Creekridge Park arrived at its most recent state. In 2010, the neighborhood population was estimated at 34 percent White, non-Hispanic; 39 percent Black; and 25 percent Latino/a.[33]

During interviews and neighborhood events, many residents shared their knowledge of Creekridge Park history. Where possible, I try to contextualize these accounts with historical data. While an in-depth history of Creekridge Park is not available (making some resident accounts unverifiable), I do present some redlining data from the 1930s that address the stories residents shared. Overall, it seems that Creekridge Park was inhabited by working- and middle-class White families from the turn of the twentieth century. There is much consensus in residents' narratives, as word of mouth seems to play a large role in how this information is transmitted. As such, Daniel, an established White homeowner, indicated that he heard a few stories about the neighborhood but was not sure of their accuracy: "Uh, you know for the first couple of years I lived there I was involved in the neighborhood association. Um, so I heard the various stories that people have told, although nobody seems to have a very definitive story about even the name or anything."

Jamie, a White homeowner and an established resident who lives on Creekridge Road, characterized Creekridge Park as historically middle class, emphasizing the occupations of past residents: "I knew that, I knew it was a, um, middle-class neighborhood. You know, the people who originally had, um, homes here were merchants and shopkeepers. And, and, you know, they weren't like, um, head of the mills or something like that. It was more middle class." Beth, a White established homeowner, shared her understanding of the development of Creekridge Park, including occupational information:

I know that, uh, it was originally platted, and that means that some kind of—here are the lines for lots that they were gonna sell, and it was originally in 1929. Um, and the first houses were built in the '30s there. They were right along Mason [Avenue]. And all that Peach [Avenue], Central [Street], all of that wasn't developed, but soon after it was. I know the land was originally a part of the Planter Family's farm, and the Carolina House restaurant on Cardinal Street is the family home. So, uh, and each area, each section was developed at different times throughout the area. The part on the east side of

Cardinal Street is much older than the west side of Cardinal Street. There's like 40 years of difference. I know the first houses were built by people who worked at the university as professors in the '30s. This would have been out in the country homes.

Although the 1930s redlining data from Groveland Estates, a more affluent adjacent neighborhood, indicate that college professors did live in the area, the data for the Creekridge Park area reveal that the small singles and duplexes were largely inhabited by clerks, mechanics, and mill/tobacco workers.[34] This occupational description was echoed by long-time resident David, who moved to the Creekridge Park area in the late 1930s. With the exception of the Carolina House, large estates are not a part of the Creekridge Park narrative.

Similar to findings in research on gentrified neighborhoods, private rehabilitation efforts supported by government funding also contribute to Creekridge Park's contemporary character.[35] This generally takes the form of individual tax credits for historic home preservation. There are a few homes in Creekridge Park that have received official historic designations from a local preservationist organization. Relatedly, there are some residents who did independent research for their own knowledge because they live in older homes. Seth, who owns a historic home on Harris Street and is an established resident, shared a few facts about where the neighborhood came from:

> The neighborhood kind of developed, um, it developed in pockets. Mostly from consolidating small farms, so, you know, there's—you drive down the street and you'll see several houses of a particular era and then you might see one that's not a particular era or you get to another section and it's obviously a much later era. And so it's, it was not only, here's this big swap of land that's gonna be laid out just like this and there's gonna be these types of houses and it's all gonna look like—there was none of that. It was somewhat hodge podge, um, but certainly right around here, um, American Tobacco was a big employer.

Cynthia, a White homeowner and established resident, agreed, stating that her house "was built in the early '30s and the houses that are, you know, are next door might be 1950, or—and different vintages." While Seth and Cynthia point out that Creekridge Park has homes built from a variety of eras that include different sizes and aesthetics, the smaller homes in particular help current residents construct Creekridge Park as an affordable neighborhood with modest and/or starter homes for working- and middle-class homeowners, especially in comparison with nearby Groveland Estates.

A few residents explicitly discussed the relationship between Groveland Estates and Creekridge Park when describing the area. Denise, a White newcomer, mentioned during her interview that "our understanding is that a load of the houses around here were looking to house people that were looking after the bigger estate places down in Groveland Estates." Sandra, also a White newcomer, shared similar information, stating, "Someone even told me—I don't even know if this is true, but that the houses in Groveland Estates were the people who had servants, like in the '50s, but that lived—I live in a little tiny house and a lot of the houses around me, I mean 720 square feet, are the same exact houses as mine and I was told that it's possible that the servants or the help might have lived in these houses. I don't know if that's true or not [*laughs*]. That's the only kind of history I heard." Bryan, a White longtime resident who lives on Pine Avenue, also described his home as a handyman's house: "Our house was built by the farmer's handyman, the house next to us— we share a driveway with the house on the corner. Across the street from the [emergency services station], that was the farm house. The farm hand bought our lot and, um, built his house there. And then he lived there and then eventually they sold off the rest of the farm and the rest of the neighborhood was built."

Russ, a White homeowner in his fifties, grew up nearby and attended Creekridge Park Elementary as a child. His description of Creekridge Park in the 1960s and 1970s is of a family-centric neighborhood: "I think it's probably more two-, two-parent, more a two-parent family neighborhood back then, um, the way things were in the '60s and '70s. Uh, and now it's much more eclectic, um, single folks, married folks, grad students, young families, pretty much everything. So it was probably more of a two-family kind of neighborhood back when I was a kid, definitely."

Pine Grove Apartments, the largest apartment complex in the neighborhood, was built in the mid-1970s and contributed to the changing landscape of Creekridge Park.[36] Although rentals were a part of the Creekridge Park locale even in the 1930s, these were largely single homes.[37] Cristina, a Latina newcomer who has lived in the Pine Grove apartment complex for a few years, shares what she knows about the large rental property:

Lo que he notado es que tengo entendido que anteriormente era un lugar mucho más exclusivo, tengo entendido que antes era muy difícil, hace unos veinte años, porque son apartamentos antiguos, tengo entendido que hace unos veinte años era difícil entrar a vivir ahí. Era difícil el criterio que usaban para que las personas pudieran vivir. Mi vecina de al lado, ella es profesora y es anglosajona y tiene veinticinco años viviendo ahí. La persona de enfrente trabaja en una clínica muy conocida acá y tiene veinte años o más viviendo ahí sola, entonces eso demuestra pues toda una longevidad, antigüedad, antigüedad en los apartamentos. Sin embargo, yo tengo entendido que últimamente han llegado más familias nuevas y más se han mudado, ya no son tan constantes y tan continuos como mi vecina y mi otra vecina.

(What I have noted is that before, this place [Pine Grove Apartments] was much more exclusive. I understand that before, it was very difficult—twenty years ago, because they are old apartments—I understand that twenty years ago it was tough to get in. The criteria they used for people to live here was tough. My next door neighbor, she's a teacher and Anglo Saxon [White], and she has lived here for twenty-five years. The person across the hall works in a very well-known clinic and has lived here for twenty years by herself, so that demonstrates a longevity—an antiquity in these apartments. Regardless, I understand that lately a lot more families have arrived and more have moved out. Now they [the residents] are not as steady and continuous like my neighbor and my other neighbor.)

Cristina's comments identify both the stable tenure of some renters in the area and the changes Pine Grove Apartments has recently experienced. Much like the neighborhood at large, Pine Grove Apartments seems to have been established with predominantly White occupants. The apartment complex, like Creekridge Park, is now much more racially mixed, with Black and Latino/a residents comprising a large percentage of the tenants.

Map 2 showcases the current amenities of Creekridge Park, including Creekridge Park Elementary, which has a predominantly Black and Latino/a student population. All of the local businesses are located on the perimeter of the neighborhood, where there is commercial zoning. These businesses include several restaurants across a large price range: Carolina

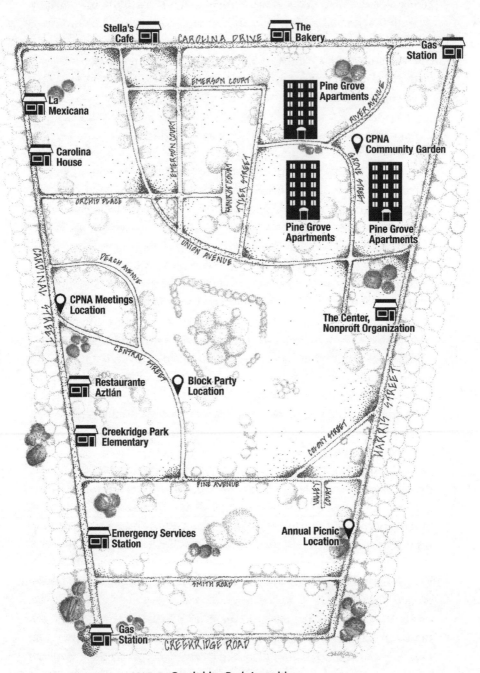

MAP 2 Creekridge Park Amenities

House is one of the city's premier fine-dining restaurants with entrees ranging between $20 and $35; Stella's Café is a gourmet bistro where an average à la carte sandwich costs $8.50; La Mexicana is a popular taquería with menu items starting at $2.50. There are no city parks in Creekridge Park, although the neighborhood is well shaded by trees. Creekridge Park is also home to an emergency services station on Cardinal Street.[38]

The White Habitus of Creekridge Park Residents

Throughout the following chapters, I interrogate how privilege operates in this neighborhood and examine how individuals understand and experience race and class privilege. I am particularly interested in how White homeowners understand their own position and how they use the resources available to them to maintain their power in Creekridge Park while simultaneously extolling the virtues of their multiethnic environment. I use social theorist Anthony Giddens's conceptualization of power: "the capacity to achieve outcomes," which is "generated in and through the reproduction of structures of domination."[39] Giddens emphasizes the importance of resources in defining and enacting power and highlights the role of individuals in reproducing and maintaining structure. This approach is particularly relevant for my study of neighborhood life and social interactions. As he clarifies, "It is always the case that the day-to-day activity of social actors draws upon and reproduces structural features of wider social systems."[40] Giddens's conceptualization of the relationship between micro- and macrolevel processes acknowledges the iterative dynamic between individuals (whose agency is defined by their capacity to do things) and structure, which is both constraining and enabling.

My analysis builds on the work of social theorist Pierre Bourdieu, whose concepts of habitus and taste (which I discuss in more detail in Chapter 2) are integral to understanding inter- and intragroup dynamics within Creekridge Park. I argue throughout this book that Creekridge Park is characterized by a white, urban, middle-class habitus. Bourdieu defines habitus as "a system of dispositions," which includes the actions and tendencies of an individual.[41] A person's habitus, however, is often experienced as a shared "way of being" based on his or her social location.[42] While Bourdieu addresses the homogenizing effects of class on habitus, I am interested in the intersection of race, class, and geography on common practices for Creekridge Park residents. This shared white, urban, middle-class habitus, which delineates certain behaviors and ways of being as acceptable, dictates many interactions in Creekridge Park—particularly those across race and class. The practices of individuals who do not subscribe to the dominant white, urban, middle-class habitus are othered; "imposing different definitions of the impossible, the possible and the probable, cause one group to experience as natural or reasonable practices or aspirations which another group finds unthinkable or scandalous, and vice versa."[43] Although those who subscribe to the white, urban, middle-class habitus and those who do not are equally capable of drawing distinctions between in-group and out-group members, this distinguishing process is more materially relevant (and potentially harmful) when it is enacted by those with the most power and resources. In Creekridge Park the privileged are White homeowners, a pattern stemming from societal structures of inequality. Using the concept of habitus, I highlight the particularly raced and classed practices and ways of understanding that White homeowners and those who embody the white, urban, middle-class habitus use to maintain their privilege in a multiethnic setting. Although I interview individuals and observe interactions at the microlevel, my analysis focuses on patterns of behavior and common dispositions that shed light on structural inequality at the macrolevel.

In combination with Bourdieu's work, research within whiteness studies provides a critical framework for understanding Creekridge Park as a *white* space that is shaped by and privileges White residents, especially homeowners.[44] As philosopher Charles Mills explains, "Whiteness is not really a color at all, but a set of power relations."[45] Over the last few decades, whiteness scholars have investigated racial identities, hierarchies, and boundary construction with a focus on power.[46] *Behind the White Picket Fence* continues in this tradition. Mills's conceptualization of a "racial contract" frames structural racial inequality as "a political system, a particular power structure of formal or informal rule, socioeconomic privilege, and norms for the differential distribution of material wealth and opportunities, benefits and burdens, rights and duties" that benefits those in the "White" category.[47] Therefore, when I use the capitalized term "White," I am specifically using it as a demographic marker; when I use the lowercase term "white," I am making an argument about a system of racial power. Although all Whites benefit from the racial contract, not all Whites are willing participants or profit from it in the same ways.[48] Some White individuals intentionally practice antiracism by acknowledging issues of power and taking action against structural racial oppression. This book is meant as a critique of whiteness and the social system that maintains and reproduces racial inequality. *Behind the White Picket Fence* addresses how certain practices veil, protect, and reproduce Whites' privileged position, while uniquely bringing to light how whiteness operates within multiethnic spaces.[49]

By using the narratives and themes repeated and shared by White Creekridge Park residents, I unpack and identify how Black and Latino/a residents are included and/or marginalized in this multiethnic space. Pinpointing how differences in power across social space are also reproduced in symbolic arenas in this multiethnic neighborhood illustrates how spatial distance is not always necessary to perpetuate privilege and inequality.[50]

A Note on the Racial Particularities of Creekridge Park

As a light-skinned woman with dark hair and brown eyes, I look like a lot of other Latinas from my hometown of Miami, Florida. When I go back home to visit my parents, store clerks do not hesitate to address me in Spanish, placing me inside a multihued Latina category. This, however, does not occur in most places outside Miami–Dade County. In new Latino/a destinations such as Durham the construction of the category "Latina" tends to be narrower than in historical Latino/a hubs such as Miami and Los Angeles. There is no room for someone who looks like me to occupy the Latina category in Creekridge Park. As such, I get placed in a category that does not match my identity or represent my lived experience: non-Hispanic White.[51] I also fully acknowledge that occupying this category situates me in a position of power in Durham, North Carolina, and other white spaces. As someone who has light-skin privilege, I have the rare opportunity as a scholar of color to study Whites.[52]

In combination with theoretical considerations and the particularities of life in Creekridge Park, I decided to focus my interviews on White residents to understand how whiteness operates in this space, "turning the lens on processes that privilege, rather than focusing on exemplars of disadvantage."[53] My decision was also impacted by the entree I had gained in White social networks, which I did not achieve to the same extent with Black and Latino/a residents. For example, after I met Roberta at the annual picnic and received a positive response to my request to interview her, I called her several times to try to meet again in person. Although I left messages and searched for her information through her employer's database, I was ultimately unsuccessful in interviewing her. I can never know exactly why Roberta did not respond to these invitations without asking her directly, although our distinct positions, the racial particularities of Durham and the CPNA, and her treatment at the annual picnic do bring up an important consideration: regardless of my good intentions in the field, I occupied a privileged position as a White-looking woman from an elite university.[54] As I discuss in Appendix A, my social location affected my conversations with respondents in important ways. The bottom line is this: good intentions do not dismantle structural inequality. This point is true when I discuss my experiences in the field, and it is true when I discuss the behavioral patterns of White residents in Chapter 3. To truly understand racial inequality as a structural and systemic social problem, we need to have tough conversations about power and how well-intentioned individuals can be complicit in the marginalization of subordinated groups. My hope is that this book contributes to that dialogue by providing an honest portrayal of life in multiethnic Creekridge Park.

Although this book is largely about whiteness, it would be a mistake to only interview White residents. Whiteness and power are relational. Identifying, analyzing, and understanding whiteness necessitates examining the experience of individuals who do not occupy (and are excluded from) the White, non-Hispanic category. As sociologist Evelyn Nakano Glenn models in her work, "We must examine not only how dominant groups and institutions attempt to impose particular meanings but also how subordinate groups contest dominant conceptions and construct alternative meaning."[55] This relational conceptualization demands the incorporation of non-White voices to inform and challenge the narrative presented by White residents. As a result, while I interviewed more than four dozen White residents whose behaviors and attitudes I discuss in Chapters 2 and 3, Chapter 4 highlights the experiences of thirteen Black and Latino/a Creekridge Park residents to further elucidate the particularities of race and class in this space.

CHAPTER OUTLINES

Chapter 2, "White Habitus and the Meanings of Diversity," begins with a discussion of why White residents choose to live in Creekridge Park and how they understand themselves and their neighbors in this space. I emphasize the importance of diversity ideology in understanding White Creekridge Park residents and how they assess their day-to-day interactions with both White and non-White residents.

Chapter 3, "Neighboring from a Distance," extends the c
Chapter 2 and highlights the behavioral aspects of life in Creek
I discuss the interracial and intraracial codes of conduct in tl
ethnic setting. Although there were some examples of reciprocal l
ships, I find that norms of high social distance and social contrc
erally dictate the modes of interaction between White and non-White
residents.

In Chapter 4, "Creekridge Park in Black and Brown," I focus on the experiences of Black and Latino/a residents in Creekridge Park. I juxtapose
their narratives with those of White residents, illuminating the similarities and differences with which these three groups navigate life in this
multiethnic space.

Lastly, Chapter 5, "Solving the Wrong Problem," offers a new definition of integration and proposes potential directions for future research.
I discuss the importance of conducting more multimethod research on
multiethnic spaces. It is imperative that we continue to understand how
both dominant and marginalized communities experience these spaces
and how power works within them. Lastly, I challenge social scientists
and policy makers to consider whether the integrative goals of 1960s social movements are adequate measures for racial progress in the twenty-
first century.

CHAPTER 2   White Habitus and the Meanings of Diversity

It's definitely diverse. It's economically diverse. It's racially diverse. It's educationally diverse.

—DEBBIE, White homeowner, established resident

It's fine dining and takeout right next to each other. . . . We have the established families that have been here for a long time, we have people who are coming in and transitional moving in and out, um, we have a wide range of ethnicities within the neighborhood, um, languages that are spoken within the neighborhood, um, house types, property types within the neighborhood.

—SHARON, White homeowner, established resident

Debbie and Sharon's characterizations of a diverse Creekridge Park area contribute important insights into the neighborhood's white, urban, middle-class habitus. Diversity across multiple axes is a prominent aspect of Creekridge Park for White residents, particularly homeowners. In this chapter I analyze White residents' definitions of diversity and the centrality of diversity ideology to this specific white, urban, middle-class habitus. Investigating what White residents mean when they use the term "diversity" helps elucidate how diversity ideology affects how Whites frame their decisions to live in Creekridge Park. I find that these definitions of diversity do not acknowledge power differentials across race or class lines, maintaining White homeowners' race and class privilege.

CLARIFYING CONCEPTS

Bourdieu's concepts of habitus and taste are essential to my analysis of Creekridge Park. A person's habitus and associated tastes are often shared with those in similar social positions. These shared ways of being, or dispositions, reflect not just class but also race and regionality. An individual's habitus is "homologous to the position they themselves occupy in social space" and includes both "the capacity to produce classifiable practices and works, and the capacity to differentiate and appreciate these practices and products."[1] This capacity to differentiate and appreciate is taste: "Taste classifies, and it classifies the classifier. Social subjects, classified by the classifications, distinguish themselves by the distinctions they make, between the beautiful and the ugly, the distinguished and the vulgar, in which their position in the objective classifications is expressed or betrayed."[2] Therefore, habitus is not just about one's own behaviors and dispositions, but it is also about one's taste and how one distinguishes between the "beautiful and the ugly" in others. Below I identify and analyze the white, urban, middle-class habitus embodied by most White homeowners who live in Creekridge Park.[3] I investigate White residents' reasons for moving to Creekridge Park, how they perceive and classify their neighborhood and neighbors, how diversity is an essential part of this contemporary white, urban, middle-class habitus, and how their uses of diversity maintain their race and class privilege.

What does it mean to conceptualize diversity as an ideology?[4] In my analysis I use cultural theorist Stuart Hall's definition of ideology: "systems of meaning, concepts, categories and representations which make sense of the world."[5] I argue that diversity ideology, much like color-blind racism, helps individuals who live within an increasingly multicultural environment reconcile a national emphasis on egalitarianism with pervasive racial inequality.[6] As part of this reconciliation, diversity ideology dictates that intentions, as opposed to outcomes, are what truly matter. As a result, those who value diversity as a concept are associated with humanist principles of equity and justice. As I indicate in this chapter, however, focusing on good intentions can obscure issues of inequality. If we are truly interested in equity, we cannot ignore inequitable outcomes— even if they are the result of well-intentioned actions.

I argue that diversity ideology does not demand that individuals take specific actions to promote inclusion or equity. Simply by being in favor of difference across a multitude of categories (e.g., race, sexual orientation, lawn care preferences), one is seen as equitable and inclusive. Emerging research evidences that while diversity initiatives were originally meant to address systemic racial and gender inequality in corporate environments, their contemporary amorphous conceptualizations have reduced their usefulness for structural social change.[7] In this chapter I identify the five ways that Creekridge Park residents define diversity and discuss how these uses, by failing to acknowledge power differentials and focus on outcomes, reinforce the race and class privilege of White homeowners.

Why should we care about this white, urban, middle-class habitus; aren't there worse, more overt perpetrators of racial inequality? Studying this white, urban, middle-class habitus matters precisely because commonsense notions dictate that those who value diversity do not reproduce inequity. We see below and in the following chapters that this is not the case. In this book I present that, even when people care deeply about issues of equity and justice, racial inequity can still be reproduced and continue to benefit those with race and class privilege. The prominence and power of diversity ideology is one important element of that contemporary stratification process. Although we live in an imperfect world with no magic bullet to eradicate inequality, highlighting stratifying processes and challenging those with good intentions to know and do better is important to achieve more just outcomes. This is the goal of *Behind the White Picket Fence*.

WHY HERE?

During interviews with Creekridge Park residents, my first questions were *How long have you lived in the neighborhood?* and *How did you go about finding your current home?* I wanted to know how residents explained their decisions to move into Creekridge Park.[8] Affordability was a common reason, although we will see that even budget constraints are presented by residents within a particular set of values. This is where Bourdieu's concept of taste comes in: many White homeowners stressed that the aesthetic and political elements of Creekridge Park and their homes were central to their home-buying process. When White homeowners emphasize these neighborhood-specific and house-specific characteristics, they simultaneously classify themselves and the residents that fail to appreciate these attributes. Below I expound on these categories and argue that the factors that White residents highlight are enactments of a particular white, urban, middle-class habitus. For ease of reading, I have omitted identifying each resident quoted in this chapter as a White homeowner. Unless otherwise noted, the reader may assume each individual discussed in this chapter is a White homeowner.

The Price Is Right

Creekridge Park's position as a working- and middle-class neighborhood is anchored in its relatively affordable housing. According to Russ, an established resident who is also a Durham-based landlord, the neighborhood is experiencing a slight economic shift. He described Creekridge Park as "fairly middle class" and "somewhat affordable. I mean, the neighborhood's, the neighborhood's not that affordable anymore, but somewhat affordable." As I mentioned in Chapter 1, Creekridge Park housing values range from about $69,000 to $201,000. According to real estate website Trulia, the median home sale price between September and November 2011 was $150,000 for the city of Durham[9] and just under $139,000 for Creekridge Park.[10] Creekridge Park's average was slightly below the city mean, although it was certainly higher than some Durham areas. For example, East Durham, which is predominantly Black, high poverty, and currently undergoing major redevelopment, had an average home sale price of $41,000 for the same time frame.[11]

Affordability is the primary criterion for many homebuyers in Creekridge Park and the surrounding areas. For Rhonda, an established homeowner in her early thirties, price was the main concern when she and her partner bought their house on Peach Avenue: "It was more, like, um, honestly it was price, because at that time I was in school full time and she was working and even though I didn't have that much left in my program, like, we wanted to have a house and then once I finished with school she went back to school, so, like, we wanted to have a house that we could afford on one income. So that was pretty much our determining factor." A few residents mentioned being able to afford their mortgage on one income as an important reason they chose their current home. Ann, a newcomer who has lived in Creekridge Park for three years and is in her mid-thirties, explained that the affordability of the area was a big change from Boston, where she and her husband, Ken, previously lived. The cost of living in Durham and the neighborhood allowed Ann and Ken to financially endure his extended period of unemployment and the birth of their first child:

> We bought [the house in Durham] . . . before people started getting laid off and, you know, Ken lost his job [a few] weeks after [our daughter] was born, so it was, like, a double blow there, you know. Just major lifestyle transitions and then not having a job, but we

managed to hang on for a year with really neither of us working. I was working part time during that year and, um, I don't think we could have done that everywhere. I know we couldn't have done it in Boston, if he'd lost his job up there, I don't know what we would've done [*laughs*]. Like, we would have had to, totally change and probably wouldn't have the baby yet and, you know, like, would've had to make other, so, you know, I feel like we came down at just the right time, you know.

Sharon, an established resident in her early thirties, was looking for an affordable fixer-upper since she and her husband could not afford their ideal home: "Price was a big, big factor. A lot of the houses we really like, like the . . . bungalows, and things like that are just not affordable [*laughs*]. Um, and so we, um, we told her [the real estate agent] our price range and we also told her we wanted a house that could, like, needed some TLC because we were looking for a house we could fix up."

Sandra, a newcomer to the neighborhood in her late thirties, was looking for a neighborhood with a few different features: "It needed to be diverse, and I like old neighborhoods and the house was—it was built in '49, so. And price, I mean price certainly had something to do with it [*laughs*]." It is worth noting how Sandra identifies the importance of price almost as an afterthought as she discusses her decision to move to Creekridge Park.

Lastly, Bryan, a longtime homeowner on Pine Avenue in his fifties, said he and his wife were looking for an affordable place they could have a good life in: "Um, at the time it was the price range that was the determining factor for where we could look. Um, and then we looked at a number of neighborhoods that met that price range and this was the one that appeared, um, the most ready to have a good life in." When I asked Bryan what he meant by "ready to have a good life in," he explained he was referring to the state of his home (he was not interested in a fixer-upper) and the condition of the neighborhood. For Bryan, unappealing neighborhoods were those that looked "a little rough," which included the presence of "vagrants" and homes with no grass in the front yard because residents parked their cars on it. So while Bryan emphasized price, we see that he still couched his home's affordability within certain value-based bounds. He and his wife did not just want an affordable place, but they wanted it to reflect the aesthetics and practices that they value, including grass in the front yard.

While some respondents explicitly discussed price, as we saw above, neighborhood residents were much more likely to discuss and emphasize the importance of aesthetic and political details when they explained their decisions to move to Creekridge Park. While price may still be important for the decision to move into the neighborhood, these residents emphasized other elements of Creekridge Park over price. Although Creekridge Park is certainly more affordable than the average housing option in Cary, a nearby town included on national "Best Places to Live" and "Safest Places to Live" lists, affordability is not brought up by White homeowners when comparing these stigmatized suburban spaces and Creekridge Park. For example, the average listing price during October and December 2011 for Cary was $376,781, which is about $220,000 more than the suburban-type neighborhoods in Durham and $248,000 more than the average listing in Creekridge Park. In fact, though all residents make housing decisions under certain constraints including income and budget, White homeowners who also occupy this white, urban, middle-class habitus generally explain their decisions as enactments of their particular taste. As many of the respondents indicated above, White residents in Creekridge Park are limited in their ability to live in other neighborhoods in Durham and the surrounding areas. By focusing on the aesthetic details and political climate of Creekridge Park, however, White homeowners redefine the presence of older housing and non-White neighbors as desirable rather than the product of constrained economic decisions. Although fundamentally about affordability, the white, urban, middle-class habitus of Creekridge Park enables White residents who are lower middle class and middle class to explain what they appreciate about the neighborhood and why they chose to live there independent of housing cost.

The Taste of Creekridge Park

Many of the conversations regarding "Why here?" became platforms for residents to explain how they view the neighborhood and interpret living in Creekridge Park. In the following sections I explore the dominant taste of Creekridge Park and its white, urban, middle-class habitus and how White homeowners make sense of their decisions to live in Creekridge Park.

Proximity to Downtown

Proximity to downtown Durham was an important characteristic of Creekridge Park. Many homeowners celebrated this as a benefit of living in the area. Sandra, a newcomer who lives on Pine Avenue, said that she appreciated the neighborhood being near downtown. She claimed, "I like urban, so that was kind of important to me." Alan, a longtime resident who was a renter in the neighborhood before he bought his current home, pointed out that while the house itself was part of what convinced him to become a homeowner, the neighborhood was also a selling point: "I liked the location, um, just because it's very convenient . . . close to Chapel Hill, close to downtown. . . . Certainly in that regard I liked it." Russ, who grew up in Durham and is in his fifties, said, "The neighborhood is the main reason [I moved to Creekridge Park]. Yeah, proximity to where I've grown up and I knew the neighborhood and was kind of comfortable there and, um, I liked Durham. It's a good neighborhood, accessible to most things."

Patty, a new homeowner in her late twenties who moved back to Durham after finishing graduate school, picked her current home because of its accessibility to Chapel Hill for work: "As far as specific location, it had a little bit to do—I work [in] Chapel Hill—ease of access to Chapel Hill, um, but also I have a lot of friends who live in this immediate area." Commuting between Chapel Hill and Durham, which is about a twelve-mile/twenty-five-minute drive, is not uncommon for area residents.

Proximity to downtown also allowed residents to participate in activities that they valued, such as bicycle riding and walking. For example, Emma, a twenty-something newcomer and graduate student, explained how her search for a home was constrained by price, a need for hardwood floors due to a medical condition, and an interest in safely biking to a local university since she either bikes or walks to school. Similarly, Ann, a newcomer on Cardinal Street, shared that she liked her current house because its location afforded her husband the opportunity to bike to work. She also explained that it is "nice to be close for a ball game or just to get downtown for a quick drink or something with a friend. It's easy to get down there." Thus proximity is not just a pragmatic factor regarding commute length; it is an enactment of a particular set of values (e.g., bike riding, environmentalism).

Rural Feel
Thirty percent of survey respondents gave "quiet/peaceful" as a main descriptor of the neighborhood (see table 2.1), a pattern confirmed by the interview data. Longtime residents in particular pointed out the greenery of the neighborhood and its quiet "rural" feel in spite of its urban character. For instance, Daniel, an established homeowner in his fifties who

lives on Peach Avenue, said that he was not familiar with the neighborhood prior to moving into it. When he first saw his current house, he enjoyed that it was off the beaten path: "My street is very secluded and even though, you know, it's right off Cardinal Street, um, it's quite quiet. Uh, it's, you know, it's only a block long, the street. Um, and it's not a very good connector, so it's not busy. Um, and it's actually the, the entrance to the street from Cardinal Street kind of looks like a driveway, you know, the trees are overgrowing and so, it's sort of set apart." Deborah, a longtime homeowner who lives on Union Avenue, stated that what initially brought her to Creekridge Park was the house. She then qualified her statement: "I have to say, too, the neighborhood appearance itself. The trees, the older homes, the general quiet feeling of the neighborhood being set back off from the busy streets, kind of in its own little closed space. That was very appealing, too. It looked like a very quiet neighborhood and the big trees on our property and around us were a huge draw." Judy, another established homeowner on Peach Avenue in her forties, shared that "the first time I drove down I felt like I was driving into the country and just, you know fell in love with the neighborhood before I fell in love in the house." This appreciation for the rural feeling of the neighborhood is noteworthy as we consider below how important its urban location is for White residents.

Urban . . . and Not Suburban

Creekridge Park residents often juxtapose their preferences with those of other White homeowners, particularly those who live in suburbs and new urban developments. White Creekridge Park residents do not see these other homeowners as participating in the same habitus. Sociologist David Hummon's analysis of Urbanists, those who prefer and are committed to living in cities, also highlights similar patterns of distinction: "[For Urbanists] the imagery of suburbia is defined through its relation to urban life, and it is difficult to understand the unfavorable portrayal that Urbanists often give suburbia unless their views are seen in the context of their beliefs about cities."[12] Creekridge Park residents believe cities and their older neighborhoods project an open-mindedness that other residential options and their inhabitants do not. For instance, Emma drew distinctions between herself and other graduate students who she believes would not enjoy living in Creekridge Park: "I feel very, you know, I enjoy living there. Um, I'm sure not everyone would. Like, if you wanted to live in, like, a ni-, super nice place with new things and, like, people who are just like you in the, in terms of your background and whatever, like, that wouldn't be a good place for you. And if you wanted to live somewhere where there aren't gonna be things that happen that are instigated by poverty, that's, you know, that's not gonna be the place for you." Emma, a newcomer, saw herself as distinct from the typical graduate student because she wanted to live in an older neighborhood rather than a new condominium with "free cable and . . . 24-hour security." For Emma, living in a new apartment complex was undesirable, and she negatively viewed those who decided to move into one.

Relatedly, Lori, a newcomer on Emerson Court in her late twenties, indicated that she was looking for three things: "Price range, location, and that it wasn't all, you know, houses that are same, the same five floor plan, plans." As she put it, "We didn't want to live in, um, like, a brand new development . . . you know, kind of suburban sort of thing." Stephanie, an established resident in her early thirties who moved to Central Street with her husband, said, "We liked that it was urban. Um, and we, we definitely liked that it's not like a, a little development with, like, a name. . . . That's not us." Ray, a longtime Creekridge Park homeowner in his sixties, indicated that he and his wife are not "suburban subdivision folk." Similarly, Cynthia, an established homeowner on Harris Street in her sixties, stated her preference for an urban neighborhood with bus access and other amenities: "I grew up in [the] suburbia of Pennsylvania and I don't—I didn't want to live in the kind of place that I grew up." Lastly, Beth, a homeowner on Emerson Court in her fifties, described the typical Creekridge Park resident as "someone who wants to live in kind of a mixed-up place. You know, as opposed to somebody who likes condos or, you know, that's what you can say about us that we have in common." In addition to wanting to live in a "mixed-up place," the White homeowners of Creekridge Park also share another characteristic: defining themselves by who they are not.

A newcomer in her thirties who lives on Cardinal Street, Julie's search for a home was closely tied to seeking out particular neighborhood-based characteristics:

I wanted to be somewhere that had sidewalks, because, um, if places have sidewalks it seems to encourage people walking around more. Um, and I wanted to ideally be somewhere where I could walk to the grocery store and would have just a very lively walking community. Um, but I also wanted to buy in like, a developing neighborhood, like, um, one of my passions is economic development, um, and like, non-gentrification economic development, and, um, I loved that. And so I wanted to be in, like, a working-class Durham neighborhood, um, which is definitely this neighborhood. And, um, it's got a huge population of Latino[s] and a huge Black population, um, and so a lot of White people often think that it's, like, gang-related or, like, it's dangerous because they're people different from them. But that, everyone's working class, so I really like that.

By describing a type of White person who interprets the presence of minority residents as "gang-related," Julie is able to classify herself by both who she is (someone who seeks out economic development) and who she is not (someone who associates non-Whites with gangs).

White homeowners move into Creekridge Park, a multiethnic, mixed-income, urban neighborhood, to distinguish themselves from the White residents of suburbs and similarly stigmatized spaces. The logic behind these decisions, however, is presented as self-evident: for example, of course Emma would never live in a brand-new apartment with twenty-four-hour security and free cable—that space is negatively valued within this white, urban, middle-class habitus. This preference for older neighborhoods and urban housing is a pattern well-established in the literature on early gentrifiers.[13] Gentrifiers and the new urban middle class view other housing options, specifically suburban and new developments, as having a spoiled identity; "the suburbs are too standardized, too homogeneous, too bland, too conformist, too hierarchical, too conservative, too patriarchal, too straight."[14] White residents who embody this white, urban, middle-class habitus tie decisions to live in Creekridge Park to their identities as individuals but also as part of a larger group of open-minded people. Their enactment of this particular habitus is experienced as individual and also shared, as Beth's comments illustrate. Their remarks indicate that part of the contemporary white, urban, middle-class habitus is identifying with urban space and living.

Unique and Older Housing Stock

The negative associations White Creekridge Park residents have with suburban living also include a distinct appreciation for older and "unique" housing stock found in urban neighborhoods. In his description of Creekridge Park, Ken expresses what he appreciates about his home and indicates how other options did not appeal to him and his wife. Ken experiences this preference as a shared way of being within the neighborhood and classifies other Creekridge Park residents as embodying it as well. Ken explains:

It's a pretty good mix of, you know, old and new families. I think it's more affordable over here and, like, Durham has a lot of great, you know, housing stock, like, a lot of great, you know, architectural housing stock and I think there are people who are drawn to that kind of, you know, lifestyle. Because I think there's, you know, probably, you know, in terms of just raw housing, I mean, you could probably find something for, you know, for the money we paid for this house in the suburbs somewhere in a quiet little thing, but people—I think people in this neighborhood, you know, know what they are getting into and, you know, are just not interested in the suburb[s] and, you know, just not their thing, not their quality of house, too isolated or, you know.

Ken's association of older housing stock with a particular lifestyle is exemplary of the white, urban, middle-class habitus of Creekridge Park. He perceives his taste as shared and reflective of a way of being among neighborhood residents.

The historic and older homes of this urban neighborhood attract many residents. Some of the characteristics of older homes that were often highlighted by White residents included hardwood floors, long porches, and general uniqueness related to age. Tammy, an established resident, stated that her house was "just charming. I mean it has three fireplaces and, um, you know higher ceilings than a lot of houses and wide woodwork and wood floors." Aesthetic details such as crown molding were also mentioned as desirable at neighborhood events. For example, at a meeting with the developer of new housing on Smith Road, residents (most of whom were White) lamented the faux crown molding that is now en vogue and insisted on the developer's inclusion of aesthetic details that reflect the age and diversity in housing across Creekridge Park. Their foundation for these demands is a list of mandates drafted by the neighborhood association and sanctioned by the City of Durham that regulates neighborhood development. I discuss this document in more detail in Chapter 3.

Newcomer Patty stated that she was originally looking for a "pre-'50s home. Um, I wanted some things, like hardwood floors and, um . . . basically I wanted some of the architectural features of that era preserved in the house." Brendan, a new homeowner in the area in his early thirties, described his and his wife's search for a historic home:

We were trying to find an older home and, uh, we looked probably, gosh, it seems like about fifty homes. I mean, it was really a lot of homes and, um, my wife, our, one day I was up here 'cause one of my friends was moving and, uh, I stayed at his house for the evening and my wife on the way back, she's like, "Why don't you look at some houses?" and so she was on the internet when I was driving around . . . and, uh, she goes, "Well, there's this house for this Preservation Durham website, it's not on any of the listings," and so I drove by it and . . . that's, you know, how we end up getting the house, uh, through Preservation Durham.

There were a few historic homes in Creekridge Park that received official recognition from Preservation Durham, a local preservationist organization.[15] Brendan went on to explain how he and his wife had to write and submit a statement to the organization on why they wanted to own a historic home before they could purchase it. Brendan then shared that he saw himself as a "steward" of the house and hoped "to do this house . . . some justice," leaving a positive footprint on it for future owners.

Julie, a new homeowner in her early thirties who lives on Cardinal Street, also expressed an affinity for older homes. When I asked what she looked for in a home, she replied, "I wanted an old house. I wanted something that had, like, fun charm. You know? Like, it had quirky things about it." Other residents also mentioned this appreciation for general quirkiness and uniqueness, which seems most closely related to a house's age. During my interview with Adrienne, a new homeowner on Mason Avenue in her early thirties, she described what she enjoys about her home: "I really like this house because it was unique. It was built in the, in 1938. Um, when I was looking around on the internet at the neighborhood and stuff like that I managed to find some history about it. . . . So it was one of the first houses on our street and there was just, I liked the uniqueness of it. I liked that it had a lot more land than some of the others [houses we considered buying]." Ruth, a homeowner in her fifties who lives on Harris Street, shared what she likes about her home, emphasizing familiar characteristics of this white, urban, middle-class habitus: "It's funky [laughs]. We like funky. The neighborhood's funky. Um, and the house just, you know, it's like a little cabin in the woods but we're right in town. I like being close to downtown. Um, and all the stuff happening." As Ruth details, the uniqueness of the neighborhood and the homes, in addition to their location and the ability of residents to easily participate in activities downtown, allow White residents to present Creekridge Park as a self-evident choice within this white, urban, middle-class habitus while simultaneously deemphasizing their financial considerations.

DIVERSE MEANINGS

Diversity and Taste

Several of my respondents described Creekridge Park as a microcosm of Durham because of its diversity. As Russ explained, "Durham's very eclectic, so you have all kinds of folks, you know, so, it's a mixture of everybody basically." He goes on to describe the residents of Creekridge Park as "very eclectic, um, fairly middle class and fairly well educated, very typical Durham. We've got everything from, um, single adults to families with young kids to retired people, all ethnicities, uh, a very mixed neighborhood. Very typical Durham. If you don't want to live with different kinds of people, don't live in Durham. I mean that's, you know, that's pretty much the case. Very mixed." The most common label residents used to define Creekridge Park when I asked them to describe the neighborhood to someone who was not familiar with the area was "diverse" or a similar term. Beth, an active Creekridge Park Neighborhood Association (CPNA) member, responded, "Oh gosh, it's everybody," when I asked her who lives in Creekridge Park. Similarly, when describing what kind of neighborhood Creekridge Park is, Luke stated, "This is that kind of neighborhood, where, like, we want you to keep it clean, and we love it when you plant something, um, but, we just like to have, you know, your own space and have nice people and have diversity, well, it's also a really diverse neighborhood for that matter. Age, race, sexual orientation, we have it all here and I like that a whole bunch, too." Luke's comments about having "your own space" are noteworthy considering the social control practices he participates in, which I discuss in more detail in Chapter 3.

As part of the household survey, I asked respondents what three words they would use to describe Creekridge Park. Those results are in table 2.1. "Friendly/neighborly" was the most common set of descriptors. As I showcase below, references to friendliness and openness are directly related to White residents' conceptualizations of diversity in Creekridge Park. "Eclectic/mixed" follows. I separated "diversity" from "mixed" and "eclectic" to see how often residents specifically referenced diversity, even though respondents commonly used these terms as synonyms in my

TABLE 2.1 *Most popular neighborhood descriptors based on survey data*

How would you describe the neighborhood?

Eclectic/mixed/diverse		42% (36)
Eclectic/mixed	22% (19)	
Diverse	20% (17)	
Friendly/neighborly		35% (30)
Older/historic		12% (10)
Convenient		19% (16)
Safe		12% (10)
Cheap/affordable		8% (7)
Quiet/peaceful		30% (26)
Comfortable/cozy		11% (9)
General positive adjective		16% (14)
N		85

interviews. Collapsing these two categories makes these terms the most popular descriptors. Considering the multitude of ways that White residents understand and define diversity, the three most popular characterizations of Creekridge Park (i.e., friendly/neighborly, eclectic/mixed, and diverse) are references to neighborhood diversity.

Residents provide insight into what matters to them with the neighborhood descriptions they choose. When they describe Creekridge Park, residents not only classify the neighborhood, but they also classify themselves. For example, Terry, another homeowner in his fifties who lives in an adjacent neighborhood, agreed that the Creekridge area is a microcosm of Durham, which he contrasted with the homogeneous fictional town from the television show *Weeds*: "That's one of the good things about living in Durham is the, it's a diverse community. You're not in a cookie cutter, everybody looks just the same, you know, like the—did you ever see *Weeds* [on Showtime], you know? . . . That's what it's all about, that suburbia where everybody drives the same kind of car, everybody looks the same, everybody's got the same income level, blah blah blah. This neighborhood is not like that. Everybody's different."

The categories White residents used to define axes of difference varied. It is interesting that when residents described the neighborhood as diverse, they almost always mentioned race and ethnicity. They often also included references to class, sexual orientation, age, and family type. Some residents also discussed housing tenure, occupations, educational attainment, and housing stock. It is notable that although many respondents discussed the inclusion of gay and lesbian residents in Creekridge Park, they rarely discussed sexual orientation beyond a mention in a list of categories of difference. White and non-White residents alike were much more likely to expand on issues related to race and ethnicity than other markers of difference during our interviews. This creates a process by which a variety of categories are used to justify a "diverse" description, but race and ethnicity are the most salient descriptors for initially designating a neighborhood as diverse. For example, Emma, who lives on Colony Street, described the neighborhood thus: "Probably it's still majority white, but in general there seems to be a lot of diversity there both in terms of age group, ethnicity, families or single people or couples, um, that sort of stuff." Here we see how Emma first discusses race, acknowledging that the neighborhood is "probably . . . majority white," and then she includes other categories to support her definition of a diverse neighborhood. This pattern is interesting because while it shows that conceptualizations of diversity are expanding, diversity is still primarily associated with race.

Below I investigate the emphasis on diversity by White residents, presenting the multitude of ways diversity is defined and how those definitions interact with the white, urban, middle-class habitus of Creekridge Park. These definitions include diversity as (1) proportionality, (2) acceptance of difference, (3) a commodity, (4) reinforcing the status quo, and (5) a liability for White homeowners.

Diversity as Proportionality

In my conversations with White residents I found that some of them used proportionality to frame neighborhood diversity, much like the social scientists who study statistical integration. The incidence of the diversity-as-proportionality framework is in part related to the number of residents with advanced degrees who live in the neighborhood. Although not all master's or doctoral degree earners used this framework, every respondent who brought up issues of proportionality held an advanced degree.

Denise, a newcomer and renter on Central Street who completed her advanced degree in a natural science field, described Creekridge Park as diverse but also gave a caveat to her description: "But I think this idea of diversity and being mixed . . . comes with the caveat that it is this sort of street-by-street, block-by-block thing and perhaps there are these patches that are not more—homogeneous inside the neighborhood and maybe we don't do such a good job of integrating between those social status." Charles, an established homeowner who also lives on Central Street and earned his advanced degree in a social science field, echoed Denise's views: "I mean it's a diverse neighborhood in the aggregate, parts of it definitely skew demographically different. Some of them are pretty, pretty just mixed."

Patty, a newcomer on Harris Street in her late twenties who also earned her advanced degree in a natural science field, specifically identified the role of statistics in how residents view Creekridge Park's demographics: "I would say that . . . this is a classic example of statistics and mapping and what not. Where if you look at the sum certainly you see diversity, but I do think that there's a, a line. . . . Um, the part of [the neighborhood by] Union [Avenue] here versus . . . towards Smith [Road] and the uh, definitely into the Peach [Avenue], um, that street area . . . that is more, um, probably White and middle class, whereas . . . towards [the northern part of the neighborhood] in this direction it's probably more African American and working class." While the neighborhood is statistically integrated and has low-moderate dissimilarity indices, not every street has the same percentages of Black, White, and Latino/a residents.[16] In map 3 and table 2.2, I divide the neighborhood into seven subregions based on census block designations and how residents spatially described the neighborhood. I indicate the racial-ethnic makeup for each area to give a better indication of how Creekridge Park is spatially organized. What we can see is that the northern part of the neighborhood, which includes Pine Grove Apartments, is majority Black and Latino/a, while the southern areas near Peach Avenue and Central Street are majority White. Interestingly, the acknowledgment of these racial spatial dynamics generally does not negate Creekridge Park's diversity designation for White Creekridge Park residents. For example, Alan, a longtime resident on Emerson Court, describes the kind of people who live in the neighborhood as follows: "I mean, oh, it's such a, it's so diverse. I mean, there's so many different kinds of people and there's kind of, you know, middle-class people and there's, you know, some poor people and, um, Black, White, and Hispanic. Um, so it's really hard to pin it down and even like within a block, um, I mean my particular block is actually all-White, except the one rental, is all-White. Um, but then you know, just around the corner in either direction it's, you know, just all sorts of folks." In this quotation, Alan's "all-White" block in subregion five did not prompt him to question

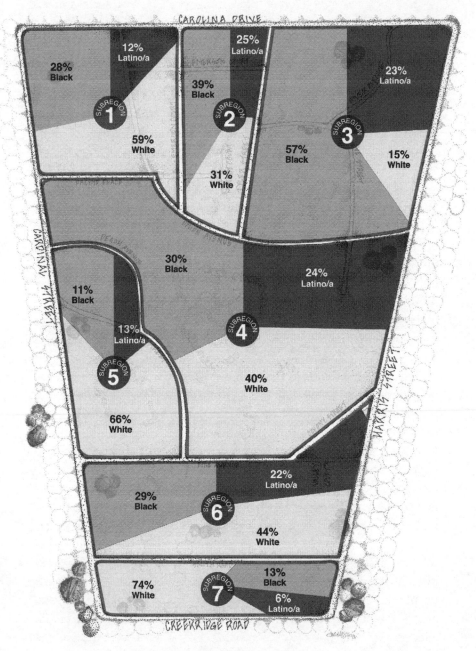

MAP 3 Creekridge Park Demographics

TABLE 2.2 *Creedridge Park demographics by subregion*

	Total	White	Black	Latino/a
Subregion 1	71	44	21	9
Subregion 2	193	62	78	50
Subregion 3	601	96	355	142
Subregion 4	369	155	116	92
Subregion 5	160	110	19	21
Subregion 6	30	13	9	7
Subregion 7	147	109	19	9
Total	1,571			

his description of Creekridge Park as diverse. This seeming contradiction allows us to see the multiple, sometimes opposing, ideas encompassed by diversity ideology. For example, while diversity ideology highlights the importance of inclusion and equality (which remarks about proportionality seem to reference), it also defines the mere presence of non-Whites in a predominantly White area as diversity. Contradictions are very important to the study of ideology; as social theorist Stuart Hall argues, contradictions "function both as vehicles for the imposition of dominant ideologies, and as the elementary forms for the cultures of resistance."[17] So while these contradictions function, in part, to maintain the control of diversity ideology across multiple scenarios (i.e., it is relevant regardless of the racial makeup of a space), by identifying these contradictions we can begin to challenge diversity ideology's hegemonic control.

Similarly, when I spoke with Tina, a newcomer who lives on Smith Road in an adjacent neighborhood, she described the area as follows: "I would say pret—like, not super diverse but friendly diverse, like they're—they're racially somewhat diverse, depending on sort of block by block. But there's a bit of racial diversity. There's a lot of—there are several gay and lesbian couples. Um, and then there are retirees, old people, young couples, not—actually not a ton of kids but some kids. So there's—there's nice diversity in that sense and a really—a really nice community spirit." While Tina acknowledges that racial diversity may fluctuate from block to block, the area still has a "nice diversity" for her. So although the racialized spatial dynamics of Creekridge Park may cause some residents to qualify their description of Creekridge Park as diverse, in general the neighborhood's diversity is not negated for White residents because of these patterns. Despite diversity being conceptualized in relation to proportionality by some, it is also more broadly used to signal an acceptance of difference and overall "friendliness," as Tina indicated. In the next section I describe how difference is conceived of by White Creekridge Park residents and how diversity as acceptance is valued within this white, urban, middle-class habitus.

Diversity as Acceptance

I argue that diversity ideology generally dictates the promotion and maintenance of egalitarianism through the acceptance of differences in others. Historically, diversity was understood as strictly referring to racial and ethnic differences, since diversity initiatives were an extension of multiculturalism and the civil rights movement in the United States.[18] Current interpretations of diversity, however, do not focus solely on the acceptance of racial and ethnic minorities. Everyone's differences are accepted—whether across race, sexual orientation, or as I found in my data, lawn maintenance habits. Established resident Beth gave us some insight into how she conceptualizes neighborhood diversity: "It's houses everywhere from the '20s to very recent stuff. Um, we're majority Democratic, as is the entire county, [laughs] though we got some Republicans. We got one or two and some Independents and people who participate and people who don't participate and people whose yards are filthy with weeds and people's whose yards are completely immaculate, people who take their trash can as soon as it's emptied and people who leave it there all week."

We see with Beth's examples that diversity is a synonym for difference, mixture, or variation. This shift in meaning matters. By broadening what diversity means, we minimize and neglect the issues specifically related to processes of systemic inequality, such as the underrepresentation of women and racial minorities—as sociologist David G. Embrick has found in his work on diversity in corporate environments. By counting more categories for inclusion, corporations and other organizations are able to escape strict scrutiny of their practices in regard to structural inequality.[19] So while expanding what diversity means may seem innocuous, this expansion actually reduces the efficacy of diversity programs in achieving their original goal of institutional social change. The focus then becomes labeling and commodification—"Who has difference so we can laud it?" While the inclusion of other systemically marginalized groups in diversity initiatives, including sexual minorities and the poor, is not counterproductive and should be supported, the inclusion of other forms of difference should not be encouraged. For example, while lawn maintenance habits may seem like strictly class-based behavior and one way to incorporate a variety of income brackets, my interview data indicate that this traditional relationship is not present in Creekridge Park. In fact, some middle-class White homeowners, particularly those with artist backgrounds, have some nontraditional approaches to lawn care that have resulted in violations from Neighborhood Improvement Services, a city agency, because of overgrown lawns. It is important to note that because of the resources available to them as White homeowners, those who received violations were able to resolve the situation quickly. As longtime resident Bryan explained, "[It] all got worked out kind of a deal . . . just one of those, if you know the right person to squawk at and or talk to, you know, you can work things out." So while Beth may be referring to more traditional class-based divides when she discusses the difference in lawn care habits, she is likely referencing more recent issues among White middle-class homeowners in regard to aesthetics. As a result, if residents include lawn care habits along with class, sexuality, and race when describing neighborhood diversity, it reduces their ability to highlight structural issues of inequality. It reframes systemic issues as individual idiosyncrasies.

An acceptance of individual preferences and difference is central to how many homeowners frame Creekridge Park. Ruth, an established homeowner on Harris Street, described Creekridge Park as "a neighborhood that you live and let live. There's not a lot of poking into other people's business, which is nice. Um, and I, I think it's a really friendly neighborhood." In Chapter 4 I discuss how these accounts of neighborhood friendliness expressed by White residents differ from the experiences of Black and Latino/a residents. Deborah, a longtime homeowner who participated in the neighborhood association, said that most people in the neighborhood love it because of its green spaces. She followed that by saying, "But it's also the diversity. I think people come here for that, too. They just feel comfortable here. You can be anybody, you can come from anywhere."

Many residents stated that Creekridge Park is a place for people who appreciate diversity or, as Beth previously commented, who want to live in "kind of a mixed-up place." Interestingly, White residents used diversity and its affiliated political stances to decipher who in the neighborhood could be a potential friend. An appreciation of difference is a similarity many White residents sought out in their neighborhood friends, particularly other White homeowners. In the following example, Ann, who is a recent addition to Cardinal Street, describes the neighborhood and its residents. Her remarks juxtapose the sameness and difference that frame White intraracial friendships in Creekridge Park. She characterizes the neighborhood as diverse and a place where everyone is not the same: "[Creekridge Park's] ethnically diverse and, um, it's not the kind of place you want to look if you want to live in a gated community, where everyone's exactly the same. This wouldn't be for you." Immediately following her description of difference, Ann highlights a "core of people" who have "similar" values:

> I think it's [a] pretty friendly neighborhood and you know, if you want to get involved with a neighborhood association, it's, like, very easy to do that and I think there's a lot of civic-minded people here who get involved with social justice causes, too. Like, the same people you see at the neighborhood meetings are also the ones who are campaigning for Obama, including us, and, like, they're always, you know, dealing with the, whatever issue is up, you know, environmental problems are up for debate in Durham. They're always— the same crowd is at those meetings, too, and so it just seems like a pretty neat core of people that tend to have similar liberal-leaning values around here, you know.

Although Ann discussed the importance of difference, she also emphasized the importance of sameness in this space, particularly for White homeowners. Interpreting diversity in this neighborhood in similar ways indicates that you are a part of the same white, urban, middle-class habitus. As Ann specified, if you do not have that same mindset, Creekridge Park "wouldn't be for you." In Chapter 4, we will see how conceptualizations of friendliness and inclusivity expressed by Whites do not extend to their Black and Latino/a neighbors.

Repeatedly using "diverse" as a neighborhood descriptor was a classifying practice among White residents. Appreciation of diversity situated Creekridge Park's White homeowners as distinct from other types of White homeowners who live in racially segregated, suburban, or newly developed housing. At the same time, while White homeowners have the broadest range of residential options and mobility among neighborhood residents, they still are restricted by their lower middle-class and middle-class social locations. As we saw at the beginning of the chapter, White residents had real financial constraints that brought them to Creekridge Park. At the same time, within the white, urban, middle-class habitus, a multiethnic and mixed-income neighborhood like Creekridge Park is highly valued. In addition to positively classifying the neighborhood space, this particular white, urban, middle-class habitus positively classifies its White residents. White Creekridge Park residents, as a result of the neighborhood's diversity and their appreciation of it, framed one another as open-minded and sensitive to issues of inclusion. Terry, who praised the Creekridge area for not emulating the homogeneous setting of *Weeds*, continued his comment by stating his preference for this kind of neighborhood: "Personally, we like the fact that we live in a diverse neighborhood where people are comfortable with that diversity. You know, that's, that's the positive thing about Durham in our opinion . . . as opposed to somewhere like Cary where everybody's, you know, wanting to be with, living next to people who are all like them."

Creekridge Park residents marked Cary as outside their particular white, urban, middle-class habitus. Residents read that particular residential space as closed-minded, conformist, or simply "blah" and "boring," as homeowner Judy described living in Raleigh. White homeowners in Creekridge Park were looking for other White homeowners who also appreciated "difference" in the form of non-White residents and unmanicured lawns. They sought out other individuals who enacted the same white, urban, middle-class habitus. As we see in the household survey data, Whites generally list other Whites as their closest friends.

The practice of lauding diversity while having mostly homophilous friendships may seem contradictory, but it is not. Diversity ideology demands acceptance of difference and nothing more. Under the guidelines of diversity ideology, the equitable incorporation of non-Whites into White networks is unnecessary, as we see when residents discuss the predominantly White neighborhood association in Chapter 3. White homeowners positively classify their homophilous White neighbors as potential allies when they observe them enact practices that are integral to this white, urban, middle-class habitus, such as appreciating diversity.

As a result, White residents who embody this white, urban, middle-class habitus classify the Creekridge Park residents who do not share these same ideas about diversity and acceptance as outsiders. Charles, an established homeowner in his early thirties who lives on Peach Avenue, stated that one of his neighbors has a "suburban mind-set about what constitutes, um, proper behavior for . . . property owners," which includes call-

TABLE 2.3 *Racial-ethnic identity of five closest friends based on survey data*

What is the racial-ethnic background of your five closest friends?

	White (N)	Asian (N)	Black (N)	Latino/a (N)	Other (N)
White residents					
Friend 1	53	2	4	4	0
Friend 2	53	2	1	2	4
Friend 3	55	0	2	2	3
Friend 4	50	0	3	5	2
Friend 5	51	1	3	2	1
Total (%)	86%	2%	4%	5%	3%
Non-White residents					
Friend 1	4	0	9	2	0
Friend 2	3	1	8	2	0
Friend 3	4	1	5	2	0
Friend 4	6	0	3	3	0
Friend 5	6	0	4	1	1
Total (%)	35%	3%	45%	15%	2%

ing city agencies, such as Neighborhood Improvement Services, to report his neighbors. He followed by clarifying, "I would say that that generally isn't the vibe that people have [in this neighborhood]." Charles's comments both affirm the normative nature of diversity ideology in Creekridge Park and point out that not all members of this neighborhood interpret living in a diverse neighborhood the same way. In my analysis, this difference in habitus is largely associated with a difference in perceived class position among White homeowners, since "[agents] choose, in the space of available goods and services, goods that occupy a position in this space homologous to the position they themselves occupy in social space."[20] At the end of the chapter, we meet Keith, whose experience in Creekridge Park elucidates this relationship between social position and habitus.

We see below that residents who enact the white, urban, middle-class habitus of Creekridge Park compare these in-neighborhood transgressors to other undesirables, such as White homeowners who live in Cary. As Alan stated, "Some people get upset about lawns and all that and grass cut and I just, to me, that's why I don't live in Cary, you know. And so, I don't care what people do with their lawns." Daniel affirmed that he finds these kinds of suburban regulations downright cruel and described his feelings toward homeowner association lawn regulations: "When I think about you know, the regulations they have in Cary and places like that or one of my co-workers is on the homeowner's association for her neighborhood, which is down by Southpoint [Mall] and it's a new neighborhood and you know, children's toys left in the front yard overnight is a violation and so, that seems so inhuman to me. Um, and it's, like, you know, you're so, you have so much extra time that in addition to keeping track of your own yard, you're keeping track of your neighbors' yards, too." Finally, Julie drew similar contrasts between Creekridge Park and newer developments: "We always joke that, like, someone who would choose to live in this neighborhood—like, we're not competing with Southpoint. Like, nobody would be like, 'Hm, like, a three bedroom tract house in Southpoint or live in Creekridge. I wonder.'" Drawing these distinctions between insiders and outsiders is inherent to any habitus and are "common sense" for those embedded in its practices. As participants in this white, urban, middle-class habitus, White homeowners in Creekridge Park continually distinguish between themselves and their suburban counterparts. By understanding diversity as acceptance, White residents of Creekridge Park classify themselves as accepting of difference and those who live in stigmatized areas as close-minded, concerned with conformity, and boring. At the same time, because of diversity ideology, those who enact this white, urban, middle-class habitus are able to laud diversity without focusing on outcomes or their own privileged positions. This process is largely unconscious due to the commonsense nature of diversity ideology within this habitus. By focusing on intentions and acceptance, deeper conversations about power are silenced before they even begin.

Diversity as Commodity

In Creekridge Park, White residents also perceived diversity as a commodity. In this white, urban, middle-class habitus, one of the normative responses to non-White bodies was a commodification of their otherness. By commodification I mean that non-Whites are treated as objects rather than people and are used by Whites for their own benefit and satisfaction. In Creekridge Park, what was most often commodified was the presence of non-Whites. The presence of Blacks and Latino/as in Creekridge Park is attractive to some White homeowners because it facilitates the definition of this multiethnic space as desirable. Philosopher Shannon Sullivan's work on whiteness identifies similar patterns. She writes, "Forbidden longings for contact with the non-white other that are generated out of habits of white domination paradoxically receive an expression that renders them invisible because they are consciously experienced as a wholesome desire for diversity."[21] So while inequitable power relations are at the root of commodifying practices, because of the diversity ideology these roots are obscured and the desires are framed positively by Whites. This is a great example of the "naturalness" of whiteness—Whites do not see themselves as oppressors and do not interpret their commodifying practices as such. As a result of the privileged position of Whites, the narrative that explains their desires and values as normal and universally beneficial becomes dominant.

Julie, a homeowner and newcomer who lives on Cardinal Street, mentioned her appreciation of the diversity in Creekridge Park:

> So what I love about, like, the Creekridge Park, like, most of the people around here, um, and most the people I know, like, love the fact that we have such a huge Latino population. Like, they love the restaurants, they love that the Food Lion [a regional grocery store generally located in lower middle-income neighborhoods] is stocked with, like, spices that you wouldn't normally get at a Kroger [a regional grocery story generally located in upper middle-income neighborhoods], and . . . that's like, a neat part about living here and not a drawback. And that most people in this neighborhood think that's fun.

The use of the word "fun" to describe the existence of the Latino/a communities in Creekridge Park is an excellent example of commodification. Julie and "most people" in Creekridge Park are pleased by the presence of Latino/as in the neighborhood because they influence what products are available at the neighborhood grocery store. Creekridge Park Latino/as provide both literal and figurative spice to the neighborhood.

The use of non-White bodies by Whites to designate neighborhood space as distinct from racially segregated suburbia is an important commodifying and classifying practice of this white, urban, middle-class habitus. Important to note here is that in Creekridge Park very few White residents have relationships with their non-White neighbors. Whites did, however, regularly refer to non-Whites during our interviews to signal neighborhood diversity and interracial interactions. For example, Ruth, an established resident who lives on Harris Street, listed several of her neighborhood friends by name throughout our conversation. When I asked her about interracial interactions, she responded that they occur around the neighborhood. I followed up by asking for specific examples of where she saw these interactions, and then she clarified:

RUTH: Well there's an interracial couple that lives right next door, so there's that. Um, I don't really see, no, I don't see it. I have to say I don't see it.

SARAH: So you don't see it, okay.

RUTH: I mean, I think it's, um, yeah that's an interesting thing to me. That, that's always been interesting, that there isn't that much mixing really, I guess. Well, there is some, um, my friend, our friend, here's another friend up the street—of course I keep coming up with more. Jill Lewis, who is African American, she's a good friend and comes to the parties at Kathleen's and then with Deena and um, but, none of the other. There's Hispanic families, you know, there's interaction in that, you know, I talk to Mr. Cameron across the street and these guys over here, and Kathleen, but not—I wouldn't say so much socially, other than Jill.

After she tried to remember more examples of interracial interactions, she identified Jill Lewis as her friend. This is not a question of whether Jill is actually Ruth's friend or not, but an example of a larger discursive pattern where non-Whites are used by White respondents to denote neighborhood diversity. This commodification of the presence of non-White residents allows White residents to positively classify themselves within the bounds of this white, urban, middle-class habitus by affirming that they live in a diverse neighborhood. This also happened when I spoke with Seth, an established homeowner, who described the neighborhood as diverse and immediately named the two African American women he knew on his block as evidence. I argue that the commodification of Blacks and Latino/as occurs when non-Whites are viewed as evidence of diversity in an environment that values diversity, such as the one created by this particular white, urban, middle-class habitus in Creekridge Park. This is troublesome because non-Whites are then seen as objects and symbols that represent an ideal (e.g., neighborhood diversity) rather than as individuals with varied interests, needs, and ways of being who may connect with White residents across a multitude of points. Commodification is a product of diversity ideology and its insufficient conceptualizations of diversity. In current discussions of diversity, non-White presence becomes the measuring stick rather than reciprocity, power-sharing, and other benchmarks of equity. By idealizing diversity without understanding power relationships, I argue, we objectify blackness and Latinidad, simultaneously valuing and devaluing them.

Diversity and the Status Quo

As an ideology without clear directives for structural change or a discussion of power differentials, diversity ideology serves as another framework that maintains the structural status quo. Without any emphasis on how race structures life chances or how equity should be guaranteed across groups, calls for diversity become a celebration of difference for the sake of difference. At the same time, acknowledgment of diversity and the importance of multicultural representation serve as markers of political progressiveness and membership in this particular white, urban, middle-class habitus. Since contemporary formulations of diversity do not connect to any real action, however, White residents only need to acknowledge the importance of diversity and its benefits to be classified positively within this white, urban, middle-class habitus.

The CPNA is a particularly good example of a group of residents who celebrate the neighborhood's diversity yet remain a white group—both demographically and politically. By demographically white I mean that the CPNA's membership is made up mostly of White residents; by politically white I mean that the CPNA's practices by and large exclusively support the interests of White homeowners. When I spoke with Beth, an active CPNA member, she explained why she thought Latino/a and Black residents were not actively involved in the neighborhood association or its board:

I mean to a certain extent it's, um, I mean, all of us got involved because we had a particular issue that the association helped us with. So maybe, to a certain extent, it's because, um, we haven't had folks, um, in the Latino community and Black community call on the association to help or that sort of thing. Um, but, you know, it's certainly is something that in—and associations can get kind of embroiled in zoning and police stuff and there might be. That's one of the reasons we liked the [community] garden [in Pine Grove Apartments]. We kind of envisioned the potential for the garden to be a place where we could diversify a little bit more. Um, but we haven't really figured out how to do that. Um, so it's something, you know, we gotta keep—

and then the block parties and stuff like that are a way to kind of seeing if we can get neighbors who are kind of averse to not, too busy
to join something can still be connected and know that they can call
somebody and voice their opinions.

Beth highlighted the entry point for White association members and
speculated why non-White members have not followed suit. She hypoth-
esized that certain political issues are not of interest to non-Whites in the
neighborhood, yet she never wondered how the CPNA's approach to subjects such as zoning and crime may affect non-Whites. The question for
the CPNA rarely, if ever, seems to be *What is the association doing that marks
this space as white or exclusive?* Rather, the failure of non-Whites to participate in the CPNA is presented as the issue. As long as predominantly
White organizations do not have explicitly exclusionary practices, diversity ideology protects them from having to question the lack of minority participation in their groups. Acceptance, however, is a measure of
intent—not of outcome. I discuss the CPNA in more detail in Chapter 3.

Since diversity ideology highlights presence and not power, living in a
multiethnic neighborhood can still reinforce the inequitable racial contract. In fact, because non-White, urban neighborhoods were (and still
are) consistently undervalued and disinvested in, being a White middle-
class homeowner in a mixed-race and mixed-income neighborhood has
some economic benefits. The financial gains gentrifiers have experienced
over the last few decades in the United States and abroad are a testament
to this pattern, as are the "affordable" mortgage rates and rents current
Creekridge Park residents claim.[22] During his interview, one real estate
agent stated that Creekridge Park was a good neighborhood for starter
homes. Starter homes, of course, provide an avenue for first-time homebuyers to build equity. The assumption is that young homeowners will
not permanently settle in their first home but see it as a temporary investment. In fact, a handful of the young White homeowners I interviewed
in 2010 and 2011 no longer live in Creekridge Park. Some relocated due
to work and others left because of their growing families. As household-
ers that do not need child-related amenities, young homeowners who
buy starter homes reap the benefits of their location and its affordability
without paying a premium for the well-funded schools generally found
in suburban areas or more affluent and less racially mixed urban neighborhoods.[23] This is a trend that economists Dan Black, Gary Gates, Seth
Sanders, and Lowell Taylor also identify for childless gay couples who

TABLE 2.4 Racial-ethnic composition of Creekridge Park Elementary

	Percentage
Black	47
Latino/a	45
White	8

TABLE 2.5 Type of school attended by children of White survey respondents

Type of school	Total children
Public	11
Charter/magnet	3
Private	7

"sort away" from suburban areas with high property taxes and property values that reflect resource-rich public schools.[24] In fact, when we look at the demographics for the children who attend the one neighborhood elementary school, they are overwhelmingly Black and Latino/a. None of the children of the White families I interviewed attended Creekridge Park Elementary School, even if they attended a public elementary school. In table 2.5 we see what type of schools the children of my White survey respondents attend.

Interestingly, one White resident did identify that some Whites use diversity to affirm their progressiveness without an interrogation of their own privilege. In a critique of another Durham neighborhood, Rhonda, an established resident, said she sees a problem when White homeowners fail to acknowledge their power in multiethnic spaces:

> Like this is what I really ran across, um, like, a lot of White families that wanted their neighborhood a certain way and they were definitely liberal, um, and, like, if, I just didn't like—they were all about diversity or, like, "look what we're doing," but almost in a "I'm better than you because," or not "I'm better than you," but, like, "look how great I am because I'm this liberal." Durham Elementary is changing, but when I was there or at least for the five years that I was there, like, it was 80 percent free and reduced lunch, so it was high poverty and so, like, the White families that would send their kids to Durham Elementary were like, "Oh, look at us, we're doing this great thing."

Like, I, just the sense of entitlement and privilege that sort of came with that neighborhood, I didn't really like. Where I don't feel like we have that as much in our neighborhood.

Although she says she does not find this kind of behavior as much in Creekridge Park, Rhonda did identify the privilege White residents wield in multiethnic environments and the social benefits they gain by living in traditionally undervalued locations. They not only dictate what they want their neighborhood to be (as we saw earlier with the neighborhood mandate enacted by White residents in regard to new housing developments), but they also distinguish themselves from other White homeowners by not participating in white flight. As cultural critic bell hooks states, however, "Meaningless commodification can remove the 'political integrity' of formerly meaningful signs of political/collective action."[25] Most Whites continue to live in highly segregated neighborhoods, so many White homeowners who choose to buy their home in a multiethnic space see it as a distinguishing political act.[26] Rhonda notes, however, that some White residents who commodify the presence of non-Whites and positively classify themselves within this white, urban, middle-class habitus fail to acknowledge their unique racial and class privilege. Therefore, the distinguishing act of living in a multiethnic space does not carry the same political meaning it would have in 1960, for example. In that sense, living in a multiethnic neighborhood has suffered from "meaningless commodification."

Here we see the importance of moving beyond good intentions. Instead of viewing living in a diverse neighborhood as a discrete act that fits in with one's identity as a good person, we must study the outcomes of our behaviors, regardless of intentions. By doing so, we see how specific actions, such as moving into a diverse neighborhood, may or may not challenge inequitable structural relations. In this way, studying outcomes is a counterideological act; diversity ideology dictates that all that matters in regard to race and ethnicity is intention. As my analysis shows, however, just because someone has good intentions (e.g., I want to live in a multiethnic rather than a racially segregated neighborhood) does not make him or her immune from reproducing race- and class-based inequality. In fact, the logic of diversity ideology enables White residents to reinforce the racial status quo by not acknowledging power differentials and only focusing on intentions. To further elucidate this point, in Chapter 3, I focus exclusively on the practices of White residents.

Diversity as Liability

The last form of diversity is invoked by White homeowners who interpret racial and economic diversity as a potential threat to their bodies and self-interests. Some residents see the downside to diversity as inevitable and integral to life in multiethnic spaces. There are generally two responses to this definition: (1) accept the downside as part of the character of Creekridge Park or (2) actively work to combat the negative by-products of diversity.

Ann, who moved to Creekridge Park from Boston with her husband, stated that they had a pattern of living in mixed neighborhoods:

> We always have gravitated towards that kind of, you know, kind of funky, diverse, affordable, you know, which also sometimes means that there's a lot of economic diversity, too, which is good and bad because I guess you're dealing with, um, you know, some people who are in real dire poverty living next door to houses that are, you know, really well taken care of and so, you know, which isn't always a bad thing, but sometimes I think there's some cultural clashes on the street because of that sort of issue. Not so much about race, it's more about really loud music and people who, you know, mow their lawns, and people who don't and people, you know, it's just kind of cultural behaviors, I guess, that al-, aren't always, you know, tied to ethnic backgrounds. It's just, I think it's more of a, a socioeconomic difference, maybe and some of the houses that, um, there's, there's places that there's just a whole lot of people living in a very small area and, and that always, kind of, can be problematic, noise-wise and stuff like that, but luckily we haven't, it's not really been a big deal for us.

Here Ann points out that when you live in an offbeat, diverse neighborhood, you encounter some predictable issues around cultural behaviors and class differences. Jamie, an established homeowner in an adjacent neighborhood, shared similar thoughts: "One of the joys of living in the neighborhood is how diverse it is. It also means that it's one of the challenges of living in the neighborhood because not everybody has the same investment in how the neighborhood is." As previously stated by other residents, accepting these "challenges" is generally part of this white, urban, middle-class habitus. There was some divergence in how residents approached these issues, although many adhered to some variation of established resident Ruth's proffered "live and let live." The individuals who took this approach were less likely to see non-Whites as a threat; as Ann stated, "It's not really been a big deal for us." Yet some White residents who accept the "liabilities" of diversity in the abstract nevertheless enact practices of interracial social control and social distance, as I will discuss in more detail in the next chapter.

Conversely, a subset of White homeowners agreed that these issues should not go unaddressed, especially since they affected the financial bottom line of residents. Brendan, a new homeowner in an adjacent neighborhood, belonged to the latter group:[27]

> I don't wanna live in a neighborhood of, you know, just, you know, manicured lawns and, like, well, nobody does in our neighborhood, you know. That's why we all live in the neighborhood, but, you know, we all want our neighborhood value to continue to rise as well. Deena, she's against gentrification in the neighborhood and there's a, big contingents of us that are for gentrification [laughs] in the neighborhood. You know, we don't want the neighborhood to, to go downhill and so, you know, there's a, there's a lot of us who, you know, there's some in the neighborhood, like Deena and others, who are constantly, you know, harping on any time anyone wants, you know, complains about another neighbor. And it's like, well, we have bad neighbors and, you know, we have trouble houses in the neighborhood and we, you know, you have to make those complaints for the neighborhood to get better and so she's always thinking that people are just targeting people and it's like . . . I think she, her and others have a big chip on their shoulder for something. . . . It's still a neighborhood that's you know, all on the rise, but it's not there yet. . . . I think everybody's kind of in consensus with that, you know, I mean, people are in, you know, um, in a mood to keep the neighborhood growing. I think Deena does too, I don't, you know, I don't think they want it to be a slum area, but, you know, I think she needs to realize that sometimes you do have to complain about your neighbors.

Brendan was happy to be in this diverse neighborhood without the manicured lawns, but he wanted to make sure that he controlled its growth and future. He does so by calling city services to report transgressions by his neighbors, such as weedy yards and presumed gang activity.

Lastly, living in an older and/or diverse neighborhood does not interest all Creekridge Park residents—a characteristic that classifies those individuals as outside this white, urban, middle-class habitus. Keith, an established homeowner on Peach Avenue, expressed his relationship to the neighborhood as follows:

KEITH: I ended up in this neighborhood because I was in [dire] financial straits. Um, I got a house just about as cheaply as you possibly could and not be in a bad area. Uh, otherwise I would probably not pick a neighborhood like this. . . . I like newer houses. Um, so the people that, that live in this neighborhood are the sort of people who would buy a house made in 1950 or older, something like that.

SARAH: Right, but that's not really, that wasn't really your initial interest.

KEITH: No, it was more, uh, necessity.

SARAH: Okay, do you see yourself potentially moving out of this neighborhood?

KEITH: No, I'm gonna work 'til I'm 150 probably, because of the financial duress [of my divorce] [*laughs*]. So, I'm gonna stay in a cheap house and there's no reason [to move] now that I'm by myself. It just makes more sense as long as, yeah.

Keith's description of the area and his admission that he does not appreciate the older homes that dominate the Creekridge Park landscape are excellent examples of Bourdieu's argument that "a work of art has meaning and interest only for someone who possesses . . . the code, into which it is encoded."[28] For White homeowners, the "beauty" of Creekridge Park—their ability to perceive it as beautiful—is in large part what comprises this white, urban, middle-class habitus; their taste furnishes that ability. Keith's situation also clarifies how one's habitus is intimately tied to one's structural position. Although Keith is a White homeowner just like Ruth, Emma, and Terry, his financial situation (both real and perceived) affects his dispositions, taste, and ways of being.

Keith's recounting also revealed his discomfort with other neighborhood elements:

Just out of convenience there's a gas station [on Cardinal Street], which I hate. Every time I go there I hate it, 'cause you, you can't get the guy's attention to turn the pump on and then there's a schizophrenic guy that hangs around. Just people that I don't feel safe around. So, I just kind of have and sometimes I feel, like, there's a racial thing. Like, I was driving through that area one time and there were these three girls walking out across the street and I'm slowed

down and they were, like, cursing at me and everything because I,
I don't know why, I mean they were walking across a busy street.
So, I feel, like, the reason that I get bad treatment at the grocery
store sometimes [is] sort of a reverse discrimination kind of thing.
Um, so, I'm just, I don't like that area over there, so I worry a little
bit, you know, about the neighborhood maybe bordering on some
not so good areas.

Keith is the only respondent who mentioned reverse discrimination specifically. He also is one of the only White homeowners I spoke with who
did not laud Creekridge Park as his ideal neighborhood. Although he does
not specify which groups he encountered, the area he referred to in his
quotation is predominantly Black and Latino/a. Toward the end of our
interview, I ask Keith if he sees interracial interactions across the neighborhood. He responded,

Like I say, I um, it doesn't seem like there's many Black people [in
the neighborhood]. I mean, I lived in a neighborhood before that's
one of the things that I really liked about it, 'cause it was just, it was,
like, the churches I've gone to that are just, like, they're like fif—
practically fifty-fifty. Um, I don't feel comfortable going to, like, a
church that's all White people. There's something wrong with that
to me, um, but it does just seem that, um, I'm trying to think, I don't
know. It just doesn't seem like there's many Black people, but maybe
it's just a little strip close to where I am.

Keith's quotation is a great example of the complexity of racial ideologies.
Through his remarks he illustrates that individuals can use multiple interpretations of non-Whites and diversity at the same time and that there
is never just a single dominant ideology.[29] At the grocery store and other
area businesses, Keith, using a frame of reverse discrimination to understand his experience, feels like a target because he is a White male. At
the same time, he enjoyed living in a neighborhood with Black residents
and sees interracial churches as normative. Keith's interpretation of a predominantly White Creekridge Park is most likely influenced by his location in majority White subregion five (see map 3). Despite being an out-
sider to the white, urban, middle-class habitus of Creekridge Park, Keith
still occasionally used diversity ideology frames to positively classify his
interracial experiences. This emphasizes the control and pervasiveness
of diversity ideology among White homeowners in Creekridge Park and

its reach beyond those who embody the dominant white, urban, middle-class habitus of the neighborhood.

CONCLUSION

Although many White homeowners in Creekridge Park chose to move to the neighborhood in part because of its affordability, it was not the only explanation that residents gave for their decision. Throughout the interviews, residents shared with me what the neighborhood was like, simultaneously telling me something about themselves. With these descriptions, I sketched a picture of the neighborhood's contemporary white, urban, middle-class habitus, which includes older housing stock, urban living, and diversity.

Diversity meant multiple things for my White respondents: diverse housing, lawns, sexual orientation, language, age, and skin color, to name a few. White residents lauded these elements of diversity as positive features of their neighborhood but sometimes saw them as unfortunate downsides of an affordable neighborhood. The presence of non-Whites marked this neighborhood as a desirable space in line with the taste of a particular type of White homeowner. It simultaneously marked other spaces, whether new developments or racially segregated suburbs, as undesirable, conservative, and sterile.

I argue, however, that the acceptance of non-White bodies in this neighborhood does not signal a change in the racial structure. Residents of Creekridge Park used the "difference" found in cities and their choice to participate in it as a signal of status and taste. Some also gained wealth through the purchase of starter homes in this changing neighborhood, which we know is an important contributor to contemporary racial inequality.[30] In contrast, the narratives residents used to explain their move to Creekridge Park largely emphasized taste rather than economic processes. For those who embody Creekridge Park's white, urban, middle-class habitus, diversity ideology redefines the presence of non-Whites and attributes desirable political and social standing to them. By drawing upon contemporary cultural values, such as diversity and inclusivity, White homeowners are able to reap the social and cultural benefits of inhabiting this space, positively classifying themselves as open-minded in contrast to the boring, close-minded residents of suburbia. In addition, White homeowners in Creekridge Park are able to collect the economic benefits of buying property in this "affordable" neighborhood. Although

Creekridge Park is not a gentrified neighborhood in the traditional sense, White residents still use the language and behaviors researchers generally associate with those areas to mark this urban space as desirable. The distinctions drawn between themselves and their suburban counterparts, however, are not performed with the intention or acknowledgment that these actions will make them "different."[31] These distinctive dispositions and the white, urban, middle-class habitus that includes them are understood as "naturally" occurring by residents. Therefore, those who embody this habitus are not necessarily aware of the inequitable ramifications of their way of being—they do not have to be. As a result of their social position and the tenets of diversity ideology, White Creekridge Park residents can maintain their privilege while positively classifying themselves as open-minded and accepting.

Diversity ideology does not dictate any political action or economic restructuring, so living in a multicultural environment is enough to act in accordance with the tenets of the ideology. Based on the logic of diversity ideology, since living in this neighborhood solidifies one's commitment to inclusivity, having non-Whites in your social network is a nonessential practice. Some residents do acknowledge that there could be more interracial interactions, but their evaluation ends there. In general, residents do not acknowledge their power as White homeowners in this multiracial neighborhood. For example, Bryan's explanation that addressing violations posted on some White homeowners' yards was merely a matter of knowing "the right person to squawk at" did not acknowledge how race and class privilege undoubtedly impacted the unfolding of these events. Being listened to, taken seriously, and not seen as threatening when challenging an authority is not a privilege shared by everyone. This enactment of privilege is not viewed as such when the resolution is described as a result of individual-level knowledge rather than structurally organized processes. In a multiethnic and mixed-income neighborhood where social life is structured by large processes of inequality, failure to recognize differential power produces a situation where truly equitable interracial interactions are not possible. Although White residents occasionally acknowledge their privilege as Whites in an abstract way, they do not see themselves as wielding advantages on a day-to-day basis. Knowing whom to squawk at is deemed idiosyncratic rather than structurally grounded. White residents are, therefore, able to maintain their dominance within the neighborhood association and the neighborhood without questioning their own social location. The neighborhood association, as you will soon see, is not just a social organization that plans picnics and block parties. It brandishes real power at the city level. Its members are embroiled in Durham political discussions: writing letters, as neighborhood representatives, in support of or against legislation; speaking at city council and other local political meetings; and even passing a neighborhood mandate to regulate neighborhood development. In the next chapter, I discuss how diversity ideology impacts neighborhood-based norms of interracial and intraracial contact to preserve White homeowners' race- and class-based privileges.

CHAPTER 3 *Neighboring from a Distance*

> *I'll definitely infringe upon people's, maybe people's sense*
> *of uh, space. . . . A lot of the properties that I walk right*
> *onto and pick up trash they're all rentals, so I could care,*
> *you know. 'Cause it's my neighborhood.*
>
> —LUKE, White homeowner, newcomer

The more time I spent in Creekridge Park, the more apparent the prac-tices of the white, urban, middle-class habitus became. In the epigraph, Luke, a newcomer on Colony Street, highlights an important aspect of life in Creekridge Park: White homeowners, many of whom are recent ad-ditions to the neighborhood, not only assume they are entitled to set the norms of the neighborhood but, because of race and class privilege, are able to do so.

In this chapter, I describe the different interracial and intraracial codes of conduct White individuals and groups enact in Creekridge Park. I call these "white codes," a reference both to the black codes of the 1860s and to the group they benefit. Although the state does not legislate them, white codes mimic the control of non-White bodies and the maintenance of the racial status quo achieved by black codes after the Civil War.[1] White codes, which in this context dictate appropriate neighborhood behavior between and among racial groups, produce mostly monoracial social net-works and maintain high social distance despite physical proximity be-tween White, Black, and Latino/a residents. I focus on these codes be-cause they constitute the dominant mode of interaction as a result of the race and class privilege of Creekridge Park's White homeowners. I also discuss the experiences of some White residents who have more contact with their non-White neighbors than the average White resident. These relationships, while still impacted by a stratifying social structure, were more intimate and reciprocal.

This chapter is not meant to include an exhaustive list of white codes. Rather, the codes discussed below are examples of three main processes that maintain social distance between racial groups: (1) seemingly nonracial practices produce racialized outcomes; (2) nonracial narratives are used to obscure racialized practices; and (3) non-White racial-ethnic status acts in conjunction with other markers of status (e.g., real or assumed class) to maintain high interracial social distance. For example, because of differential power across race and class lines, well-intentioned actions by White homeowners, including efforts to "green" the neighborhood, marginalized non-White residents and negatively marked their behaviors and spaces. Not only do these three processes and the codes of conduct they encompass maintain high social distance between Black, Latino/a, and White residents, but they also fail to provide the positive interracial interactions traditional segregation and integration research promise.

WHITE IS UNIVERSAL

The Creekridge Park Neighborhood Association (CPNA) served as a rich site of residential socialization. It taught residents how to interact with neighbors, city officials (e.g., city council members), and city services (e.g., Neighborhood Improvement Services). For example, when a new class of fraternity members from a local university moved into the neighborhood in the fall, CPNA board members went over with a welcome letter that included information on how to be a good neighbor.[2] The association also instructed members about the range of entitlements they shared. For instance, the CPNA reminded residents via the online listserv that they should call the police when they have noise complaints to create a record of incidents. The neighborhood association and its members believed that the CPNA was a universally beneficial organization that all residents should support. Its history, a board membership that included only White homeowners, and a general membership comprised predominantly of White homeowners, however, made it neither universal nor apolitical, but white.

One entitlement of CPNA membership is the ability to represent neighborhood interests. Below is a quotation from Beth, a White CPNA board member, who responded as follows when I asked her if the board represented the association or the neighborhood: "We speak for the whole neighborhood. . . . Because I know there's plenty of people who are paying attention who are not a part [of the CPNA] or a member and that sort of thing and that's the way it's set up and the organizational structure in the city. Um, and so, you know, um, just because you don't write your senator and your congress about something doesn't mean that they're not representing you. . . . It's how local stuff gets done." Beth saw herself and the CPNA board as a continuation of local politics and the democratic process. Neighborhood association members elected the CPNA board every year, although no position had more than one person vying for it while I was in the field. Traditionally, outgoing board members first decide whether they want to run again, and then the nominations committee, which is comprised of nonboard and board members, identifies Creekridge Park residents who may be positive additions and willing to participate to fill the remaining positions. As described in Chapter 1, association members in attendance vote on the new board slate every fall at a neighborhood picnic; between thirty and forty neighbors came to the neighborhood picnic during my fieldwork. If we use households as the unit of analysis, forty represents less than a 7 percent voter turnout. Those who voted on the board were not demographically representative of the neighborhood: at the neighborhood picnic I attended, over 90 percent of the attendees were homeowners and over 85 percent were White.

During our interview, Beth continued to discuss neighborhood representation:

BETH: If we have a diverse enough board and we have people who would
   do a good enough job, we're gonna have a good difference in opinion
   arise and arrive at a reasonable opinion. So, that's, I guess I trust
   the process of everybody kind of pitching in with their feelings and
   their thoughts and you work it out and you educate each other and
   you make a decision. And you make, you know, I think we've been
   careful that our board always has people from different parts of the
   neighborhood. Um . . .
SARAH: Like geographically you mean?
BETH: Geographically, yeah. And we don't have African American, we
   don't have Hispanic and that's something we're aware of that we
   need to be paying more attention to, and I don't think we necessarily
   represent those issues and needs.

This quotation indicates Beth's confidence in the organization and its ability to properly represent the neighborhood. She acknowledges that the association does not represent the "issues and needs" of Black and Latino/a residents, but she does not present this as a challenge to her previous statement. The lack of minority representation could have represented a threat to the legitimacy of the board, but ultimately, the *universality* and *neutrality* of the organization trumped any potential conflict.

Beth interprets the association as a universal and race-neutral organization, not a white one. Those who support and implement seemingly race-neutral policies, however, often ignore how race already affects the creation and application of these policies. Race-neutral policies, because of the inequitable structural organization of race in the United States, produce racialized outcomes and maintain the status quo.[3] So while the CPNA may present itself and its practices as value-free, neither can be universal within our racially structured society.

As our conversation continued, Beth pointed out that Black and Latino/a residents did not use the neighborhood association as a resource. She viewed the lack of minority involvement as a reflection of the personal choices of non-White residents rather than the political climate of the organization. Work on predominantly White spaces, however, has helped elucidate the particular politics of predominantly White organizations, underscoring and challenging important facets of white privilege—including the assumption that all-White spaces are inherently welcoming to non-Whites.[4] Yet Beth did not see the racial makeup of the CPNA as a problem it needed to solve; if residents of color wanted the association to better represent "those issues and needs," they could have chosen to participate in the existing organization.

While other White residents did not think the neighborhood association represented all neighborhood residents, their critiques of the organization's limited representation were not connected to the organization's whiteness. For example, Ray, an established White homeowner and CPNA member, said that the association is representative of "the people who show up. I think any pretense that it's representative of the neighborhood would be completely crazy. It's people who want to do the work." Similarly, White newcomers and renters Thomas and Denise explained that they thought the neighborhood association only represented part of the neighborhood. They connected this pattern to certain "barriers to involvement," including the association's reliance on online communication and some residents' lack of leisure time. Denise elaborated: "I mean if I was holding down two jobs to make ends meet, this would not be a high priority." Although Thomas and Denise identify important class-based obstacles to participation, they, along with Beth and Ray, do not make the connection between the racial state of the neighborhood association and why non-Whites were less likely to participate. In contrast, my interviews with non-White residents indicate that being the only non-

White person at a CPNA meeting influenced their decisions not to attend events. See Chapter 4 for more on this topic.

A corollary of the universality of whiteness is the normalization of whiteness and all-White spaces. All-White spaces in Creekridge Park include neighborhood events, informal social gatherings, and neighborhood businesses. For example, the neighborhood association meetings I attended in Creekridge Park were consistently all-White meetings. Unarticulated whiteness allows Whites to mark these spaces as universal and generic. Whiteness scholars have pointed out that race may not be directly addressed, but it is understood as "subtext" in white, racially segregated spaces.[5] This subtext, however, is readable when non-Whites enter these spaces. Jerry, a Black established homeowner, provided an example: "I notice that even when, a lot of times I go over there [to my White neighbor's house], it's only me, the only Black person there. You follow what I'm talking about? And so, I'm always like [taps], all—these—folks [laughs], you understand what I'm talking about? Suppose they just have a flashback, and I'd be hung from one of them trees back here? You follow where I'm coming from? So, I don't know what's on their mind. I know what's on mine [laughs]." So while Whites may view all-White spaces as safe and comfortable, non-Whites may find them alarming. Jerry went on to describe his feeling at these all-White events as "apprehensive," particularly because of the constant potential for microaggressions, including conversations with racial undertones that reference "them people" and "crack heads." Jerry's experience, which parallels those described in studies on minorities in predominantly white spaces and institutions, presents a challenge to the universality and inclusivity of these white gatherings.[6]

HOUSING TENURE

White residents in Creekridge Park had a set of narratives they used to explain their social relationships in the neighborhood. I found that although their claims capture important patterns of relationship building, they also obscure the racialized processes that perpetuate all-White social networks. For instance, many White homeowners stated that they only invested in neighbors they thought would be around for a while, specifically naming other White homeowners as examples. A few also mentioned that they only invested in neighbors with whom they shared a common interest, such as dog walking or gardening.

TABLE 3.1 Attitudes toward renters based on survey data

Do you think the percentage of renters should increase, stay the same, or decrease?

	Percentage of Creekridge Park Residents
Renters	
Increase	55
Stay the same	14
Decrease	32
Owners	
Increase	2
Stay the same	53
Decrease	45

Housing tenure (i.e., whether you own or rent your home) was one of the central ways that residents described one another and assessed class and value similarities and/or differences. I found a generally negative attitude toward renters in the survey data. Homeowners were more likely to state that they would prefer the number of renters to decrease, as table 3.1 shows. In contrast, based on my interview data, renters tended to distinguish between good and bad neighbors rather than the renter-homeowner divide that some homeowners use. When describing why their relationships with their neighbors were generally monoracial, White homeowners mentioned the transitional nature of renters. Graduate students at one of the many nearby universities comprised an active subset of White homeowners in Creekridge Park. These owners, however, generally stayed in the area for only three to six years, depending on their program of study. This was a short stay in comparison with some renters who have lived in the neighborhood for ten, fifteen, or twenty years. At the same time, these homeowners were some of the best-incorporated and most well-known across the neighborhood. Many of the White graduate student homeowners involved themselves in the neighborhood association and took positions as board members. Other residents even referred to the inevitable relocations of these graduate students as a "loss" for the neighborhood. Their short tenure, in turn, was clearly not an impediment for the establishment of relationships between them and other neighbors. Consequently, length of tenure on its own is not a sufficient explanation for Whites' monoracial networks, but when we consider it along with racial-ethnic identity, it helps unfold important relational dynamics in Creekridge Park.

Data from non-White residents indicate that residents constructed judgments about similarity, difference, and neighbor compatibility using dominant ideologies and contextually specific data about race and class. For example, Cheryl, a Black homeowner and established resident who lives on Pine Avenue, shared a story of how her neighbors did not greet her until her fifth or sixth year in the neighborhood, when she started planting flowers in her front yard. Her work schedule had kept her from doing so beforehand:

> When I started doing stuff in my neighborhood, my neighbors knew me so little that they stopped to introduce themselves to me and welcome me to the neighborhood. Now what was interesting is that nobody did that when I moved here. But when I was—and now, a number of reasons that that could've been. Because these same folks, many of whom were here when I moved here, started welcoming me. And I'm talking about not just this street [Pine Avenue], but people down on Harris and, and on, Cardinal Street. . . . And so they saw me in, working in the yard and they'd stop and they commented about the yard and commented and introduced themselves and asked how long I had been here because they couldn't imagine that the person that had been here for five years and hadn't done anything was now doing something [*laughs*].

Cheryl's neighbors, most of whom are White,[7] did not greet her until she shared a safe and familiar practice: planting in the front yard. Gardening, however, is not a value-free practice. Gardening and community gardens in particular are commonly associated with contemporary urban neighborhoods, especially those with gentrifying elements.[8] It is part of the white, urban, middle-class habitus. Cheryl's neighbors filtered their interactions with Cheryl through cultural schemas of blackness as well as neighborhood-specific understandings of blackness. Members of the dominant group viewed Black residents as renters, lower income, and disinvested. By challenging her neighbors' assumptions about who she was by working in her garden, Cheryl became approachable and someone worth engaging with. Although Cheryl's example indicates how a multiethnic neighborhood could potentially produce positive interracial interactions, it also shows how the basis of these interactions must be presumed similarity. In this case, home investment, gardening, and assumed class served as the bridging elements.

HOMEOWNER DOMINANCE

White homeowners also participated in practices that established and maintained their control of Creekridge Park through the neighborhood association and as independent actors. This establishment of homeowner dominance was based in White homeowner entitlement. In this next section, I problematize the normativity of the interests of White homeowners and question the assumptions that are taken for granted about homeowners and renters.

Scott, a White established homeowner and CPNA board member, mentioned during his interview that homeowners were more likely to invest in the neighborhood and the neighborhood association. As a follow-up question, I asked him if other people in the neighborhood felt the same way about renters. He responded,

> I would guess, I would think that a lot of the people in the neighborhood are um, pragmatists, but they also, I mean, there's a lot of um, bigger sort of social understanding and a desire to kind of not live in a gated neighborhood. Um, so I think people recognize that that's a positive thing, but, um, it's probably one reason also people are a little bit more politically involved and a little bit more involved in the neighborhood association because it's not the type of neighborhood where you just sit back . . . and let a set of rules sort of take care of everything. You have to kind of continuously be involved and be sure that, um, with all that change going on that, that there's, um, that you're watching out for the quality of life in the neighborhood. So it takes a little bit more effort maybe to live in the neighborhood like ours.

This quotation highlights the importance of relationality, a concept sociologist Evelyn Nakano Glenn uses in her integrative framework for race and gender analyses. Glenn proclaims that generally in discussions of inequality "the dominant category is rendered 'normal' and therefore 'transparent' while the other is the variant and therefore 'problematic.'"[9] Hence "relationality helps point out the ways in which 'differences' among groups are systematically related" and problematizes the dominant categories.[10] Using relationality to understand the renter-homeowner relationship, we can question some of the taken-for-granted assumptions about renter engagement. Rather than accept that renters are less likely to be engaged in neighborhood issues, we can interrogate why homeowners participate in neighborhood associations. For example, does "pragmatism" in the form of neighborhood engagement serve specific race and class agendas? Indeed, Scott's quotation indicates that involvement in the CPNA is very closely tied to class- and race-based goals: White homeowners in Creekridge Park want to live in a neighborhood with mixed housing that is different from "cookie-cutter" or "gated" suburbia, reflecting their white, urban, middle-class habitus and distinguishing them from other types of White homeowners. At the same time, their neighborhood must also grow in the ways they dictate to preserve their race and class privilege. One way White homeowners are able to accomplish this is by controlling the neighborhood association. If the CPNA, therefore, functions as an organization that maintains the race and class privileges of White homeowners, it fundamentally excludes renters as an independent interest group. The association could incorporate individual renters if the renters reflect the appropriate race-class agenda, but not as people with independent, let alone opposing, needs.

One way homeowners maintain control of the neighborhood association is through the CPNA's advertising practices: (1) the online email listserv and (2) the quarterly newsletter. There are limits to the reach of the online listserv, which numerous residents also pointed out to me. In addition to needing a computer to subscribe, many residents are not even aware it exists. For example, during our interview, Michelle, a newcomer but a remote White homeowner, stated that she did not know there was a listserv until I mentioned it. She had told her new tenants that there was no listserv when they asked. The online listserv is currently comprised of over 250 members, although some of these are nonresidents, including Durham officials, who update subscribers about city matters, and representatives from local universities, whose students reside in the neighborhood. About 50 percent of my survey respondents and 55 percent of my interview respondents subscribed to the listserv.

The CPNA also had a quarterly newsletter hand-delivered by volunteers to houses across the neighborhood. Both owners and renters occupied these houses. Inside the neighborhood, however, large complexes, including Pine Grove Apartments, hold hundreds of apartments. Volunteers did not deliver the newsletter to each apartment; they placed it in common areas within the complexes. This meant residents had to notice it and stop to read it. Charles, a White former CPNA board member and established resident, elaborated:

CHARLES: I mean, so, certainly, certainly there's kind of a communication gap with Pine Grove [Apartments], I mean, I think that certainly anybody who wanted to shell out a membership, $5 for a membership would get a vote, even though there's a really, a huge concentration of people there, right, so, if everybody in Pine Grove voted and wanted to vote in representatives or board seats from Pine Grove, you know, it could really be the Pine Grove neighborhood association. Um, in practice that doesn't happen and it's, there may be a part of that that's about the incentive structure and, you know, the fact that they're renting means that they're not as engaged. Um, that's your economist views of things. I think that's a little bit, rough, as an understanding of how this stuff works. I do think though that the people who are in the single-family duplexes or single-family houses or duplexes seem to be the ones who come regardless of whether they own or rent. Um, part of that, part of that is communication. Um, we have a, we distribute newsletters four times a year to the owner-occupied houses and we post them in Pine Grove, but we don't give every single person a copy, um, part of that's logistical, part of it's financial. You know, and I, you know, that, that probably is problematic. Um . . .

SARAH: How so?

CHARLES: Well, it just in terms of you know, extending the franchise equally across, across the area that we cover, that we represent, that we claim, you know, if you come home at night and there's a newsletter hanging on your door you're probably going to read it. If you come home at night and there's no newsletter hanging on your door and you pass the manager's office and there's, there's a newsletter posted on the bulletin board, you might read it or you might just sort of go, oh, huh. And keep going and so, I guess there is . . . Do newsletters facilitate engagement? I don't know.

Charles acknowledged that the advertising practices of the CPNA had the potential to disenfranchise the residents of Pine Grove Apartments. He then questioned the importance of newsletters in eliciting participation, despite the fact that he recognized that residents of single-family homes and duplexes participated because they received direct communications from the neighborhood association. Non-White residents were less likely to get the newsletter and were subsequently less likely to be aware of the association and neighborhood events and therefore were less likely to participate. Charles might have hesitated to say firmly one way or the other whether newsletters facilitate engagement because he realizes the inequity of the distribution process. Charles, reflecting national conversations on equity, seems to have concerns over the lack of equal opportunity in this case, not the unequal outcomes. In the end, these advertising practices, however, were not a major enough concern for Charles or the neighborhood association, as the CPNA maintained the same procedures and continued to primarily function as a homeowner-based association.

In addition, some White homeowners used their privilege to assert their dominance over renters independent from the CPNA, as White newcomer Luke describes below. During his interview, he boasted about how he cleaned up the neighborhood and picked up trash whenever he saw it, including going onto neighbors' lawns: "I'll definitely infringe upon people's, maybe people's sense of uh, space. . . . A lot of the properties that I walk right onto and pick up trash they're all rentals, so I could care, you know. 'Cause it's my neighborhood." Luke's comments indicate a clear privileging of homeowner interests over renters' rights, seemingly contradicting his previous statements that in Creekridge Park "we just like to have . . . your own space." Luke's assertion of his right to pick up trash is a clear endorsement of the neighborhood's homeowner dominance code.

LATINO/A INCORPORATION

During interviews or board meetings, CPNA board members occasionally mentioned the need to involve the neighborhood's Latino/a communities. After a year of repeating the same goals, however, no Spanish translation for the newsletter existed, and all board meetings and neighborhood events were held in English with no Spanish translation.[11] One White homeowner who was more active in the association a couple of years ago stated that during his involvement with the CPNA "there was a lot of, you know, sort of appropriate interest expressed in having the association reflect the demographics of the neighborhood, so, you know, I can't remember if it's like that, but talk about having the newsletter in Spanish and English, having some Spanish-speaking to invite people to come to events, that sort of thing. Um, nothing ever happened actually as a result, as far as I could tell." This emphasis on the incorporation of the Latino/a community was part of a larger citywide narrative of inclusion across neighborhoods, universities, and employers. For example, Duke University's Office of Durham and Regional Affairs, which managed all of the university's community involvement, had a program especially for Latino/a community outreach and engagement.[12]

Bilingual flyers for neighborhood events became a more common practice toward the end of my fieldwork. One neighborhood block party even included representatives from a local Latino/a nonprofit organization. A folding table with information on drunk driving, a practice commonly attributed to Latino male drivers in Durham, and small plastic baggies were the extent of the nonprofit's presence. These plastic baggies contained a bilingual pamphlet on drunk driving laws, a Spanish pamphlet on alcoholism, a business card for an outreach coordinator at the nonprofit organization, and two condoms. Based on the contents of the baggies, it seems unlikely that the nonprofit knew the purpose of the event, which was a family-oriented block party, and they simultaneously reduced their efficacy and stigmatized Latino/as at this event. In addition, within this white space, the narrative of Latino/a drunkenness is perpetuated and Latino/as are inaccurately marked with these negative behaviors. The number of local DUI arrests for Latino males is not due to a higher rate of Latino/a drunk driving in comparison with other racial-ethnic groups, but to the gender and age composition of the Latino/a population in Durham, which skews younger and male. Young men, regardless of racial-ethnic identity, are the most at risk for driving under the influence.[13]

Only one Latino family was in attendance that day—they rented a home a few houses down from the party's location on Central Street. When I later interviewed newcomer Juliana, the female family member, she stated that she was unfamiliar with the neighborhood association; she went to the block party because the flier was in Spanish and it said they were invited. She also said the presence of the Latino/a nonprofit organization positively influenced her and her husband's decision to attend. At the event, Juliana and her husband stood by the nonprofit's table while her son, Marcos, played. Juliana said her son and the other kids at the party had some trouble communicating, but Marcos was still able to play some of the games that had been set up by party organizers. This block party, which took place on the street rather than in a single home, seemed to attract a more multiethnic crowd than the annual picnic, although it was still predominantly White. As I was leaving, I noticed that a block party attendee, who I believe was a Creekridge Park resident (there were some nonresidents in attendance), began to talk to Juliana, who had until that point stood quietly with her husband on the party's perimeter. When I asked Juliana later on during her interview if she would attend the block party again, she said she did not know. She did not seem particularly enthusiastic about her experience, but she may have felt uncomfortable saying so since she initially assumed I was affiliated with the block party organizers.

GOOD INTENTIONS

In the United States, we often understand issues of race and inequality in moral and individualistic terms—good and bad people do good and bad things, respectively. This isolationist framework, however, fails to capture the systemic nature of racial inequality and contemporary racial matters and how well-intentioned people in positions of power can produce inequitable outcomes when they fail to consider power differentials and their own privilege. Similarly, when my White respondents enacted good intentions, their actions—which may seem benevolent from their perspective—were actually ways to control non-White renters and homeowners. This is, in part, because White homeowners failed to understand how their actions were not universally good. Their lack of understanding could have been avoided had they engaged in a more thorough reflection of their power and social position and had more intimate and reciprocal relationships with the residents of color they were interacting with.

In 2008, the CPNA applied for and received a grant to create a community garden in the middle of the neighborhood's largest apartment complex, Pine Grove Apartments. Two White female homeowners from the neighborhood association spearheaded the effort. After getting approval from the property manager, they advertised the plots, had a local nonprofit organization till the soil, and created plots for each participant. They saw this as an opportunity to connect with the mostly non-White apartment residents, potentially diversify their organization, and continue to stabilize what was once, according to one of the organizers, a "gang-ridden and drug-ridden" complex. They ran into a few issues, however. Sharon, one of the current organizers and a White established homeowner, explained:

> And we were trying to foster some leadership within the garden or the participants, trying to get them to take it over because there's also this dynamic where it's us versus them, like I've talked about

our side and their side of the neighborhood. Like, there's Pine Grove Apartments and there was, like, CPNA coming in, like, the home-owners coming in and telling the renters what to do and so it was the dynamic between the two groups. Um, and uh, so it's, it's really hard to keep it going. . . . We haven't been able to identify a true leader within the participants who wants to take it on, like they, it's one of those things where they just want to show up and do it. They don't wanna take it to that next step. Um, so and there were some other issues. This one lady, she turned out to be great, but whenever Ruth [the other organizer] was getting it started it was that issue of, um, "you White people are coming in and telling us what to do" kind of dynamic and, um, I don't know what happened but when-ever I came in and started working with them she was very apprecia-tive and it was like nothing, no bad ill will had even been there so there was that issue, too.

When I interviewed Ruth, a White established homeowner and one of the initial organizers, she elaborated on what happened: "[One apartment resident accused the organizers] of being racists because we, I mean she [Harriette, the apartment resident] came in without following protocol, you know. We have contracts, you sign and you pay for your plot and its very minimal, but you pay for your plot and she just ignored all of that and came and showed up, with her tiller. So they called me, I couldn't be there that evening and it was a pretty horrible conversation with her telling me it was none of my business that us White people should, you know, we, its none of our business." Sharon and Ruth explained that Harriette was given a plot after contacting a local nonprofit organization to plead her case and threatening legal action. Harriette then gardened without any further issues, although according to some of my White respondents, a couple of apartment residents refused to return to the garden while Har-riette was a participant.

I recount this event because it highlights how Ruth assumed good in-tentions were enough to avoid any inequitable outcomes in the commu-nity garden. She was clearly upset by Harriette's accusation of racism. Harriette's reaction, however, highlights how planning the garden with-out input from Pine Grove residents exacerbated existing racial and class inequities. The project did not really belong to the residents of Pine Grove Apartments but, rather, to the members of the CPNA. This may also ex-plain why Sharon did not find residents willing to take on the organizational responsibilities of the garden. In the end, the community garden fulfilled the CPNA's agenda of outreach and did not take into consideration the ideas or practices of Pine Grove residents. In this way, it also reflects larger patterns of paternalism between White homeowners and non-White renters, which I discuss later in this chapter.

In another instance, Tammy, a White established homeowner, began watching an unknown neighbor's backyard with binoculars to observe how the family treated their dog, Minnie. Tammy reported that after watching the dog, she went over to the house of the Latino/a family in question, introduced herself to the male head of the household, and offered to build her neighbors a bigger doghouse. Tammy described the situation as follows:

> But that one [dog], um, I just, I was going there, I went in the backyard with binoculars cause I, cause their, I couldn't see the dog from the street. I didn't even know they were tying her up and, um, they had her in a box. Um, a wooden box they cut out a hole for, I guess when she was really little. But I mean, the box was as big as underneath this chair and she couldn't fit in it [*starts crying*]. So, I was trying to see for myself what the deal was and so, there's a woods behind there, so I went there with binoculars and the dad came home just as I was looking [*small laugh*] and I was also trying to find another dog that was barking incessantly and I thought, "There's something wrong with this dog," and everybody was complaining about it, but nobody knew where the dog lived. And, and from here I couldn't tell where the barking was coming from and they also kept it kinda hidden, so I couldn't tell. So I was trying to see both dogs and the dad came home, so, I lied and I just said, you know, "I'm just trying to look at the other dog to see what the deal is." And he spoke some English, but it's not like you could have a whole conversation with him. He understood some but like not every word and the mother understands only a little, tiny bit and, um, so I asked him if he wanted a doghouse and he said yes, so he came by and picked up the doghouse and so that's the way I started with that. And then I, and then I said, "Would you like me to take her for a walk? It seems like she's tied up all the time," and he said that, that I could. And then, then when I'd come in the afternoons and they'd [the kids] come running up to me and they'd say, "You're gonna take her for a walk?" They loved her. They just didn't . . . know . . . what to do with her.

After Tammy took over dog-walking duties and started watching Minnie all day while the kids were at school, the Latino/a family asked Tammy for help with placing her in another home. When I interviewed Tammy, Minnie was under her care while she tried to find Minnie a suitable home; Tammy's requirements included a fenced-in backyard, doggie door, another dog to play with, and young, active owners. She mentioned that there was an older, active couple who wanted to adopt Minnie, but she did not allow it because they were too old for a young dog.

Tammy felt justified in judging her Latino/a neighbors' pet care as inferior because she had good intentions. Her candidness in our interview about her initial dishonesty with the neighbor and her standards for dog care indicate that she expected me to understand and sympathize with her concern for Minnie over her treatment of her Latino/a neighbors. Her interactions with this Latino/a family were also not an aberration, as she regularly intervened when she felt people mistreated their dogs around the neighborhood. In fact, during the interview she mentioned that the Latino/a family that owned Minnie got another dog after they gave Minnie to Tammy, and she "got involved with him," too. Tammy explained, "It's a different story every—every time [I approach a family], but basically it's the same reason." She failed to see her views and expectations of dog care as culturally specific and not universally good. Although it is possible that Tammy may intervene when she sees White residents mistreating animals, the two examples she shared with me during her interview were of Latino/a families. Tammy sees these racialized outcomes, however, as the results of nonracial processes (e.g., well-intentioned interventions for inadequate dog owners). This finding is in line with previous research on the relationships between pets and their owners, which indicates that what dogs mean to families and the ways they believe they should treat dogs can differ across race and class lines.[14] Using her race and class privilege, Tammy attempted to shape her neighbors' pet care behavior through daily interventions. This resulted in her neighbors offering Minnie to her so Tammy could place her as she saw fit. Both Ruth and Tammy illustrate how individuals, by not taking power differentials into account, can enact whiteness through well-intentioned actions.

GREENING CREEKRIDGE PARK

The community garden, which I previously mentioned, is just one example of a larger commitment to "greening" the neighborhood by the association and its members. Regardless of the intentions of White home-owners, non-White spaces, including Tyler Street, were negatively framed by their narratives about neighborhood green space. Although a seem-ingly universal good, within this neighborhood context, the emphasis on green space and landscaping exacerbated other neighborhood issues related to development and homeowner-renter relations. Ideas about crime and traffic reduction also informed some proactive ventures to create and protect green spaces across the neighborhood. Some respon-dents pointed to landscaping as an important way to indicate that resi-dents watched over and cared for the neighborhood. Residents also cited it as a speed reduction measure on busy roads. Beth, who lives on Emer-son Court, mentioned the importance of planting trees to maintain the residential-commercial border in Creekridge Park after a planning devel-opment dispute with a local business: "One of the things the neighbor-hood has done, the neighborhood association, we've gotten plants and, um, trees donated and we planted them kind of to celebrate winning here [on Mason Avenue]. . . . So there's daffodils blooming that are all from our yards and we, you know, share bulbs and we all got out and dug and we get out every year and mulch and weed it and stuff like that."

Additionally, the neighborhood association barred certain types of de-velopment and mandated the maintenance of green spaces and trees in 2009. A group of neighborhood residents, mostly from the neighborhood association, worked for two years to create these mandates. These con-struction directives resulted from the cutting down of several trees in a wooded area during the development of Tyler Street; the neighborhood mandates currently protect undeveloped green areas in the neighborhood.

These protections articulate the neighborhood association's view on neighborhood aesthetics and negatively frame some of the more recent Creekridge Park developments. For example, many neighborhood associ-ation members and White homeowners viewed Tyler Street, which houses a large portion of the few non-White homeowners within the neighbor-hood, disapprovingly. Longtime White homeowner Alan described the construction on Tyler Street as awful "because they razed everything. I mean, there's . . . some trees now, but it was just terrible. I mean, they just went in and cut everything down." Charles, a former CPNA board member, elaborated: "The city said, you know, 'We don't like the way you did this, but we're happy that you're putting in housing that's affordable.' Um, almost everybody's had some sort of problems with their house due to sort of shoddy construction, but that, that, the loss of that, the sort of trauma of that street going in the way it went in, there's a lot of like, the impetus for the [neighborhood construction mandates]." Charles sees the construction of Tyler Street almost as a cautionary tale, one that helped the neighborhood association acquire the city's approval for the neighborhood's mandates against clearing trees for new developments. While the construction of Tyler Street brought new affordable housing to the neighborhood, Charles also reframes the neighborhood mandates as protecting future lower-income residents against the type of "shoddy construction" associated with the development of Tyler.

The residents of Tyler Street, however, expressed satisfaction with their homes. In fact, after one of the CPNA board members offhandedly mentioned on the online listserv that she did not want the soon-to-be-constructed houses on Smith Road to include "matchy homes" like those on Tyler Street, one Tyler Street resident contacted her and informed her that she was very pleased with and proud of her home.[15]

Besides poor development and "trauma," the only other characteristics White residents associated with Tyler Street were the presence of Black and Latino/a families and children. Black established homeowner Cheryl raised important questions about the undertones of these aesthetic concerns. While she affirmed that they may be legitimate and that builders should always consult with neighbors before construction, she declared, "I would question when people have concerns about trees versus housing for folks. What's really at the root of people's concerns, whether it really is about the loss of trees or whether it's about who they think is gonna be moving into that housing." Cheryl's comments point to the ways that nonracial narratives may sometimes camouflage race- and class-based concerns. Regardless of intention, White homeowners' narratives about green space in Creekridge Park adversely characterize the homes on multiethnic Tyler Street.

FRIENDS AND NEIGHBORS

During their interviews, many White Creekridge Park residents stated that they had friends who lived in the neighborhood.[16] Some of these friends were people they met outside Creekridge Park, but others were friends they made as a result of living in the neighborhood. The survey data also indicate that neighborhood friendships are common; 45 percent of survey respondents replied that they have at least one friend in the neighborhood.[17] In addition, when I asked residents who their five closest friends were in their lives, 15 percent responded that one of their five closest friends also happened to live in Creekridge Park. Most friendships in Creekridge Park were monoracial, particularly for White homeowners. When we consider the practices that friends participate in (e.g., sharing real estate listings), we see how seemingly nonracial practices can produce racialized outcomes.

Five White residents specifically indicated during our conversations that their involvement in the neighborhood association helped them form their neighborhood friendships. Ray, a White established homeowner, lives on Union Street, which includes a mix of residents across race and housing tenure. He said that his neighborhood friends tended to live on Central Street and Peach Avenue, which are predominantly White streets in subregion five: "You know, our friends don't live on our street, they live on Harris Street, they live on Central, and they live on Peach, and probably wouldn't have known those people without the neighborhood association. We don't run in the same circles outside of that. And, um, you know, I see my neighbors, I'm friendly with my neighbors, I can negotiate with my neighbors, um, whether they're selling drugs or not. Uh, but those aren't my friends." Throughout his interview, Ray described the range of neighbors that have lived in the rental units next to and across from his home. He said he and his wife had "a couple of good neighbors" and some who he claims sold drugs and were petty thieves, but he has generally gotten along with most of them. As he indicated, however, these are not his friends.

Bryan, a White longtime homeowner who lives on Pine Avenue, said he had "lots of friends" in the neighborhood and specified a few avenues through which he made neighborhood friends: "Well, one of the houses—actually somebody from work moved into a couple doors down. Um, and they lived there for a long time. They've since moved on, but, um, lots of folks we met through the neighborhood association or just, um, walking the dog and that sort of thing. Um, but a lot of contacts through the neighborhood association at this point. Um, my wife is a big, um, gardener and so she's got gardener friends all around the neighborhood and that sort of thing."

Other residents also mentioned gardening and dog walking as popular avenues for establishing neighborhood-based friendships. When I asked Ruth how she became friends with Sharon and others, she stated, "Hanging around, you know, walking dogs. That's a big—Laura and Ron we met them through, um, walking dogs and then Chris and Trish through them and then—yeah. I think a lot of it, excuse me, is probably through the dog, what we call the dog park down at Groveland Estates." Russ, a White established homeowner who lives on Central Street, also mentioned dogs as pivotal to his neighborhood friendships. He explained that "none of my neighbors were my friends before they moved in, so they have all been neighbors who have become friends. . . . [We] talk politics, go to ball games occasionally, um, do dog stuff, walk dogs together, walk dogs together a lot. It's a big deal. The dogs, politics, go to ball games, um. . . . We mostly just talk in the street. Stand on the street and talk, it's very, it's a Central Street thing to do."

Defining what constitutes a friend is difficult because of the heterogeneity of friendship. The characteristics one resident uses to describe friendship another resident would use to define neighborship.[18] One general theme, however, is that if someone has friends outside the neighborhood, they are more likely to differentiate between friends and neighbors. Those without strong friendship networks outside Creekridge Park are more likely to describe neighbors they interact with as friends. White homeowner Seth, for example, distinguished between neighborship and friendship:

> What I've sort of learned over the years is that just because you're not, you know, close personal friends with your neighbors doesn't mean that you can't—I mean, to be a neighbor can be a distinct relationship from being a good personal friend. I mean, my next door neighbors here, we've had a key to their house for twelve years now. Um, I can go into their house any time I want to. They'll let me borrow anything I want to. Um, to interact with them socially outside of work, outside of anything that we might have going on here, I mean, we'll include them if there's a, you know, my, you know—I turned forty last year and I had a fortieth picnic and stuff and of course my neighbors were invited, but as far as eating together regularly and talking about non-neighborhood stuff, no.

In contrast, Robin, a White established homeowner, provided a different understanding of neighbors and friends:

> I would say my neighbor Tracy is a friend. Um, um, we don't—I guess it's sort of—um, but it's different I guess—the late in life friends are different than, um, when you're friends—when you make friends in your twenties or thirties. So, uh, in that—you know, you tend not

necessarily—we've gone out to dinner together and stuff like that, but it's not, um, it's—it's—it's more a different type of friendship as I said than when you're in your twenties and thirties. And then, um, Tammy I would—I consider, um, with helping her walk her dogs and, you know, someone I would ask if I felt that she could do the favor or that—you know, I would ask her to do it, yeah.

For Robin it seems that age and life stage are important factors in determining friendships, and if she spends time with a neighbor now, in her early fifties, she is likely to consider that person a friend.

The features of neighborhood friendships also differed across individuals. Some people got together regularly for drinks, as late-twenties newcomers Tina, Eric, Thomas, and Denise described. Tina and Eric own their home, while Thomas and Denise rent theirs. Some neighbors also got together for vacations. For example, Tina and Eric indicated that they recently rented a lake house with one of their neighbors. Ruth, who is in her fifties, also mentioned that she biennially joined her neighbor on vacation in New England. Spending time together at home was also an important social activity in which many White residents participated. Urban geographer Tim Butler's work on gentrifying London neighborhoods similarly concludes that "the home is a crucial element in middle-class notions of friendship and asking people into it for dinner is probably the best single indicator of 'becoming friends' which is also a crucial means of belonging in a middle-class community."[19]

Although concrete data on the race of these neighborhood-based friendships are not available, we can infer that they are same-race friendships, based on interview patterns. When I asked White residents about interracial interactions in the neighborhood, they identified the non-White neighbors they interacted with or knew, if any, as I discussed in Chapter 2. We can, therefore, argue that because there was very little overlap between the individuals White residents mentioned during responses to the question on interracial interactions and the question on neighborhood friendships, very few White residents had neighborhood friendships across racial groups.

The most common form of neighborhood friendship was one that began outside Creekridge Park; these were generally intraracial friendships. Robin affirmed that these types of friendships were normative in the neighborhood: "Um, I know that with a lot of the young couples . . . it does tend to be the case where they've known them previously from a university connection or a work connection, and you know, a house has opened up, so someone moves in and they already know maybe two or three folks that live in the neighborhood." Relatedly, Emma described her new neighbors as friends from her former apartment complex: "Aaron and Jane came over and of course we could basically vouch for the neighborhood, that like 'Oh okay, you probably have some noise over here.' Then, in general, 'We've lived here we haven't had any trouble, it's a nice neighborhood.' So, um, we encouraged them to look at the house again and they really liked it once they looked at it." Emma's example corroborates Robin's point about the impact of preexisting relationships on Creekridge Park–based friendships and the active role current residents play in recruiting their friends to live in the neighborhood.

A number of respondents said they found out about the neighborhood because friends sent them information about a particular house listing. For example, Charles, who first rented in Creekridge Park before buying a home on Peach Avenue, shared that his "dog walking buddy" was the main reason he owns his current home: "The reason that I own that house is because our neighbor who was a dog walking buddy, uh, and he posted a flier on our door, a note on our door one day when he found out how much the sons [of the deceased owner] were going to ask for the house and it was really, really cheap." Similarly, Stephanie, a White homeowner who lives on Central Street, indicated that she had several good friends in the neighborhood, most of whom were colleagues of her husband, John, that she helped recruit: "You know, we've whenever, um, the neighborhood has a strong listserv, so whenever people, um, you know, put that their house is up for market we shoot it off to, you know, people at [a local university]. We wanted to make sure we have great folks that live around us, so it's been nice that way." Other White neighbors lauded Stephanie and John's practice of "promoting" the neighborhood to their friends. For example, Tammy stated, "John has brought a lot of his friends to the neighborhood to live here. That's how many of the—many of the people who live on Central [Street] are there as a result of him telling them when the houses become available. He should be in real estate." Michelle, a White homeowner who no longer lives in Creekridge Park, explained that she believed her friend moved to the area because of her recommendation: "I think my friend who's living on Cardinal Street . . . I think actually moved from Chapel Hill to Durham into that area based on my recommendation, spending time at my house and getting a feel for the area."

Similarly, White homeowner Rhonda shared during her interview that "our really good friend lives on Central [Street] and he's in a rental property, and he . . . probably rented it because we live so close." Though potentially harmless, these behaviors replicate the social networks of White homeowners in the neighborhood, which we know, based on interview and survey data (see table 2.3), are mostly White. As White homeowners replicate their social networks, owner-occupied housing in Creekridge Park will continue to be predominantly inhabited by Whites, and there will be fewer owner-occupied residential options for non-White residents in Creekridge Park. This is one way that seemingly nonracial processes (e.g., telling your friends about available homes) can help maintain the racial status quo (e.g., predominantly White homeownership in Creekridge Park).

OBSERVE AND REPORT

Almost 90 percent of my survey respondents said they felt safe in Creekridge Park. The majority of Creekridge Park residents also did not believe there was a crime problem in the neighborhood. At the same time, as we see below, discussions of crime and the reporting of undesirable residential behavior were prevalent in Creekridge Park. Anthropologist Sally Engle Merry's work on urban danger argues that an increase in crime reporting happens in urban neighborhoods as a result of the relations between "racially, culturally, and economically distinct" groups within a single environment. Her crime analysis, which focuses on power and inequality, is applicable here: "Members of a dominant group may denounce a subordinate group for its criminality rather than denounce it for the real threat it poses to the perpetuation of the existing social order and continued elite dominance of that order. Concern about crime thus justifies and reinforces the hostility that stems from class conflict and racial and ethnic differences. Discussions of danger often focus on aspects of the dangerous group's social life that are perceived as bizarre and immoral."[20] As we have already seen throughout this chapter, White homeowners participate in social control practices that include the surveillance and reporting of neighbors. These white codes are a response to the social and political climate of an area and a way for the dominant group (White homeowners) to maintain the status quo. So while the presence of city agents in Creekridge Park may be in response to criminal activity, punishing the violators is intended to protect the interests of White homeowners within a multiethnic space.

TABLE 3.2 *Attitudes on neighborhood safety based on survey data*

Perceptions of neighborhood safety	Percentage of Creekridge Park residents
Do you feel safe?	
Yes	89
No	11
Do you think there's a crime problem?	
Yes	37
No	63

At a joint meeting with an adjacent neighborhood, Creekridge Park residents met with the local police captain and two area police officers. Captain Hanks, a muscular, middle-aged Black male, addressed the crowd of White residents, giving tips on how to reduce crime and gun violence as part of Project Safe Neighborhoods, a City of Durham and Durham Police Department initiative. Along with other advice, Captain Hanks encouraged residents to "take the risk" and call 911 if they saw anything out of the ordinary around the neighborhood. He explained that he did not want residents to take the law into their own hands, but that they should be aware of what was going on around them. From his point of view, "neighbor means something"; you do not necessarily have to have cookouts with your neighbors, but you should be nosy. Throughout the presentation he mentioned what he does to protect his home as a homeowner, which seemed central to facilitating a class-based rapport with the White homeowners in attendance. At one point, while telling a story about someone stealing from Dollar General, a discount retailer, Captain Hanks added, "Why anyone would steal from a dollar store is beyond me." His comment was followed by laughter from the crowd, expressing their shared dismay and class solidarity. Later he explained, in regard to a problem house adjacent to the neighborhood, "Disruptive people are good at going far enough. . . . I'll stop short of calling them uncivilized." The whiteness of the neighborhood association and its dominance by homeowners—which based on Captain Hanks's comments is endorsed by the police—allows White homeowners to be the main beneficiaries of these intimate gatherings with local law enforcement.

There are multiple avenues through which the police and the neighborhood association encourage residents to observe and report undesirable and criminal behavior. Through the increase of intentional surveillance, residents are participating in opportunity reduction. Criminologist Dennis Rosenbaum identifies that these tactics are often associated with neighborhood organizations: "Collective anti-crime measures that emerge from the opportunity reduction approach often involve surveillance, crime reporting, and target-hardening activities designed to control or deter crime in specific settings. Neighborhood Watch is the prototype of this approach, and often serves as a vehicle for encouraging a range of opportunity-reduction behaviors."[21] Rosenbaum's description encapsulates the dominant practices of crime prevention in Creekridge Park. As such, I learned the ins and outs of neighborhood surveillance and the expectations associated with neighborhood watch via CPNA meetings, neighborhood events, and reading the CPNA's online listserv—as residents do. This speaks to the normalization of neighborhood surveillance and the prevalence of neighborhood watch logic in this neighborhood. As a result, White residents participated in these codes of conduct, rarely challenging the logic or the racialized outcomes of these "nonracial" practices.

Important catalysts for phone calls to the police and other services are interneighbor conflicts. Many residents said they dealt with neighborhood conflict by speaking with the appropriate neighbor first. I found, however, that when White residents described specific conflicts with non-White neighbors, White residents usually involved the police or another authority. In part, this occurs because, as we established, White residents are less likely to know their non-White neighbors. As one White homeowner described, "I would say if they were people that we knew, could trust, and feel safe talking to, probably most people for one, would've already talked to them if there was gonna be an issue that would bring, potentially bringing up a problem. But then for people that I didn't know I'd probably just call the police [laughs]." When White residents are more likely to know and be friendly with other White residents, however, these social control practices reinforce high interracial social distance.

Sometimes neighbors called the police to curtail physical violence, in the case of a fight breaking out, for example. Established resident Sharon explained:

Actually I think I called the, um, the nonemergency police number.
It was, um, there were a lot of people out, in the summer there's a
lot of, people that spend time out kind of in the parking area in front

of the quadriplexes [rental properties on Harris Street] that are up there and this is right after probably the first summer we had moved in and maybe that first year after and, um, there's just a lot of fights that would happen. It was just like people kind of congregating and then all of a sudden this woman started like body slamming this one girl, ran out of her house with a bat and I was like "oh this is not good," so, um, I don't think I called 911. I might have called 'cause everyone by the time I realized what was going on it had dispersed so I just wanted, I called the nonemergency phone number. Um, and I've called it, I've had to call it a couple of times that summer just to, like, congregations kind of getting out of hand. Um, and to the point where something bad was happening.

Although Sharon did not fear for her own safety, she was concerned that someone could be hurt. This prompted her to call the police nonemergency number to report the incidents.

In other cases, no threats of violence were imminent and the interactions had racial undertones. One example comes from Mary, a Black retiree whose son littered a White neighbor's yard a few years ago. Mary, a longtime renter in Creekridge Park, described the incident as follows: "[My neighbor Mark] went and called the guy . . . that owns the house in Mebane [a nearby city] and tried to get him to make us be moved. And I didn't like that because, what kind of neighbor is that? He could've came and talked to me and told me and I could've made my son stop doing that, you know, so, but I didn't like the fact that he went behind my back and he supposed to be a neighbor. And he's gonna go behind my back, and he called [the property manager]. . . . 'Cause to me that, that to me was being mean and hateful. I mean, it was being very mean." Mary said that she did not think this incident with Mark was racially motivated, but she went on to describe another incident where Mark, unlike her other neighbors, never stopped to give her a ride when she walked home from the bus, regardless of how many packages she was carrying. He saw her and waved as he drove to his house, which was directly across the street from hers. Mary speculated that this interaction was likely fueled by Mark's desire not to have Black people in his car. Mark has since moved to Pine Avenue because, according to Mary, "he don't want to live across the street from us no more." She explained that her landlord did not kick her and her son out because she always pays her rent on time, but Mary was dismayed with her neighbor's actions. Since Mary did not have a particularly close relationship with Mark, which at least on his part seemed intentional, his procedure to address the trash issue maintained their high interracial social distance.

Many residents went to the CPNA listserv to announce a violation they observed (e.g., an abandoned car, trash in a front yard, or loud music at night), to ask questions about the proper avenue of reporting, and to get more information on the situation. Some respondents mentioned that they did not want to inundate the police with unnecessary calls. The sentiment the police shared during community meetings and via the listserv was that residents should call in anything that concerned them and the police would decide how to respond. For most of my White respondents, more police presence in the neighborhood was a good thing, especially since the police clearly expressed positive attitudes toward homeowners—reinforcing their sense of entitlement within the neighborhood—and did not associate their bodies with criminality.[22]

Posts to the listserv and concerns shared at community meetings are extensions of the social control practices that city agencies and law enforcement themselves practice; that is the logic and power of organizations such as neighborhood watch. While having a Black police captain may have been an opportunity to build a multiethnic and cross-tenure coalition in the neighborhood and the CPNA, Captain Hanks's explicit alliance with homeowner interests barred that from happening. Social control practices also reinforce high interracial social distance and low intraracial social distance. Important to note is that not all White homeowners appreciate Neighborhood Improvement Services or regulations on lawn care; some actively dislike them. When I say that White homeowner interests are aligned with Neighborhood Improvement Services, I am speaking in an aggregate sense—regulations against overgrown lawns exist to protect the interests and financial bottom line of homeowners, most of whom in Creekridge Park are White.

The cultural deficiency White homeowners associate with renters creates additional opportunities to observe and report non-Whites. In particular, White homeowners scrutinized non-White childrearing and pet care practices during interviews and neighborhood events. One White homeowner described her calls to the police in regard to a particular neighbor:

> We do have another neighbor that we have called the police on and animal control multiple times because of noise problems and, like, letting their dog off lead and I got chased by their dog once and we

saw them beat that dog with a belt one time, so we've called animal control on them before. But we don't know them. Frankly, I don't really wanna know them if you're the kind of person that you're gonna beat your dog and scream at your children at 11 o'clock at night. It's just, you know, um . . . I walk my dogs regularly and frankly they yell so loudly that we can hear them most of the time.

Emma places her neighbor outside the white, urban, middle-class habitus. She views this neighbor's behavior toward her dogs and her children as beyond the bounds of what she considers acceptable and appropriate, prompting Emma to control her neighbor's behavior via city authorities.

Another White homeowner, Terry, mentioned that "we have a lot of dysfunctional parenting and behavior in the parking lot of the apartments behind us, and there has been a lot of drug activity there and gang activity there." He indicated that he and his wife, through an adjacent neighborhood's association, were in contact with the property manager and that the manager was making efforts to "kick people out who are problems." This example shows that the CPNA is not an exception and that other neighborhood associations also serve to protect White homeowner interests in multiethnic settings.

PATRONIZING PRACTICES

While White homeowners tended to include White renters across social lines, such as inviting them over for dinner, White homeowners tended to interact with non-White renters in paternalistic ways. First, the non-White renters that were incorporated into White networks were usually elderly and female. Second, the relationships were based on White assistance to non-Whites. When White homeowners solely dictate the terms of their relationships with non-White renters, there is no reciprocity, a key element of egalitarian relations, friendships, and bridging social capital.[23] This dynamic is important, of course, because bridging social capital is one of the positive outcomes social scientists attribute to multiethnic neighborhoods and policies, such as the Hope VI and Moving to Opportunity programs.[24] Sociologist Mary Jackman's work on paternalism helps us to fully understand this type of interracial dynamic. According to Jackman, "Subordinates do not demand something unless they define it as a need. Dominant groups thus mimic the traditional father-child relationship by claiming superior moral competence and attempting to define the needs of subordinates. They can then provide—with pleasant sentimentality and with a satisfying *feeling* of benevolence—for the fulfillment of those needs."[25] Some White residents saw themselves as helping their non-White neighbors by calling the police and city agencies, for example. Brendan, a new homeowner in the area, spoke about how recent phone calls to the police in regard to pit bulls and a gunfight at a Latino neighbor's house benefited the children in that home. He cited their playtime activities, which he said included jumping out a window and into a garbage can, as evidence that a change in the living situation was beneficial. Brendan shared this story at a neighborhood event after Emma said that calling the police helps everyone, but probably not the families in question. Although calling the police in regard to his Latino/a neighbors reflected larger social control practices, Brendan frames his phone call as a benevolent act.

Similarly, while interviewing Emma, I asked if she had contact information for Mr. Cameron, her elderly Black neighbor whom she referenced as someone she was in contact with relatively often. She proceeded to explain:

> Yeah, I'll actually, let me ask Luke [Emma's partner] about whether he thinks that, 'cause I think that, the thing is that I think Mr. Cameron would do it, it's that, maybe that sounds like really patronizing, but I'll just ask him to see what he thinks. He's got a lot going on with his wife being really sick and I think that he would probably do it, but I'm just not sure it would be a good idea. Um, simply because like if something happens to her while he wasn't there you might not be able to hear it or he might not be able to hear it, um, but anyway I'll ask Luke. It might be fine, I just, I'll ask him what he thinks about that.

By attempting to define what would benefit Mr. Cameron without consulting him, Emma simulated a traditionally paternalistic relationship.

Patronizing practices, of course, varied in degree. In the example above, Emma acknowledged the potentially problematic relationship with Mr. Cameron and recognized their differing social positions during her interview: "[Mr. Cameron's] always been really friendly to me, which I find incredibly impressive because he was in Durham sixty years ago. The amount of [sighs] racism that he probably endured as a consequence of that, I can't see how anybody would be, like, just so open and friendly to White people. Um, if that were [sighs] if that were me, it would be hard to have that." On the one hand, Emma's reflection on Mr. Cameron's position as an elderly Black man in a southern U.S. city indicates that she is aware of the historical context of race relations in Durham and is sensitive to how non-Whites may perceive White individuals as a result. Luke, on the other hand, saw his relationship with Mr. Cameron as entirely positive and commented to me at a neighborhood event that he was happy to help him and Mary, another Black neighbor. The basis of his relationship with the Camerons and Mary was his assistance to them. When I interviewed Luke, he described Mary's situation as follows:

> Frank Hill Realty, who also owns our poor neighbors Mary and [her son] Philip's house, which just looks like Boo Radley's shack [from Harper Lee's book *To Kill a Mockingbird*], it's just falling down on them. If you've been inside, if you get to go inside it's just as bad on the inside as it is on the outside. But they don't feel like they have the power to fight anybody. She's an elderly Black woman who's retired and sick. Her son is sick. They can't afford to fight anybody. They can't afford to push on anyone and you get that sense when you discuss it with them. You know, she really gets passion—in passionate, you know, mode about talking about it when you talk to her, but she, but she kind of backs off if you say "I'll help you, you know, I'll help you talk to them, I'll help you deal with the situation because it's unfair and there, there, you know, there's codes all over the house being broken," but um, they kind of back off and I think that's part of the issue, too. I mean, we have, we definitely in this community people who don't feel empowered to you know, serve their own rights, really.

When I spoke with Mary, she mentioned that her house definitely needed a coat of paint. She also, however, addressed the cost of asking Frank Hill Realty to take care of it. As a retiree, Mary lives on a fixed income and cannot afford to pay more in rent to cover the cost of her landlord painting her house. She also cannot afford to cover the cost of independently hiring someone to do the job for her. This highlights the tensions that can exist between homeowner ideas and renter realities in regard to "quality of life" improvements. Often these improvements more readily benefit homeowners than renters because while homeowners are concerned with housing values, renters are more immediately concerned with maintaining their current rental rates.[26] By not asking her landlord to paint her apartment and refusing Luke's intervention offer, Mary is exercising her constrained agency. From our conversation it seems Mary is perfectly capable of advocating for herself, but she also understands her limited options. Her issues boil down to economic resources and the rental housing system.

During our conversation Luke also mentioned how he helped Mr. Cameron and his wife: "Um, and he [Mr. Cameron] can't really do anything, but when, when I can and I, and I get the chance, I help him clean up stuff out of his yard, people always pitch garbage out at the base of our hill, that's where people throw their garbage out before they go through the stop sign, so there's always trash in his yard. Um, so I pick up his trash, um, I help him with his wife a few times." Luke described Mr. Cameron as incapable of doing anything, despite the fact that he provides full-time care for his ailing wife.

The Camerons elderly age and Mrs. Cameron's and Mary's chronic illnesses make them nonthreatening to Luke. He takes a lot of pride and enjoyment from assisting them. This differs greatly from his interactions with another, younger Black neighbor, who Luke said did not want to be helped. His interactions with this house centered on complaints to the police, Neighborhood Improvement Services, and the neighborhood association listserv. His repeated calls to Neighborhood Improvement Services also defined his interactions with his Latino/a neighbors, who were of working age. He proudly explained during his interview that he spent about three weeks "sending extremely well-thought-out and well-written letters to everybody in Neighborhood Improvement Services" in which he openly disagreed with the inspectors who came by, citing specific municipal codes that he says his Latino/a neighbors violated. From our conversations, Luke seems to take a lot of pride in both aiding and reprimanding his neighbors. Patronizing responses, however, are dependent on the subordinated status of others. As such, the social position of each neighbor seems to dictate which approach (assistance or punishment) Luke takes.

CHALLENGING PRACTICES?

Although most White respondents had predominantly White networks, there were a few exceptions. Below I outline the normative practices of Esther and Lois, two older White female renters whose neighborhood networks included non-Whites. Although they had more intimate relationships with their neighbors of color, because of their social positions as vulnerable (in Lois's case financially and in Esther's case physically), elderly women renters who lived in predominantly non-White areas, their cases do not challenge the racial status quo. Although they may not embody the dominant white, urban, middle-class habitus of Creekridge Park, their social positions and behaviors are still structured by a larger system of whiteness.

Esther was an elderly White widow who lived in one of the large apartment complexes within Creekridge Park.[27] She had been renting an apartment in the complex for nineteen years at the time of our interview. As she described her social circle, it became clear that she spent time with Pam, her Black female neighbor, and her two daughters fairly regularly. Esther stated, "My neighbor upstairs I just, I can't tell you how much I appreciate her. . . . Those are the sweetest girls you could ever meet. And I've adopted them as grandchildren." She explained how one of the girls has an autism spectrum disorder and that she read books on her condition so she could better understand it. Esther concluded, "They do family things with our family, too. You know, they're part of our family." When I asked her whom she spent the most time with in the neighborhood, Esther replied

> I do more with Pam and the girls. And then I've learned so much from them. Um, you know, think about getting along with no checking account, um, when I have extra money I take them out to dinner. They had never been to a Japanese restaurant, Chinese. These things that they had never experienced and I thought, these are things we did with my boys when they were small and they grew up with it and these, you know, have never had that so I've had a really good time exposing them to some of those things. And so, you know, I'm learning what it means to not have, to have to watch every single penny and that's, I can't imagine.

Her characterization of the relationship pointed to some economic inequity, but Esther's interactions with Pam and her children were some of the most consistent interracial interactions that my respondents reported. Although I was unable to interview Pam, she and her daughters also provided aid to Esther, who used an oxygen machine and whose mobility was limited, indicating some semblance of reciprocity. As discussed earlier, most White residents said they had friends or acquaintances of other races when I specifically asked them about interracial interactions, but very few originally named non-Whites among their list of friends, a pattern in line with contemporary interracial friendship research.[28] From her description, Esther maintained a more regular and intimate interaction, beyond the typical "hi" and "hello," indicating higher friendship closeness.

Lois lives in one of the large apartment complexes with her adult son and husband. Also an older White female, Lois seemed to have more interactions with her neighbors of color than her homeowner counterparts did, despite saying she would not call any of them friends. For example, when I asked Lois to tell me about her neighbors, she mentioned each of her neighbors of color by name and followed with an anecdote about each one. White homeowners rarely knew the names of their non-White neighbors, let alone had regular enough interactions with them to share any personal details. Lois described how nice her Sudanese neighbors were and how she shared produce from the community garden with them. She also recounted a story of how her female neighbor from Sudan came over one day asking for "grandma," which is what she called Lois: "She gave me, um, about four bags of goat. You have to be nice about it, you know, and, uh, or maybe it was lamb, I don't know. Goat, lamb, what's the difference, I don't want any of it [laughs]. It was lamb because my husband and [my son] Simon love it because, in fact, they like goat meat because they eat at the Indian restaurant so much and, they, not me. Uh, but I cooked it for them 'cause I knew she would ask me, you know, how it was, yeah."

Lois also provided child care for a former neighbor's biracial child named Lizzy. She shared that over the past two years she had grown very close to Lizzy and described Lizzy's White mother as her best friend in town. Lois recounted that Lizzy one day said to her, "Grammie, I'm brown," and Lois replied, "You sure are, but you're a beautiful brown." On the one hand, Lois used language that is taboo in the twenty-first century (e.g., she used the term "colored" rather than "Black" or "African American") and her statement to Lizzy reinforced racist ideas about skin color and beauty. On the other hand, her life was much more embedded with her neighbors of color than the White homeowners who praised the diversity of the neighborhood but lacked multiethnic social networks. Her hesitance to call any of them friends, however, may be due to her situation in North Carolina. Originally from Oklahoma, she planned to return home when she could. She moved to Durham to be close to her granddaughter, whose father was completing graduate work in town. She said all of her close friends were back home and she did not want to make new ones. Her resistance to making new friends locally, however, may also be because she was situated in a predominantly non-White area. The presence of non-Whites may have served as a reminder of her current status (she shared that money did not go as far in Durham as in her hometown) and her inability to change it any time soon.

Lois's and Esther's incorporation into non-White networks was a result of multiple processes. Unlike the rest of the neighborhood, which is majority White, they lived in apartment complexes that were predominantly non-White. At the same time, Lois and Esther were elderly, relatively immobile, and female, all statuses that limit their power. Additionally, because of their immobility, their networks are somewhat limited to individuals in their immediate proximity. Lois's financial vulnerability also impacted her ability to move beyond the confines of Pine Grove Apartments, as she desired. The multiethnic nature of Pine Grove Apartments was in some ways a reminder of her downward mobility in North Carolina in comparison with Oklahoma. Overall, Lois's and Esther's stories provide a different angle of Creekridge Park, showcasing how Pine Grove Apartments could potentially be a location for multiethnic coalitions across class lines. Based on my interviews, however, this possibility was not reality. The impact of larger social systems must also be considered, as Esther's and Lois's interactions with non-Whites were structured by white paternalism and high interracial social distance.

CONCLUSION

In this chapter I present several white codes that residents described and enacted in Creekridge Park. These codes of interracial conduct, which dictate appropriate neighborhood behavior, help explain why White residents had mostly monoracial social networks despite living in a multiethnic, statistically integrated neighborhood. In this white, urban, middle-class habitus, white rule is customary and "fair." As a group with class and race privilege, White homeowners are able to control the neighborhood association and the resources it entails, including legitimacy as an organization and attention at the city level. They also exclude non-Whites and renters as claims-makers and justify the lack of minority participation as individual choice and disinterest. White residents gave several explanations for their social networks, but these explanations fail to include the important racial dynamics that produce predominantly White friendships. White codes maintain white values and privilege, regardless of the intentions of White residents. Their explanations call upon dominant ideological schemas that support the view of race and class subordinates as culturally inferior. They highlight parenting styles, neighborhood investment, and other behaviors to solidify white control in this neighborhood. In order to challenge these "commonsense" notions, we must include concepts such as relationality and power to present a more accurate, nuanced, and complete vision of life in Creekridge Park and other multiethnic spaces. In the next chapter, I present the voices of non-White residents to provide a more comrehensive picture of this multi-ethnic space.

CHAPTER 4

Creekridge Park in Black and Brown

Now, what do they mean by that?

—**MARY**, Black renter, longtime resident

Mary's quotation introduces us to a central concern of this chapter. Mary, a Black longtime resident, was responding to one of my standard interview questions: *The neighborhood association claims that the neighborhood is mixed income and diverse; do you think that is true?* "Mixed income" and "diverse," phrases commonly used in the sociological literature and newspaper articles on urban development and eagerly endorsed by White residents in Creekridge Park, were questionable to Mary. Mary's query highlights how diversity may function as a "code word." A code word, as defined by sociologists Michael Omi and Howard Winant, is the "non-racial rhetoric used to disguise racial issues."[1] Rather than explicitly referring to power, inequality, and structural racism, "diversity" is a catchall category that allows Whites to discuss race, along with other categories of difference, in a manner that is nonthreatening to themselves. This, as I discussed in Chapter 2, is one way that diversity reinforces the racial status quo.

Based on interviews with thirteen residents and twenty-one survey responses, this chapter highlights the particular experiences of Blacks and Latino/as in Creekridge Park and the meanings they attached to living in a multiethnic neighborhood. Overall, material gains and social costs marked the experiences of non-Whites in Creekridge Park. In the following sections I discuss why Black and Latino/a residents say they live in Creekridge Park, their varied neighborhood relationships, and their experiences with race and racism as well as with interracial interactions in Creekridge Park.

WHY HERE?

Diversity

I started all of my interviews the same way, asking residents why they chose to live in Creekridge Park and how they found the house or apartment in which they currently resided. Overall, Black residents used diversity to signal that a space was not predominantly White, although in some cases it was used to describe nonracial characteristics (e.g., presence of gay and lesbian residents). Although Mary was not familiar with the term, "diversity" or "mixed" living was one characteristic that many non-White residents referred to when they described what they liked about Creekridge Park. For example, Angela, an established Black homeowner in her late forties who lives on Creekridge Road, mentioned the appeal of living close to downtown and neighborhood diversity: "I wanted to live close to downtown because we're from Philadelphia. I don't want to be way out in some subdivision somewhere where you can't get to anything. And then my husband works at [a local university], so we wanted to be close enough to work and to have my daughter in a neighborhood that was, uh, uh, diverse enough so that she can have experience with multiple issues that she should be familiar with. Uh, so it was just—it was just right for us; let's put it that way." It is unclear what Angela meant by diversity. During our interview, she seemed to equate diversity with sexual orientation. In fact, when I specifically asked her about interracial interactions in the neighborhood, she said they were very common. She then proceeded to discuss the presence of lesbian and gay couples in the neighborhood. Perhaps she felt sexual diversity was the most pressing issue she wanted her daughter to be familiar with, or perhaps Angela did not think the Creekridge Park area was racially diverse.

While a few other Black female homeowners also mentioned diversity as a positive neighborhood trait, their use of the term differed from that of White respondents. For example, Cheryl, whom we heard from in Chapter 3, stated that she wanted a mixed-race neighborhood because homes are assigned higher values in them than in predominantly Black neighborhoods. Connie, a Black longtime homeowner in her late fifties, also mentioned the diversity of Durham at large as a plus, although she moved into Creekridge Park when it was a predominantly White neighborhood. Connie mentioned that Creekridge Park was now "just a mixed bag," but she initially wanted to stay in the predominantly Black area where she first lived in Durham. She moved to Creekridge Park because it was more affordable: "That is what I liked when I moved from Chapel Hill because I had gone to school there then worked there for three years. Everything is just so homogenized; when I just moved to Durham I was like 'this feels so good,' because I was over by [North Carolina] Central [University]. I want to say the first week that I moved in Maya Angelou was speaking by Cen-

tral. It was like the Harlem Renaissance. It felt nice being near this historically Black college and working in the park. Because that's where I worked
when I first moved to Durham. I just had a mixture of everything." For
Connie (and according to neighborhood demographics), Creekridge Park
only recently became a mixed neighborhood. As someone who has lived
there for several decades, Connie felt that Creekridge Park did not originally meet her definition of diverse. At the same time, she explained that
moving into a predominantly White neighborhood did not bother her,
since she was used to those kinds of environments after living in Chapel
Hill.

Diversity also mattered to Lawrence and George, who intentionally
sought out a multiethnic area while looking for a house to rent. While
both men are Black North Carolina natives and work in the arts, Lawrence
is in his early thirties and George is in his late twenties. They are newcomers and live in the Creekridge Park area. During our discussion of how
they ended up in the area, I asked them if a diverse neighborhood was
something they specifically sought out. George responded:

> Yeah, I mean—I'm the kind of person, I don't like to live in any
> neighborhood that is any too much of one something. It's not, like,
> I want to live in an all-Black neighborhood or an all-White neighbor-
> hood or anything. I like the diversity of this sort of—it feels, like, it
> puts everybody on better footing because I grew up in a mixed neigh-
> borhood sort of, like, from age zero to nine, zero to ten, sort of more
> similar to a neighborhood like this. And then later when I was about
> nine we moved to sort of an upper middle-class, all-White neighbor-
> hood and it was fine for me but I'd rather not repeat that experience
> in my adult life. I think, I mean, that was fine for me growing up be-
> cause—well, I didn't have a choice. But I prefer places that are mixed.
> Because [inaudible] mixed neighborhoods of racially mixed, [inaudible]
> you start getting other sorts of alternative ways of thinking so. So,
> even to this day it is still odder to see mixed neighborhoods than it is
> to see segregated neighborhoods. It's actually an interesting thing—
> people living, based on racial statistics living where, in what parts of
> the city, so they did like San Francisco, Los Angeles, New York, blah,
> blah, and they did it by color, and it was insane, it was just insane,
> everything was so racialized, so segregated. So I actually think it's
> still the, honestly, it's still the exception to be in a mixed neighbor-
> hood as opposed to—and as opposed to not being.

George seems to be describing the color-coded maps of dissimilarity indices across different cities by digital mapmaker Eric Fischer that have been featured in national publications.[2] I followed up George's explanation by asking him if he thought mixed neighborhoods were the exception or the rule in Durham. He said that it was much harder to find all-White spaces in Durham. Lawrence added, "I think it's a product of Durham's past." George concluded, "So I mean that's part of the reason why I like Durham because I can name every other city just about in North Carolina and I can point out to you the Black and White parts of town, or the Hispanic parts of town or whatever. But you'd have a much harder time doing that in Durham." Lawrence's framing of Durham is noteworthy, since he seems to view Durham's contemporary multiethnic state as a historically established one. Based on demographic information and contemporary research on multiethnic spaces, however, the creation of multiethnic neighborhoods, particularly in southern cities, is largely due to new immigration from Asia and Latin America. Durham has several multiethnic neighborhoods due to the post-2000 Latino/a population growth spurt, but as I discussed in Chapter 1, historically it was a very racially segregated city.

For the most part, the Black residents that mentioned neighborhood diversity when discussing Creekridge Park were seeking areas that were not predominantly White. This finding is in line with sociologist Camille Zubrinsky Charles's work on residential preferences, which finds that Black residents' desire for some Black neighbors is more about avoiding White hostility than about ethnocentrism.[3] Although some of the definitions of diversity used by Black residents were ambiguous, like Angela's, they generally referred to racial issues. At the same time, Black residents were looking for an affordable area where the value of their homes could be retained. Creekridge Park was the compromising option for their various needs.

Neighborhood's Political Identity

While drawing the parallel between Durham and the Creekridge Park area was something White residents did as well, Lawrence and George framed their fondness for Durham a bit differently than White residents did in Chapter 2. For example, while they highlighted the economically mixed nature of Durham, they framed the mix as a conduit for interclass acknowledgment and power-sharing:

GEORGE: Durham's a great place, mix of, like, sort of conservatism and liberalism, I mean it's definitely slanted more toward the liberal side but there are folks—it's not, like, is this enclave where, like, you're not going to hear any opinion that is different from yours, and I like that. I mean I may not agree with it but that voice needs to be there and it needs to—we need to continue to challenge each other, like, on all sort of levels, social and political and, you know, economic. It's also what I like about Durham is that it's sort of— there are very few neighborhoods in the city anyway that are sort of, like, these gated communities. Like most communities, even in, like, Groveland Estates, the houses are enormous and they are worth who, God knows how much money, but they back up right to our neighborhood. And everybody is just sort of okay with that, and I like that—those kind of—they call it mixed income, well it's not exactly that but it's pretty close.

LAWRENCE: Well, I mean in the sense that you—that neither one of those groups of residents can ignore the existence of the other. Like you're always aware, you know, of either disparity but also of variety, that you are not the sole makeup of this place.

GEORGE: Yeah, you are not the only thing that defines this because other places like Raleigh you can drive around all day and not see anything that sort of challenges—like this is how everything is, on sort of either side whether you're sort of the lower middle or upper, like you're always sort of seeing some [inaudible] it looks like this now but that doesn't mean that it's always going to look like this [inaudible] that it will always look like this for you or whatever. So I really like that, it just seems like a place that is a very—it's a mix of old stuff and a lot of brand new stuff. Durham feels less like the old South than some of the other cities in the South that I have been in that consider themselves to be South. Like Raleigh for instance, Raleigh just feels—and places like Atlanta, just really tout themselves like being really progressive and really doing new are just stuck in these really old, really entrenched sort of this is the way that things have been done kind of thing and those people are still in power, where I feel in Durham that there is—some of that mentality is certainly still there but there are enough other voices and other sort of forces working that is like wow, yeah, that is a way to do it but why don't we try it this way.

For George and Lawrence, Durham represents the new South in a way that feels authentic. It does not just tout itself as progressive while continuing its entrenched practices. It is a mixed space where different types of people, across class lines especially, cannot ignore one another. This is in contrast to the way White respondents described Durham, which touted difference as the desired outcome. George and Lawrence connect the juxtaposition of economic difference to the maintenance of Durham's authentically progressive identity.

As part of Durham's queer community, George said he and Lawrence actively sought out "alternate . . . social structures" and saw Durham as a great location where "a lot of social activism" took place. As some White residents shared as well, they felt Durham's current state provided residents an opportunity to impart their influence. George explained: "It feels like a city that is in some sort of transition which I really like because if you're here during that transition you can shape what it will look like. Because, you know, other cities are more established or other forces are sort of controlling how they grow." And although it was not perfect, in their eyes Durham was "pretty damn close."

Lawrence and George were the only non-White residents I spoke to who used aesthetic features, such as lawn care, to extrapolate residential political attitudes:

GEORGE: And so we went there [to their neighbor's party] and we was like, "Wow, we live in a gayborhood."

LAWRENCE: Yeah, because, like, I knew—like, we had a hint of it because knowing that we were getting Bea's house and knowing that, like, her daughter and her daughter's partner live nearby, we're, like, "Oh okay, we will be near, you know, queer people." But we got here and we're, like, "Oh, wow."

SARAH: You weren't expecting.

GEORGE: [*inaudible*] I mean we weren't surprised but we certainly weren't expecting.

SARAH: Right. So it wasn't necessarily something that you were seeking out or was Betty's daughter a slight comforting?

GEORGE: Their presence was comforting.

LAWRENCE: Yeah, you know, I guess I don't think that we were, like, explicitly seeking that out, like, in the sense that we were looking for a neighborhood with that makeup, but I think on some level.

GEORGE: And you sort of have an idea just by looking at the houses, like, which types of neighborhoods are going to be a little bit more flexible, a little bit more quote/unquote "alternative" just by how the people keep up their yards. I mean you see a house with a really crazy yard that is clearly maintained somehow but not in, like, a conventional sort of [inaudible].

LAWRENCE: You can tell where people are less conservative.

GEORGE: Yeah, and people who basically are less concerned with conforming to what your mainstream suburban house should look like. Like, painting it purple, for instance.

George and Lawrence were pleased that they moved to a "gayborhood" although they did not actively seek one out. George and Lawrence interpreted the offbeat aesthetics of their neighborhood as representative of liberal and progressive politics—one thing they appreciated about Durham as well.

Most Black and Latino/a residents did not frame their choice to live in Creekridge Park or the surrounding areas as a reflection of their own identities and political affiliations. During our interview, I asked longtime homeowner Connie why she chose to live in Creekridge Park. Rather than list all the reasons she loved her house or how the neighborhood reflects her political ideals, she responded candidly, "I've got to live somewhere and here it is. I've got it. It's mine." Connie's response highlights the limitations in which she could exercise her own political ideals. While she praised the predominantly Black area she first lived in as a renter ("It was like the Harlem Renaissance, it felt nice"), she explained that it "seemed more and more run down" after her apartment was broken into, and she was happy to move from those apartments into a house. She then stated, "Believe it or not those houses cost more in that area of houses that appealed to me [than in Creekridge Park]," indicating the importance of affordability in her decision to move to her current home. Here we see how Connie, unlike most of her White counterparts, was unable to achieve her desired neighborhood outcome. For her, Creekridge Park was a fine substitution, but it did not reflect her identity or her ideal predominantly Black neighborhood. Using social theorist Anthony Giddens's definition of power, this difference in achieving outcomes is a textbook illustration of a difference in power.[4]

Neighborhood Upgrade

The experience of Latino/a renters in the area varied slightly from that of homeowners and other renters. Many Latino/as explained that they chose Creekridge Park because they had to leave their previous inadequate housing. Three Latino/a respondents described cockroach infestations in their former dwellings. Martín, a newcomer and painter in his early forties from Mexico, stated that he had lived in terrible situations before moving into a house on Orchid Place: "Y te digo que he vivido con varia gente, pero ha sido lo mismo; siempre, siempre lo mismo. O sea, realmente aquí el hispano, el hispano vive muy mal fíjate, Sarah. No sé por qué." (And I'm telling you that I have lived with different people, but everything's been the same; always, always the same. In reality, the Hispanic here, the Hispanic lives very poorly, Sarah. I'm not sure why.) In contrast, Marta, a Mexican migrant in her late twenties, explained that she had to leave her house in Creekridge Park because it was in terrible shape:[5]

> La razón de mudarnos [es] porque no iban a pasar inspección y habían muchas cucarachas. Nosotros echábamos líquido, y vamos a decir allá, porque a mi niño, el más grande, se le metió una en su oído. Y yo iba allá que vinieran a, pero nunca vinieron. Entonces por eso nos mudamos.

> (Our reason for moving was because they weren't going to pass inspection and there were a lot of cockroaches. We would put pesticide and tell [the property manager]—because my son, the older one, a cockroach crawled into his ear. And I went to them to tell them to come, but they never came. So that's why we moved.)

So while moving into a house in Creekridge Park was a sign of upward mobility for Martín, the apartment that Marta lived in within Creekridge Park was in violation of city housing codes and was run by unresponsive management. This prompted her to move her family to an adjacent neighborhood.

Latino/a residents also mentioned that they chose to live in Creekridge Park over other neighborhoods because of neighborhood-specific factors, such as noise and delinquency, in predominantly Latino/a and Black apartment complexes. Below Martín describes in more detail how Creekridge Park was in better shape than his previous neighborhoods:

MARTÍN: Sí, ya como uno quiera vivir. Ajá, pero como soy pintor, Sarah, pues yo agarré y la pinté bien, la arreglé, arreglé la cocina, pinté los gabinetes, los cambios—o sea lo dejé accesible, o sea bien bonito lo dejé, para vivir un poco decente.

SARAH: Okay. ¿Y está feliz con el?

MARTÍN: ¡Oh sí! Una zona muy tranquila, porque mira, en las zonas donde yo he vivido son zonas que se llega viernes, sábado, y domingo, y es un desastre; ruido, carros pasan—arrancones, gente tomando, más que nada hispanos es lo que vive ahí. Entonces es imposible vivir. Y dentro del lugar donde vivimos es lo mismo, o sea hay gente que vive con uno, y es gente que toma, que le gusta el escándalo, cosas así; entonces no puedes vivir tranquilo, tienes que buscarle otro lugar si quieres vivir bien.

(MARTÍN: Yes, however one wants to live. Yes, but since I'm a painter, Sarah, well, I grabbed and I painted [the house] well. I fixed up, I fixed up the kitchen, painted the drawers, the—so, I left it. I left it very nice, to live a bit decently.

SARAH: Okay, and are you happy with it?

MARTÍN: Oh, yes! A very quiet area, because, look, in the areas where I have lived, they are areas that when Friday, Saturday, and Sunday arrive, it's a disaster. Noise, cars passing, engines revving, people drinking, more than anything it's Hispanics that live there. Therefore, it's impossible to live. And inside the place where we live it's the same, rather the people that live with you are people that drink, that like to be scandalous, things like that. Therefore, you cannot live peacefully. You have to look for another place if you want to live well.)

Martín's comments reveal his view that Creekridge Park is better than the previous neighborhoods he lived in because it is quieter, more *tranquilo* than those predominantly Latino/a areas. In contrast to his living arrangements in the previously described apartments (he lived with other migrant men), Martín lives in Creekridge Park with his wife and daughter.

Peace and Quiet

Overall, Latino/a and Black residents described Creekridge Park as quiet or *tranquilo*. Martín stated that he really enjoyed living in this neighborhood. He described it as follows: "Este barrio es muy tranquilo, demasiado tranquilo. . . . Te digo que ni sale la gente en este barrio. Tú pasas por ahí a las ocho de la noche, cada quién en sus casas; no se escucha ruido." (This neighborhood is very quiet, extremely quiet. . . . I'm telling you, that the people don't even go out in this neighborhood. You pass by at eight o'clock at night, everyone is in their house; you don't hear a sound.) For Martín, one of the major benefits of living in Creekridge Park is the silence at night. Cheryl, a homeowner on Pine Avenue, also stated that Creekridge Park's quiet nature is her favorite part of living there: "I like my neighborhood. I really do. I tell you the thing that I find most appealing about my neighborhood is how quiet it is. It is one of the quietest neighborhoods. It's a tranquil place. People come to my neighborhood to visit me and they are like, 'Where did this place come from? I am so surprised that—.' Like they had no reason to come through this neighborhood so they don't know about it and they are always struck by how quiet it is, which I love." When I spoke with Mary, a longtime renter in Creekridge Park, she explained that she was not familiar with the neighborhood before she moved to Creekridge Park nineteen years ago, despite frequenting the area: "I didn't even know [laughs] this was, this was, this street was Colony. I didn't even know if this house was on Colony, 'cause when I used to walk up, down Harris Street going to the movies, I didn't pay no attention. You know, this is a nice, quiet neighborhood. It's quiet; some people stick to their own business around here." Connie also described Creekridge Park as quiet: "Generally it's quiet. Which I like. The older I get the more, you know. I'm thinking even if you're young you don't want to hear that. Sometimes I come home from a music event, having listened to something. You know you come home and it's one o'clock [in the morning]. It can be disconcerting to see a bunch of cars out or whatever. People loitering or lingering. But I don't see stuff like that much." Lastly, Jerry, an established resident and retired Black homeowner, described why he chose to live on Tyler Avenue:

> Well, actually, I would have preferred to be, like, out where there's not too many houses, that type of situation. But since we moved here and, um, our daughter live here, I don't—I only have one first cousin live here, and she's a professor at [a local university]. And so well, we decided that—well, we needed to look at more homes because I was more interested in, like, a ranch or something, like, a brick house or something like that. But this is the type that they was building at the time, and—and the amount that we were willing to pay at that

particular time, it was either too much or it was—it was too little or too much. So I did decide that we always wanted, like, a two-story or something like that. And so we looked at a few houses, and then I'm just an impatient person. So we saw this one. Being since it was just the last one, and there wasn't anybody on the other side, we decided on this one. And so—so it's all right.

For Jerry, his home's location on Tyler Street gave him some semblance of the privacy he was seeking, within his and his wife's budget.

Family Recommendations

Juliana, who is Mexican and whose husband is Salvadoran, moved to Creekridge Park from Virginia and relied on her sister's help to find housing in Durham. As a newcomer, she explained that there were certain areas in Durham her sister warned her against. When I asked what specifically was the issue with these other areas she said,

> Era porque nos dice que es muy mal, mal, mal lugar porque hay mucho—Ahí hay gente que . . . Que a veces la gente—hay mucho moreno, que vive mucho moreno y que es malo; bueno, será verdad, ¿no? Como no conocemos, apenas venimos llegando aquí, pues nomás le dicen a uno eso. Pero este—pero ahorita ya que vivimos aquí pues ya conocemos mucho, ya conocemos muchas áreas y todo eso; pero nos gusta vivir aquí.

> (It was because they [Juliana's sister] told us that it is a very, bad, bad, bad place because there are a lot of—There are people that . . . Sometimes the people—there are a lot of Black people, that a lot of Black people live there and that it's [the area's] bad. Well, could it be true, no? Since we didn't know the area, we had just moved here, so they just tell you that. But this—right now, now that we live here and we are familiar with many things, we know a lot of areas and all that; but we like living here.)

Juliana's stop-and-start quotation indicates her hesitance in sharing the housing advice her sister gave her, perhaps because of its basis in anti-Black prejudice. Many researchers that study Latino/as in the United States and race in Latin America have documented the prevalence of anti-Black attitudes and structural racism.[6] These studies remind us that migrants, regardless of their country of origin, come with already formed ideas about race when they arrive in the United States.[7] An important facet of the experience of Latino/as in Durham, however, is their relative social isolation from other racial-ethnic groups. So while some Latino/as share negative views of Blacks in Durham, their social isolation along with their limited resources and power inhibit their ability to restrict or affect the life chances of Blacks. This is in contrast to the power White homeowners hold in Creekridge Park, as we saw in Chapter 3. According to research by political scientist Michael Jones-Correa, Latino/as similar to the majority of my Latino/a respondents—who have mostly Latino/as friends and coworkers and are foreign born—are less likely to feel commonality with Blacks and Whites.[8] A sense of commonality with Blacks in particular is more likely to emerge among Latino/as who speak English and are U.S. citizens.

Like Juliana, Marta and Diana found their apartment in Creekridge Park via a family member. Marta told me that she discovered her former home through the help of her cousin who used to live there. Héctor, an established renter and fifty-year-old migrant from Honduras, explained how he has lived in multiple Creekridge Park apartments. Although Héctor first lived with other Hondurans in the neighborhood, he now lives across the street from his former apartment on Cardinal Street. He decided to stay in Creekridge Park when his original roommates moved. The importance of family and compatriot networks for Latino/a migrants is not surprising and is in line with sociological research on recent immigrants.[9]

Overall, the neighborhood's multiethnic and quiet nature motivated non-White residents to live in Creekridge Park. Recommendations from friends and family, which were embedded with anti-Black prejudice, were important to the decisions of Latino/a migrants to live in Creekridge Park. Only one Black couple discussed aesthetic details reminiscent of the white, urban, middle-class habitus as an aspect of neighborhood life they appreciated. Most other Black residents discussed some feature of Creekridge Park they enjoyed, although they did not describe it as their ideal neighborhood or with the same fervor as White homeowners. For many it was a compromise of their ideal neighborhoods and their limited power. Like Connie said, "I've got to live somewhere and here it is."

NEIGHBORS, FRIENDS, AND OTHERS

The relationships Black and Latino/a residents had with other Creekridge Park residents ranged in closeness, reciprocity, and warmth. The three main types of relationships were neighborship, friendship, and ambivalent/antagonistic relations. Neighborship encompasses relationships where neighbors greeted each other but did not spend time together. Friendship describes residents who spent intentional social time with each other. Ambivalent relationships include neighbors who did not greet each other or neighbors who have had negative encounters with their neighbors in the past, but whose relationships are no longer antagonistic. Antagonistic relationships are those characterized by interneighbor conflicts and other negative issues. Since ambivalent relationships were sometimes formerly antagonistic, I analyzed both categories together. Why some relationships were friendly and others were antagonistic is outside the scope of this project, although my sample indicates that antagonistic relationships among non-Whites included issues of power and exploitation involving Black men and Latino/as.

Neighborship

Most residents seemed to have neighborly relations with their neighbors. Across all racial groups, most people I interviewed said they at least greeted their neighbors when they saw one another. Table 4.1 illustrates this trend. Most survey respondents indicated that the statements that best describe their relationships with their neighbors are "We say hello when we see each other" or "We have conversations outside our homes when we see each other." Since these characterizations are based on the neighborhood context, I describe them as neighborship, rather than friendship. (See Chapter 3 for my discussion of friendship and neighborship).

Most Latino/a respondents indicated that they thought Creekridge Park was a very friendly place. They based their characterization of friendliness on greetings, as very few Latino/a residents engaged in full conversations with neighbors. For example, when I asked Juliana, who rented on Pine Avenue, if she spent time with any neighbors, she responded, "Pues no, solo con la tía la que vive allí en frente, y a la par vive también un tío mío. Solo con ellos platico y todo, solo ellos." (Well no, only with my aunt, the one who lives here across the street, and an uncle of mine lives next

Which statement best describes your relationship with your immediate neighbors?

	Across-the-street neighbor (N)	Right-side neighbor (N)	Left-side neighbor (N)	Total (%)
White residents				
Do not talk	6	7	6	11
Say hello	21	21	20	37
Converse outside homes	27	19	16	37
Once-in-a-while plans	6	4	10	12
Regular plans	0	4	2	4
Non-White residents				
Do not talk	0	1	3	11
Say hello	7	7	4	50
Converse outside homes	5	3	4	33
Once-in-a-while plans	0	1	1	6
Regular plans	0	0	0	0

door. I only chat with them, only them.) She also revealed that the basis of her interactions with other neighbors were *saludos* (greetings). I asked her if there were neighbors who spoke Spanish, and she explained that her neighbors' Spanish was limited to *hola* (hello) and *¿cómo estás?* (how are you?). Therefore, so were their conversations. Héctor's experience echoes Juliana's; as a renter in Creekridge Park, he stated that his neighbors were generally friendly, but there were limits to their interactions:

HÉCTOR: Por ejemplo, las señoras que viven a la par ahí—"Hey [inentendible] . . ." Y yo digo, "bueno," medio nos saludamos. Ella tiene unos perros y muchas veces me cuenta las historias de los perros y así ¿verdad? Pero, no es así pues, nos saludamos ¿verdad? Y con los otros de allá lo mismo, bueno es la gente muy amable, bueno, para otra gente que no habla ellos, ah. Y los del frente pues también, así están.
SARAH: Okay, se saludan pero no hablan mucho.
HÉCTOR: Pero no, no.
SARAH: ¿Y te hablan en inglés o en español?
HÉCTOR: En inglés, ellos son americanos.

(HÉCTOR: For example, the ladies that live next door there [say]—"Hey [inaudible] . . ." And I say, "good," we halfway greet each other. She has dogs and a lot of the time she tells me stories about her dogs, and it's like that, right? Well, it's not that way, but we greet each other, right? And with the others from over there it's the same, the people are very friendly, and there are others who don't speak. And those directly across [the street], those also are like that.

SARAH: Okay, you greet each other, but you don't say much.

HÉCTOR: Well, no, no.

SARAH: And they speak to you in English or Spanish?

HÉCTOR: In English, they're American.)

Héctor characterizes his White neighbors as friendly because they say "hey" to him. Although they cannot communicate beyond preliminary greetings, he appreciates their hellos.

Martín, who lives on Orchid Place, also identified similar practices, which provides some evidence that this mode of interaction between Latino/as and non-Latino/as is normative in Creekridge Park. The way his White neighbors interacted with Martín pleased him very much, particularly since he saw these short interactions as a reflection of Creekridge Park's quiet and peaceful nature:

MARTÍN: Aquí en mi vecindario toda la gente nos saludan.

SARAH: ¿Sí?

MARTÍN: De verdad. Todos, mis vecinos—Como ven que somos muy tranquilos también nosotros, no hacemos ruido—Nosotros nos hicimos a la forma de ellos, ¿me entiendes? Aquí en este vecindario no hay escándalo, no hay carros con volumen—el estéreo a todo volumen, no hay borrachos afuera de las, de las yarditas; y nosotros nos hicimos igual. Como somos nada más nosotros, bien tranquilos; nos tomamos unas cervezas tranquilos, hasta ahí; y nosotros nos hicimos como ellos. Entonces por eso ahí todo mundo nos ve: "Hola, hola, hola." Hasta ahí. Sí, cómo ves.

SARAH: Okay. ¿Y eso ha sido desde el principio que todo el mundo lo saluda y los trata bien?

MARTÍN: Desde que llegué ha sido así digo, no cambia.

SARAH: ¿Y ustedes tienen conversaciones? ¿Usted habla inglés?

MARTÍN: Hablo muy poco, muy poco. Pero en este vecindario casi no hay mucha conversación, todos en su casa. O sea, llegan, te ve: "Hola, hola," y a su casa.

SARAH: Y se meten a la casa.

MARTÍN: No hay nada que conversemos, no. No, nada de eso.

SARAH: ¿Y cómo le parece eso?

MARTÍN: No, perfecto.

SARAH: ¿Perfecto?

MARTÍN: Sí—Sí, sí, para mí está genial. Imagínate, para qué quiero vivir en un lugar donde no pueda dormir, donde te vas a dormir y ya está el escándalo, que el vecino está haciendo escándalo; mejor así, está perfecto.

(MARTÍN: Here in my neighborhood, everyone says hello to me.

SARAH: Yeah?

MARTÍN: For real. Everyone, my neighbors—Since they see that we are also quiet, we don't make noise—we conformed to their way of acting, you understand? Here in this neighborhood nothing scandalous happens, there aren't loud cars—the stereo at full volume, there aren't drunks outside in the, in the yards; and we conformed. Since it's only us, we're quiet; we drink some beers peacefully, that's it, and we made ourselves like them. Therefore, everyone sees us and says "Hello, hello, hello." That's it.

SARAH: Okay, and have people been greeting you and treating you well since the beginning?

MARTÍN: Since we arrived it's been that way, no changes.

SARAH: And do you guys have conversations? Do you speak English?

MARTÍN: I speak very little, very little [English]. But in this neighborhood there's hardly any conversation, everyone's in their house. So they come home, they see you, they say "Hello, hello," and to their house.

SARAH: And they go inside their house.

MARTÍN: There is nothing we talk about, no. No, none of that.

SARAH: And what do you think about that?

MARTÍN: No, it's perfect.

SARAH: Perfect?

MARTÍN: Yes, yes, yes, for me it's great. Imagine, why would I want to live in a place where I can't sleep, where you're going to sleep and there's scandalous behavior, your neighbor is acting scandalously. Better this way, it's perfect.)

Martín's assessment of Creekridge Park is directly related to his previous housing experience. He appreciated these limited interactions because they took place in a quieter environment, free from drunkenness and loud cars. At the same time, Martín's reading of me as *americana* may have also influenced his consistent description of Creekridge Park as "*perfecto*" and the pride with which he shares that he and his family have conformed to the neighborhood's way of being. (For more on the intricacies of our interview dynamic, see Appendix A.) Martín's comments also reveal the pressure of assimilation that many immigrants are under. It seems that Martín wants me to positively judge him as the "right" type of immigrant—not like the others who fail to change their manner of behavior. This theme comes up again in my conversation with Martín, as I discuss later.

The characterization of Creekridge Park and its residents as friendly by Latino/a migrants echoes claims by White respondents. While the neighborships that Whites describe differ significantly in their intimacy, Latino/a residents do not identify this difference. Their experiences of Creekridge Park and its American residents are greatly impacted by their social positions in the United States as Latino/a migrants—some of whom are undocumented. Similarly, the scholarship of sociologists Rebecca Adams and Graham Allan on friendship explains that friendship and how individuals define friends are based, in part, on their social and economic locations.[10] Within an unreceptive national context (as Marta and others describe below), the greetings Latino/a migrants receive are perceived as a stark, "friendly" contrast.

Unlike their Latino/a neighbors, Black residents were much less likely to see Creekridge Park as a friendly neighborhood. This characterization of the neighborhood is directly tied to their experiences and their social positioning within a racialized system. Cheryl, a Black homeowner on Pine Avenue, indicated that she had hopes that more substantial neighborhood interactions would be a part of her life in this neighborhood:

CHERYL: People were not as friendly as I had hoped and thought that they would be or at least, this image I had in my head of what friendly would be like. . . . Despite the fact that I didn't have a lot of relationship with these folks, if they saw somebody walking around your neighborhood—like, I might have gotten somebody to come and do something at my house, but I wasn't here, they would come over and ask them questions or they would call the police. And so there was a way that, even though we weren't chummy, we weren't talking to each other—and some of them I had met—they in fact did look out for neighbors if there was folks looking around your house and you weren't here.

SARAH: Right. Okay. Okay. So it's still—you still sort of had some relationships even though it wasn't exactly what you expected.

CHERYL: I had people who looked out for my house. I didn't have any relationships in this neighborhood for the most part.

Cheryl mentioned that she and some of her elderly neighbors had positive relationships. As she puts it, however, these relationships were "purely based on support and intervention in crisis." Cheryl checked on her elderly neighbors when there was a storm or some other severe weather: "They would speak, you know, if they happened to be outside, but they were very rarely outside. And so that, at least, was some semblance of what I was looking for, but it wasn't even like they were in a position to reciprocate. It just was a obligation that I felt as a neighbor to them." Cheryl felt a duty as a neighbor because of her neighbors' advanced age. At the same time, when I asked Cheryl if she had any friends in the neighborhood, she responded, "Absolutely not. Absolutely not. I think, I think too much of the term 'friend' to, to, to use it lightly. So I absolutely would not say that I have any friends in this neighborhood, absolutely not." Although she acknowledged that the neighbor role has obligations, she also saw a clear distinction between friendship and neighborship. In Chapter 3, we saw how Cheryl was ignored by her neighbors for the first five years of her tenure in Creekridge Park. This changed when she began to plant a garden in her front yard. The work of Adams and Allan on friendship is helpful here. They argue that analyses of friendships and other relationships must consider the larger structural context of the relationship rather than merely focusing on the dyad alone. Cheryl's disappointment with the social interactions in Creekridge Park is inextricably tied to her social location as a Black homeowner—especially when compared with the overwhelmingly positive social experiences of White homeowners.

Lawrence, a Black renter in the Creekridge Park area, also believed there was a difference between friendship and neighborship. This distinction, however, reflects a separation he intentionally created:

It's not really a priority to me [to be friends with my neighbors].
I tend to structure my life socially in ways that are deliberate. Deliberate in some ways and then I actively resist other sorts of things. . . .
It has never for me been, like, a rule that, like, well you live . . . near

all of these people so you have to become friends with them. So I'm also that way sort of, like, in the workplace, like, it's the fact that we, like, see each other for, like, forty hours a week does not mean that we are friends, you know, like, friends are people I spend my free time with. So yeah for me it hasn't been a priority, but also I don't know just because, like, there's—because we have other social artistic recreational stuff going on, but it's just sometimes kind of hard to try [inaudible] to have time for all of that.

Similar to how he viewed work acquaintances, Lawrence hesitated to call neighbors friends and engage in structured activities meant to foster neighborhood-based friendships. Unlike Cheryl's, Lawrence's distinction between neighbors and friends was self-imposed, while Cheryl's classification reflects her disappointing social experience in Creekridge Park.

During our interview, Mary, a Black renter on Colony Street, described the different types of relationships she had with her next-door neighbors:

Like I say, I, Luke [her White next-door neighbor] he talk anytime I talk. Yesterday I was talking to his wife 'cause she out there . . . and I was talking to her a while. I was out there [in the yard] and stuff, you know, so, you know, we have a pretty good, you know, I mean they are pretty good neighbors. You know, 'cause my neighbor that lived there before them, he was a lawyer, he was all right, too, 'cause he stopped one day and gave me a ride up the street when I walked, but he didn't do too much talking like they did. He wasn't, he wasn't as friendly, although he still, he was nice enough to stop and give me a ride, but he still wasn't as friendly as they were, you know, he wasn't as friendly. . . . His son, you know, he would come and visit, whoever would come to visit, they would speak, you know, they had good manners, you know, but he just wasn't home that much [because he was a lawyer].

Mary's description identifies two ways that neighbors can be friendly: talking and giving rides. Although Mary's previous neighbor was not home much and did not chat with Mary as often as Luke and Emma, Mary does identify this previous neighbor as somewhat friendly because he offered her a ride one day. This is a particularly important act for Mary, since she relies on public transportation for her grocery shopping and other activities. Mary's distinction points to a range of friendliness—people can be polite while keeping to themselves. It is clear from our conversation, however, that Mary preferred when people regularly spoke with her. Unlike her Latino/a counterparts, a hello did not constitute friendliness for Mary.

Friendship

Many White homeowners—more so than their non-White neighbors—discussed the friends they had in their neighborhood. Some White residents, such as Seth, did perceive a difference between friendship and neighborship, as I indicated in Chapter 3. Some Black and Latino/a residents did mention that they were friends with their neighbors. Only 25 percent of the non-White survey respondents (N = 4) indicated that they had a close friend who lived in Creekridge Park. Over 50 percent of the White survey respondents (N = 33) stated that they had a close friend who lived in the neighborhood. Interestingly, of residents who claimed that they had close friends, a larger percentage of Black and Latino/a residents than White residents indicated that one of their five closest friends lived in their neighborhood.

My interview data included a few accounts of non-White residents with neighborhood-based friendships. Connie, for example, lives on Pine Avenue and occasionally got together with her White next-door neighbors, Lilith and Frank: "Like I said my friends Trent [inaudible], Frank, and Lilith—on a semiregular basis we'll, most of the time I'll email them something and give them a heads up, 'I'm thinking about doing this, are you interested?' There have been times where I might be sitting out and they might say, 'Oh were fixing to—' they're heading some place, and if I feel like it, I'll go with them. We've done that a few times. So that kind of interaction has happened. Mainly just with them. So I don't know what other people on the street do." She even described one scenario in which she stayed at their house for a week when her own house lost power after a storm. During our interview, Connie described how she befriended Lilith and Frank. It seems Connie shared a connection with Lilith and Frank before they even moved next door:

> Yeah, well, Frank and Lilith are people that have been there the least time that live right below me [inaudible]. When they first moved in, I used to see her but I didn't see her face, I only saw her back. She didn't seem to want to be seen so I didn't, I'm not that outgoing so I wasn't one to go knocking on the door and say hi. She looked like

she wanted to be in her world and that's fine because I like to be in my world. So you know I didn't say anything but one of my musician friends said that his girlfriend's cousin had moved in the neighborhood and was probably close to where I lived. But he didn't know where they lived. Anyway it turned out I knew Lilith because I used to be in a hiking club, or whatever you want to call it that every Saturday we would meet somewhere and hike. A lot of times we would come here [to Stella's Café] for lunch or we would go somewhere after the walk. So I had met her but then I hadn't been in that walking group for a couple of years and so I never saw her anymore. But then when she moved in I didn't know that was her. So, because she didn't really ever look, because we didn't look at each other. So then she got a piece of mail one day and she goes "I know that name." So that's when she and her husband came over and it turns out he was the cousin of the musician and I thought, "You got to be kidding." So we just started doing things. They were coming out to some of the music things that the musician friend of mine who is a sax player. So they came to some of the things I was doing, you know, different things. Sometimes we'll play [the board game] Scrabble. We haven't done that in a while, but we would do that when I was down at their house. They would play Scrabble by candlelight or something because the power was out. Then they would come over and play on my porch; we just haven't had a chance to do that. Not too long ago we did go to [inaudible] for dinner because a musician I know is performing there. We had a nice dinner there. You know we'd get our little outings here and there but I don't like to try to suggest "let's do this or that" because you know they have things that they do separately and together.

With this explanation, we see that Lilith and Connie were friends because of their previous, nonneighborhood connections. Their proximity to each other provided support for their friendship, but the catalyst was their hiking club association. The impact of Connie's connection to Frank's family is also important to consider. This type of neighborhood relationship was also common among White homeowners. In Chapter 3, I discussed the impact of sharing neighborhood house listings with one's social networks to increase the presence of like-minded people in the neighborhood. The new neighbors that current residents already knew were likely to become neighborhood-based friends. Again, the proximity may have helped to strengthen the relationship, but some preexisting connection assured their compatibility. These pre–Creekridge Park connections may help explain why almost half of the survey respondents said they had a close friend in the neighborhood.

Ambivalent and Antagonistic Relations

As I mentioned at the beginning of the chapter, ambivalent relationships were those where no greetings took place between neighbors or where formerly antagonistic relationships became neutral. Mary, who had positive relationships with a few of her neighbors, described her displeasure with her new neighbors on Colony Street. She stated a couple of times during the interview that this new couple was not as friendly as Luke and Emma, her other neighbors, because they did not say hello or speak to her when she and they were outside at the same time. She was clearly unhappy about it, although she did remark toward the end of the interview that they were not doing anything harmful:

> All my other neighbors are all right, 'cause one thing about those [new] people, they might not associate with nobody, but they don't do har—, mean and hateful things to me, I mean, to nobody. 'Cause they tend to their business and some people like that, they's like being to theyself, you know, like I say, Luke and them about their age. All of them probably the same age range, so mean that's what they associate theyself with, you know, that's why I, they, be friends 'cause they probably have a lot more in common than they have with the rest of us. So that I can understand, too, and they don't [have] too much in common with the Camerons, 'cause they're pretty old and they probably don't have nothing in common with me, 'cause I'm not, you know, not they age. But see Luke and Emma, they probably have a lot in common with them, so that's what they, they associate with them. You know, get along good with them 'cause, you know, 'cause they probably about the same age and they have a lot of, they probably think like on the same level about things, you know, so I can, I can understand that, you know.

In this explanation, Mary pointed to age differences to rationalize why her new neighbors did not speak to her but did socialize with Emma and Luke. The survey and interview data indicate, however, that very few of my respondents did not speak to their neighbors. Mary's initial reaction to her neighbors' lack of communication indicates that at least acknowledging your neighbor is normative in Creekridge Park and that her neighbors' failure to do so was undesirable for Mary.

I did encounter one instance of a formerly negative relationship becoming more neutral between Lawrence and George and their Latino/a neighbors:

LAWRENCE: Next door are the [*inaudible*], Rodrigo and Juana, and he works in construction and she's an advocate for the Latino community. So we had a rocky start with them and you're [George] not into them much.

SARAH: May I ask why? You don't have to answer.

LAWRENCE: Well that's why we no longer have a cat. One of their dogs got and killed the cat.

SARAH: Oh wow, okay.

GEORGE: They're not the most responsible pet owners, let's say that. Other than that they can be halfway okay sometimes. Individually I think they're fine, but there seems to be other people so they have at least two children, two school-age children living there, but there are often other people there, too, and I don't know if they live there or if they work there or what, and they have also other adult children as well. I don't know if they live there, work there, or renting rooms in there or what, so there's—and I don't really [want] to get into it, I don't care to really know what exactly is happening over there. But there's a variety of people who spend considerable amount of time there. So that's them.

George's comments about the actual event were minimal, and most of his response was about how many people lived next door. The number of Latino/a residents living in particular homes was a trope a few non-Latino/as called upon during their interviews. Although it may be true that several people lived next door and he was not sure who lived there, the connection George drew between the number of residents and their roles as pet owners was unclear. Using this trope seemed to be a way to discredit or negatively judge the Latino/a household in question.

Over the course of our conversation, Jerry, a Black homeowner on Tyler Street, discussed his run-ins with the residents of a small multidwelling rental property behind his home. According to Jerry these neighbors were noisy and even came into his backyard, which prompted him to put up a fence. Although the fence is up, he complained to the police that his neighbors would come up and hang out behind his fence, "smoking reefer and all that type of situation," as well as play their music very loudly. Although he says those living in these rentals are very transient, he did state that some of his neighbors had walked by his house in an attempt to intimidate him. After asking the police to address the threats the neighbors made to him ("[they said] they're going to shoot me"), Jerry felt frustrated with the authorities' lack of action. His antagonistic interactions with the neighbors culminated in him firing his gun in the direction of the rental property between Tyler and Grove Street. Jerry explains:

> I did it [fire my gun] for a message to the fools [who live in the rental property behind my house] that was threatening me saying they was going to kill me. And they're going to shoot me, and they're going to do all this. I just let them know "you got the wrong one because I'm not going to be a sitting little duck here." But [after I fired my gun] that's when I got in trouble—when the policemen came. They came, I didn't run and hide. I was sitting out on my, my car when they came in. He asked me whether I did it. I said "yeah." And I said, "You know why I did it? Because every time the bad guys do it or whatever, you don't do nothing. I've been telling you all for the last—what, for the longest, you never arrested anybody. But look who you arresting now. You arresting me." . . . [Let me clarify,] they didn't arrest me. They took my weapons. But I had to go to answer the charges—I got, um, letters [of support] from the neighbors [who participated in the neighborhood watch with me] and, you know, I got letters from like four, four of my neighbors, and they explained, "Look, the only thing the man do is . . . [try] to keep the neighborhood safe. It's unfortunate that he went about it the way he did, but sometimes, things happen." But I did it [fire my gun] on purpose to actually to prove a point to bring light on what's going on. . . . So I made that statement [by firing my gun]. . . . You know, I said, "I just won't do that again," and I haven't done it again.

So while White homeowners successfully called upon the police to take care of issues in the neighborhood, Jerry fired his gun in the city to get the attention of the police, who he felt were failing to address his concerns. Jerry also explained that some of his neighbors who participated in the neighborhood watch with him wrote him letters of support as part of his defense against the charges. These letters seemed to explain that he only fired his weapon out of frustration with his neighbors' threats and the authorities' lack of response. And while they disagreed with his action, Jerry's neighborhood watch supported him.

Jerry explained that the neighborhood was currently quieter and that the residents who caused trouble before no longer lived there. This was the only example of a truly antagonistic altercation involving any of the Black and Latino/a respondents and the only interaction with any respondent that included gunfire. Multiple times throughout his interview Jerry made the statement "I'm a man" or a variation thereof (e.g., "I'm a grown man"; "I'm a Black man") to explain his behavior. His comments on being a man are related to his raced and gendered social position. For Black men, particularly in the South, "I am a man" is imbued with historical and cultural meaning.[11] The word "boy" was historically used by Whites to demean Black men in the South during slavery and Jim Crow. The slogan "I am a man!" was used during the 1960s as part of various civil rights protests, most famously a 1968 sanitation workers' march involving Dr. Martin Luther King Jr.[12] Exclaiming "I am a man!," therefore, can be a profoundly countercultural act. In this historical and regional context, Jerry's refrain of "I'm a grown man" can be seen as a direct response to his patronizing interactions with the police who did not take him seriously.

Jerry's interactions with his neighbors can also be viewed as masculine performances, or as sociologists Douglas Schrock and Michael Schwalbe argue, manhood acts.[13] They explain that "manhood acts are . . . strategically adapted to the realities of resource availability, individual skill, local culture, and audience expectations."[14] Taking this information, we can begin to comprehend Jerry's behavior and his explanation that shooting at the apartment complex was the only way to get the attention of his neighbors and the police. Frustrated by the lack of response from the police and his neighbors, shooting his gun was a strategy Jerry adapted from the resources available to him.

Interactions with the police were also a topic of conversation with some of my Latino/a respondents. Martín explained that being undocumented complicated neighbor-to-neighbor issues. He stated that he would call the police if he ever had an issue with a neighbor; it was clear that he saw this as the proper behavior in American neighborhoods. Because Martín framed calling the police as the correct way to act as a Creekridge Park resident, I got the impression that he wanted to be perceived as different from the majority of Latinos in Durham because he knew how to act appropriately in the U.S. context. Again, this may have been related to his perception of me as *americana* and his desire to present himself as properly assimilated. He did, however, indicate his concern that calling the police puts undocumented migrants in a particularly vulnerable situation:

En México tenemos la costumbre de arreglar nosotros mismos nuestros problemas, y hay mucho pleito por eso. Y haz de cuenta que tú empiezas el pleito, y termina tu hermana, termina tu mamá, termina—luego ya terminan los hombres, y son golpes. Y aquí como es otra educación, yo he visto que aquí para todo llaman a la policía. No sé si yo tengo—un error, pero yo siempre veo que si hay un problema llaman luego, luego al policía, el policía arregla, ve que cosa, y lo arregla—Porque imagínate, imagínate si yo me pongo a discutir ahorita con—por ejemplo con un mollo de—perdón, con un moreno; ni yo le voy a entender, ni él me va a entender, y puede ser que se enoje él o me enoje yo. Entonces el que la lleva de perder a veces somos nosotros por ser ilegales, porque hoy a como están las cosas mejor así. Pero yo pienso que si tuviéramos un problema, pues yo pienso que con el policía; pues ya el policía verá.

(In Mexico we have the custom of fixing our problems on our own and there are a lot of fights because of it. You start the fight and your sister finishes it, your mom finishes it; afterward the men finish and there are punches thrown. And people are taught differently here and I have seen that here they call the police for everything. I don't know if I have [made] an error [in my assessment], but I also see that if you have a problem they call, the police, the police fixes—they see what happened and they fix it. Because imagine, imagine if I go ahead and start arguing with—for example, a mollo[15] of—excuse me, a Black person. I'm not going to understand him and he's not going to understand me and it could be that I annoy him or he annoys me. And so we [undocumented Latino/as] are the ones who have something to lose sometimes because we're illegal, and so because of the way things are today it's better this way. But I think that if I had a problem, well I think that with a policeman, well the police would take care of it.)

Although Martín acknowledged that involving the police is potentially jeopardizing for him and other undocumented Latino/as, he still insisted that he would call the police if he had a problem. It is also important to acknowledge Martín's casual anti-Black prejudice that peppered his example. He uses a racial epithet, and although he corrects himself, his example is based on the assumption that he and his Black neighbor will not understand each other. Although he is likely referring to an English-Spanish language barrier, one can imagine—based on Martín's comments—that he also means they will not *culturally* understand each other. This distancing from Blacks and alignment with Whites is consistent with findings on Latin American migrants in Durham who feel most close to Whites.[16] Based on our interview, I am also left wondering if Martín would actually call the police if he had an issue or if he was merely saying so because he believed it was the appropriate way to act in this predominantly White, *tranquilo* neighborhood.

Héctor echoed Martín's concerns about making a situation worse by involving the police. Unlike Martín, however, Héctor concluded that he would never call the police as a result: "Si yo le llamo la policía a las señoras [con los perros que ladran], ¿qué cree usted que puede pasar? . . . Cuando yo cometo un error por mínimo que sea, ella me va a llamar la policía y a mí no me va a gustar, entonces yo no le hago algo que no quiero que me hagan a mí. Eso está muy bien así, sí." (If I call the police on those ladies [whose dogs bark loudly], what do you think will happen? When I do something wrong, however small, she will call the police and I won't like that, so I don't do anything that I don't want them to do to me. It's very good as it is, yeah.) Héctor's sentiment acknowledged the power differential between native Whites and immigrant Latino/as and the unintended harm and racialized outcomes that these conflicts can produce. Similarly, although they said they never had any specific conflicts with their non-Latino/a neighbors, some Latino/a residents described the general political environment in the United States in regard to immigration and Latino/a migrants as antagonistic. For example, Diana and Marta framed the attitude toward Latino/as in the United States as fundamentally hostile:

DIANA: Pues nunca van a aceptar los hispanos aquí [risas].
MARTA: Aquí estamos a la fuerza.
DIANA: De aquí lo quieren sacar a uno como sea.

(DIANA: Well, they're never going to accept Hispanics here [laughs].
MARTA: We're here by force.
DIANA: They want to remove you from here however they can.)

From the point of view of Diana and Marta, conflicts underlie their time in the United States because they are Latinas. Diana and Marta's experience is supported by data presented in Chapter 1 on Latino/as in the United States, including American attitudes toward undocumented migrants (who are often associated with Latinidad). Interestingly, when asked specifically about their experiences with Black and White Americans, Diana and Marta are more positive, while their pointed criticisms are reserved for other Latino/as. I discuss this pattern in more detail in the following section.

DIVERSITY, INTEGRATION, AND RACISM

The meanings of residential integration and neighborhood diversity are central to this project. A person's racial-ethnic standpoint structures how she or he interprets the world, so it is not surprising that there were differences in how White, Black, and Latino/a residents experienced Creekridge Park. As I discussed in Chapter 2, White residents may have acknowledged inequality in an abstract manner, but they rarely saw themselves as actors with racial privilege or power. Class factors mitigated their racial privilege; even though they were homeowners, Creekridge Park was not wealthy Groveland Estates. There were other White homeowners who were better-off. In addition, they saw their decision to live in Creekridge Park as the manifestation of their progressive politics, placing them above reproach in any questions related to equality.

In contrast, many of the Black and Latino/a residents I spoke with mentioned a negative event or situation in their neighborhood life that they viewed as a result of their marginal racial-ethnic status. In this section, I present the experiences of Black and Latino/a Creekridge Park residents in regard to race and racism.

Black Residential Experiences

Cheryl, a Black homeowner who has lived in the area for several years, stated that she specifically sought out a racially mixed neighborhood when she purchased her home. Her reasons, however, were not the same as those White residents gave:

CHERYL: I was very clear that I wanted a racially mixed neighborhood. But the reason I wanted a racially mixed neighborhood was because of what I understood about the depressed values of homes in all-Black neighborhoods. But it was very important that I not be in a all-White neighborhood because—and one of the reasons I'm interested in your topic is because when I purchased my home, I specifically was interested—this was an unarticulated interest—I was specifically interested in recapturing the kind of neighborhood that I had when I grew up, a neighborhood where there were close relationships, where everybody knew each other, where people spoke to each other when they were in their yard, where people took care and looked out for each other, looked out for each other's children, 'cause that's what I grew up with. And I had been living, up until I bought this house, in apartment communities. It was closer to that in my last apartment before I moved here because they were duplexes, as opposed to those multifamily dwellings that I had been accustomed to. So what I said to him [the realtor] was it was important to me for it to be racially mixed. And I kept saying to him, "Are you sure this is racially mixed?" Because all of my immediate neighbors were White. But it wasn't until later that I discovered that the people of color that he was referring to were at either end of the street. Most of my immediate neighbors were White, but this was constituted as a racially mixed neighborhood because of the people in racial, different racial and ethnic groups in Harris Street and at the top of Pine Avenue going into Cardinal Street. I think that's basically what I was looking for. I mean, I had some characteristics specific to the house that I was looking for, but in terms of racial makeup, that was kind of a prerequisite for me.

SARAH: Okay. So he sort of couched it as racially mixed. Is that—would you have used that term then?

CHERYL: I said I wanted racially mixed, even though since then I am politically conscious of the fact that race is a myth, it's a political construct. I mean, I'm real clear about that. But I'm saying whether you call it race or ethnic mix, I specifically said that to him because of my concern about the value of my home being retained and increasing, as opposed to what happens, because of an industry, not because there's anything wrong with folks' houses, in single-race, particularly African American communities. Even I understood politically that even residents of all–African American neighborhoods pay higher insurance costs and so because I had that understanding, it was important to me making my first big, you know, and one of probably my largest kind of investment, that I make a choice that meant that I could try to mitigate those circumstances.

Cheryl's concern about property values resonates with the work by sociologist Camille Zubrinsky Charles, which concludes that Black homeowners in particular are more likely to live in segregated, poorer neighborhoods than Black renters and are the only racial group to incur financial penalties for owning a home.[17] Social scientists refer to this structural devaluation as the "segregation tax."[18]

In our conversation, Cheryl revealed the economic interests that undergirded her decision to look for a racially mixed neighborhood. Because of her position as a Black woman in our racialized system, Cheryl had a different set of concerns than her White counterparts. Although economic concerns fueled her decision and the decisions of her White neighbors, she weighed her choice to move into Creekridge Park against social costs. Unlike her White neighbors who, as I discussed in Chapter 2, had a lot to gain socially in this particular white, urban, middle-class habitus, Cheryl saw a lack of social cohesion in Creekridge Park and it disappointed her. She wanted to replicate the neighborhood-based social relationships she had when she was growing up in all-Black neighborhoods, but Creekridge Park had not met her expectations. Cheryl speculated that the lack of social relationships across the neighborhood is in part related to increasing neighborhood diversity. She also pinpointed the loss of multigenerational housing and the fluidity of some residents, particularly students, as important factors that affect neighborhood socializing. She did clarify that she has found some students to be very friendly. Unlike her White counterparts, however, Cheryl viewed all of these social interactions and lack of relationship building within the context of systemic power and privilege:

> I think all of us, by virtue of living in a racist, classist culture, that means that people of color have less privilege and less access to power than Whites do in this culture, that there are all kinds of reasons why we all are prejudiced. But Whites have, by virtue of being in economic, political, and social power, having positions of social and political power, by virtue of the fact that they control all of the institutions in our culture, even when you are working class or poor Whites, because Whites control the system, you cash in on that privilege and you have power, whether or not you recognize it, whether or not you use it, you have power. And so it is your prejudice and your power that enables you to then marginalize and deprive people of color of privilege and

opportunities and power that they ought to equally have access to. But because of your power and privilege, you get to control. And I'm saying that based on the fact that all of our institutions are primarily controlled by White men, but Whites have that power. But even when you look at the highest office in the country, the presidency, the president is a Black man. He don't have the power to do nothing outside of a corporate, economic, capitalist structure that is not allowed by the folks who actually have the power. And so I don't think about the fact that somebody has a position that is supposed to be associated with power with real power. I'm talking about people who have real power or who get the benefit of that real power and who is in control of that power. So power plus prejudice equals racism to me. And there are a number of other -isms 'cause I think the same way about class and all those other -isms.

Cheryl identified the importance of power and privilege in structuring one's life chances. We can see, based on her comments, how race and class also impacted the limited social interactions she experienced in her neighborhood. Although the loss of intergenerational homes and neighborhoods is an important consideration for understanding contemporary neighborhood relations, we can see how neighborhood interactions take place within a larger "racist, classist culture." The socializing we see in the Creekridge Park of Chapter 2 is not the same experienced by Cheryl. While her White counterparts are able to enjoy the social benefits of occupying the white, urban, middle-class habitus and living in Creekridge Park, Cheryl unwittingly chose retaining her home value over the kind of neighborhood social life she wanted. Because she is a Black homeowner in this white space, enjoying both is not an option for her.

Cheryl is not the only resident of color who shared her views on racial inequality with me. Jerry, whom we heard from earlier, lamented the current state of racial affairs both broadly and locally. Days before our interview in Jerry's home, the workers of Stella's Café, a neighborhood gourmet café, accused Jerry of panhandling from customers seated in the restaurant's outdoor area. I held several interviews with White residents at Stella's. It is a white neighborhood space White residents frequently cite as a favorite spot. Their prices also attracted a specifically middle-class clientele.[19] Jerry recounted his experience at Stella's as follows:

It's terrible. I'm—I'm 60 years old, and I—I'm visited with the same crap that I went through all my life, and it hurts. It really hurts, and there ain't nothing I can do about it because even in the—in—in my neighborhood, take Stella's [Café], for instance, up here. To me, I think they're prejudiced toward Black people. I see Black people there. But if you don't fit in that whatever they call a good Black person, then you got a problem because actually, one day last week in particular, I was walking by with a lot of people. And, um, I spotted some people talking. They had dogs. . . . I owned some dogs like that at one particular time. And I was just speaking to them. All of a sudden, I'm [accused of being] a panhandler [by the staff of Stella's Café]. Do you understand what I'm saying? [They said] "You're a panhandler," and people tell him "no, he—he didn't ask for money or anything." . . . They [the staff at Stella's Café] came out of accusing me of asking people for money. Maybe because . . . I'm a disabled vet. A lot of times, I wear my old uniform. That's me. Do you understand what I'm saying? But panhandling? No. You're wrong.

While he was at Stella's, Jerry spoke with several customers who were outside the café with their dogs. It seems, based on Jerry's suspicion, that because he is a Black disabled vet who was wearing his old army uniform, the staff at Stella's assumed he was a panhandler and was asking customers for money. Jerry's experience did not end with the accusation of panhandling. He went back the next day to demand an apology. Jerry continued:

JERRY: But I've been here [in Creekridge Park for] ten years, like I said. And I notice. No Black people [eat at Stella's]. And that tells me either Black people don't like the food, or they make Black people uncomfortable. Actually, when I asked to speak to the manager the other day, they sent me to a Black guy. I don't even think he was the manager.

SARAH: How did that go?

JERRY: "You Black, you go to"—I went. I said "I'd like to speak to the manager or somebody in charge." They direct me to a Black guy [who works at Stella's]. The only Black guy that was in there.

SARAH: Um-hum. Um-hum. How did—how was that—how was that response? What did he say? Was he helpful?

JERRY: Oh, he—he said, "Well, I will speak to them [the manager]. She's not in today." But I said, "Look, all I want is an apology or something because—because something wrong about this. There's something just definitely wrong about this. What did I do?" I'm still waiting to see what I did [to be accused of panhandling]. I spoke to the—to the owner, the manager, the owner. He came over that day. He didn't know who I was. But when I went there, and I was talking to the Black guy, he said [to me], "You were here yesterday?" And I said "yes. I was the person that was here yesterday, and I'm just trying to figure out what's going on." He said, "You have to leave the place. You got to leave the premises."

So after Jerry went back to Stella's to ask for an apology, he did not receive one and he was asked to leave the premises by the manager on duty. Jerry also explained that the police told him that if the management at Stella's does not want him at the café, they have every right to ask him to leave. Jerry was incredulous, asking how it is legal that he not be served when he has done nothing wrong. Jerry's recounting of this experience reminded him of the overtly racist treatment more common in the 1950s. As he said, he's sixty years old and is still dealing with the same type of discrimination of his youth.

Later in the interview, Jerry connected his experience at Stella's with a larger frustration in regard to race. He was particularly annoyed with how people discuss race in America today: "I'm not that person to be like 'Oh, kumbaya, I love everybody.' I don't. I do not like everybody. I do not like a lot of Black people. I'm a human being. And that's what's going on in the world today. Everybody want everybody to love each other. It ain't going to happen. It's not going to happen." Jerry spoke with candor, especially about contemporary racial issues. What he characterized as the "kumbaya, I love everybody" approach parallels common definitions of diversity, including those I discussed in Chapter 2. Diversity is positioned contemporarily as an issue of acceptance and everybody getting along. From Jerry's point of view, this is an absurd premise (e.g., "I do not like everybody. . . . I'm a human being"). As Jerry argues below, this emphasis on acceptance legitimates more conservative, racist points of view, since they can be veiled in egalitarian terms. He makes this point by using conservative talk show host Elizabeth Hasselback, who was on ABC's *The View* at the time of our interview, as an example:

This [Elizabeth] Hasselback woman on [ABC's morning talk show] *The View* . . . you can tell a person by what they stand for. . . . What she stand for to me [is], "Well, you know, we got slaves, but you know, they happy. They just love being on this plantation," that type of situation. You understand what I'm talking about? Now, see, that's the kind of fight that I—that I would jump right in. You understand what I'm talking about? Because if you don't understand something, you fall for everything. The N word. "Well, you called me the N word." Are you saying I'm nice? That's what they telling me. Well, I'm nice? Well, go ahead and call me what I am—not what I am. Call me what you been calling me. Everybody walks—"oh, the N word, the N word." Well, there's no such thing. There's no N word in the dictionary. It's N-I-G-G-A, nigga. Used to be nigger. You follow me? Tell me the truth. I mean, you know, as long as people put it out there, I know where I stand. I don't know where I stand when you're putting on airs for me.

Rather than protect marginalized groups, Jerry astutely points out that this language of diversity and "kumbaya" protects those in power by obscuring the inequitable racial status quo. As he says, when people use code words or do not say what they mean, it is harder for him to know where he stands—and challenge that standing. This "putting on airs" approach also flies in the face of Jerry's experience at Stella's Café, where we saw the salience of race in both his initial encounter and in whom workers directed him to speak to upon his return.

Mistreatment by White male neighbors is something two Black female residents described during their interviews. First, Mary, a longtime renter, cited an example of what she could only describe as racism by her former neighbor. As I mentioned in Chapter 3, Mary's former neighbor attempted to evict her and her son, and he never offered her rides in his car when she was walking home from the bus: "I try to be friendly, but deep down, I don't even know if he like Black peoples. Now, he was friendly. He probably been friendly with them [Mary's next-door neighbors], too, but yeah. But I, you know. I really didn't care because I was able to walk [from the bus], you know, so it didn't bother me and I was getting me exercise, so hey, the only person he was hurting is hisself acting like that. 'Cause like when he called those people [the property owner], you know. So that's the only one I've ever had trouble with." Mary presented an interesting juxtaposition, saying that her neighbor may have been racist but he was also very friendly. This argument that racism is "beyond good and evil" is in line with structural arguments about racial inequality. Connie, a homeowner, also had a similar experience when a conflict with a neighbor "escalated" because of racial tensions:

CONNIE: I guess I've gotten a reputation for not wanting people to park in front of my house just because part of [it] is just because when I first moved there, there was this house, I mean there was this car that was parked there right in front of my house and I didn't know whose car it was. When I was first looking at the house I guess I didn't pay any attention because I thought it was just, you know, going to move. It was chronically parked there and I thought that it belonged to this guy that lived directly across from me. Who, he had a car that was parked in front of his place, and this one never moved. So finally I addressed him about it and he was a youngish White guy who I got some very negative feelings from, like he had some racial bias. 'Cause you ask nicely but then it escalates. Finally it did go but I know I was in the house over a month before the thing left. So I got very sensitive to that space. . . . So that's why my neighbors, some new people moved in recently. They said to me, I was outside in the yard, we just introduced ourselves and they said, "Well we know that you don't like when people park in front." I said, "Well I didn't advertise it but, you know, even though I don't have a lot of company I do have company sometimes, where am I going to put them?"

SARAH: Right, right. So they already knew, who told? Who told them that? Was it the old tenants do you think?

CONNIE: I don't know, I didn't even ask. I was just surprised that they said it. I just said, "Yeah great, fine."

Connie's situation provides us with an example of how a seemingly innocuous issue, such as where a neighbor parks his car, can turn much more serious when high interracial social distance is factored in. Connie's past experience with her White neighbor also impacted her future relationships with her neighbors, as she was now more acutely aware of who parked in front of her home. This corresponds with work on racial microaggressions and the experiences of non-Whites in predominantly White institutions. As sociologists Joe Feagin, Hernan Vera, and Nikitah Imani argue, past experiences guide the responses of people of color in these spaces, not "shoot-from-the-hip paranoia," as some Whites assume.[20] Similarly, Connie based her response to her neighbors on her past experience, which was intensified by racial undertones when Creekridge Park was a predominantly White space.[21]

Latino/a Residential Experiences

When I asked Latino/a residents about their experiences with other racial-ethnic groups, they generally gave vague but positive statements about Black and White residents. Generally, my respondents were more likely to speak candidly about their negative encounters with other Latino/as. There were, however, a few instances that respondents shared of non-Latino/as treating them poorly. For example, Diana and Marta relayed stories of their mistreatment at the hands of individuals from both Latin America and the United States:

DIANA: Pues son amigables los morenos.

MARTA: O sea a veces—Hay de todo, porque hay veces que usted se encuentra—Porque yo una vez me fui a la—andaba cambiando un WIC, y me encontré una americana ahí y me dijo muchas cosas—pero yo andaba con el vecino, él me llevó, él, que le digo yo, él habla mucho inglés, y dijo que nosotros veníamos a quitarle su comida a ellos, que no sé qué, me dijo muchas cosas. Y me he visto otros americanos como muy buenos. Sí. Y hay hispanos también que son muy racistas, malos, también como que no fueran de nuestro país también. Es que hay de todo.

SARAH: Okay. ¿Y eso lo encontraron también en Honduras o creen que eso es diferente aquí en los Estados Unidos?

DIANA: No, en Honduras no es así.

MARTA: No, en Honduras no.

SARAH: ¿No es así? Okay. So, aquí hay más como divisiones.

DIANA: Eso.

SARAH: Okay. ¿Y eso le sorprendió de otra gente latina que también no se dan—que son racistas?

DIANA: Sí, el racismo.

SARAH: ¿Sí? ¿Me pueden decir un poco más sobre eso?

DIANA: Mire, supongo yo que esa gente así es racista con las mismas personas de su lugar, porque hay gente latina que también lo trata mal en las tiendas, o le dicen—porque uno no habla inglés y le dicen que ellos solo hablan inglés, que no hablan español, y tal vez el latino del mismo lugar de uno. Entonces para mí que eso es racismo.

MARTA: Mira, va pasando una calle usted, hay veces que van unos americanos que se paran para que pase usted y lo saludan y todo;

hay veces que va un latino de esos—de uno mismo, y lo está—casi le andan echando el carro encima y están pite y pite, está feo eso.

(DIANA: Well, Blacks are friendly.

MARTA: Rather, sometimes—there's all types, because there are times when you find—Because one time I went to, I was cashing in a WIC [Special Supplemental Nutrition Program for Women, Infants, and Children] and I encountered an American woman there and she said a lot of things to me. But I was with a neighbor, he took me, he, how do I say this, he spoke a lot of English, and she was telling me that we came here to take food from them, that I don't know what, she said a lot of things. And I have met other Americans that are very nice. Yeah. And there are some Hispanics also that are very racist, bad, as if they didn't come from our same country. There's all types.

SARAH: Okay. And did you also find that in Honduras or do you think that it's different in the United States?

DIANA: No, it isn't like that in Honduras.

MARTA: No, in Honduras no.

SARAH: It's not like that? Okay. So, here there are more, like, divisions.

DIANA: Yes.

SARAH: Okay. And so did it surprise you that other Latinos did not give you—were also racists?

DIANA: Yes, racism.

SARAH: Yeah? Can you tell me a little bit more about that?

DIANA: Look, I suppose that these people are racists with the people from their same country because there are Latinos that also treat you poorly in the stores, or they say to you—because you don't speak English and they tell you that they only speak English, that they don't speak Spanish, and maybe that Latino is from the same place as you. So, for me, that is racism.

MARTA: Look, you're passing on the street and there are times when some Americans will stop for you so you can pass and they will say hello and everything. There are times when a Latino, one of your own, and he's—he's almost running you over with his car and they're beeping and beeping. That's ugly.)

Unlike Martín, Diana and Marta did not use anti-Black prejudice in describing their encounters with Americans in the United States. They acknowledged that there are all types of people, including friendly Blacks and less friendly Americans. It is unclear if the woman who confronted Marta in the store was White or Black, although *americana* is generally used to refer to Whites. Diana and Marta also identified ill-treatment at the hands of their compatriots and fellow Latino/as. Diana and Marta used the word "racism" to characterize any mistreatment they connected to their Latina identities.[22] This prejudice-based definition differed from the one previously given by Black homeowner Cheryl, which was based on both prejudice and power.

During our interview, Martín explained to me how Latino/as who think Americans are racist are wrong:

> Bueno, hay mucha gente que dice que [los Americanos] son racistas; le digo, pero si no le pones buena cara, ¿cómo te van a saludar? Si tú tampoco saludas, pues no te van a saludar. Para mí Sarah, ustedes los americanos, bueno la gente americana son una gente muy amable, muy amable; los que son un poco más así, son los morenos. Son como que—como que a uno lo ven mal, ¿me entiendes? Pero en realidad no, no siento que haya mucha discriminación. Y a veces: "No, es que no me dieron trabajo"—le digo: "Pero cómo te van a dar trabajo si no tienes papeles, no hablas inglés, ¿cómo te van a dar trabajo?" ¿Me entiendes? Pero no, yo siento que no Sarah, no hay tanto. Con nosotros mismos hay racismo.

> (Well, there are a lot of people who say that they [Americans] are racists. But I tell them, well if you don't present yourself well, how are they going to greet you? If you don't greet them, then they won't greet you. For me Sarah, you Americans, well the American people are very friendly people, very friendly. The ones who are a little more like that [unfriendly] are blacks. They're like, like they look at a person badly, you understand me? But in reality no, I don't think there is a lot of discrimination. And sometimes, "no, but they didn't give me a job." I say, "But how are they going to give you a job if you don't have papers, if you don't speak English, how are they going to give you a job?" You understand me? But no, I don't feel, Sarah, there isn't a lot. Between ourselves we have racism.)

As we saw earlier, Martín continued to positively frame Americans, with an implicit connotation of *White* Americans, even giving a caveat that those who are most unfriendly are Black Americans. He also chastises Latino/as who complain that Americans (here, presumably referring to

Whites again) are unfriendly. Martín gives two examples of how Latino/as are actually to blame for their current positions, since they fail to properly engage with Whites; from his point of view the social isolation and position of Latino/as in the labor market is a result of their improper behavior. Martín once again insists on the importance of following customs and rules to get ahead in the United States—a somewhat contradictory stance, considering he is undocumented.

Like Marta and Diana, Martín also mentions how his fellow Latino/as are racist toward one another. He expands on this point below:

> Por ejemplo, tú estás trabajando en un lugar, estás—hay digamos puro mexicano, y entra un salvadoreño: "Ay, mira, ya entró ese salvadoreño menso"—"No que los hondureños no le echan ganas, que los hondureños no son como los mexicanos." Aquí el—Mira Sarah, te voy a decir algo: La mayor parte . . . la gente más, más huevona son los hondureños, no sé por qué; y casi nadie los quiere, entre nosotros ¿eh? Entre los latinos. Dime si no es discriminación eso.

> (For example, you're working in a place and you're—let's say it's all Mexican workers and in walks a Salvadoran. "Ugh, look, no a Salvadoran is here." "No, Hondurans don't work hard enough, Hondurans aren't like Mexicans." Here the—look Sarah, I'm gonna tell you something: the biggest part . . . the most lazy people are Hondurans, I don't know why. And almost nobody likes them amongst us, amongst Latinos. Tell me that that isn't discrimination.)

There are obvious contradictions in Martin's comments. Martín, a Mexican migrant, criticizes the discriminatory attitudes that exist between Latino/a communities by matter-of-factly expressing prejudiced attitudes toward Hondurans. He continues:

MARTÍN: Entonces te digo que entre nosotros mismos hay eso también, por nuestras razas. Y no de—hablemos eso también de México, a nosotros no nos quieren, Sarah, a nosotros nos llaman "chilangos," a los de la Ciudad de México. Nos dicen "chilangos." Fíjate que a nosotros no nos quieren. Nosotros es que, mira, nosotros tenemos otro nivel de vida, venimos de una ciudad, ¿me entiendes? No venimos de un pueblo. Y lamentablemente en un pueblo son cosas muy diferentes a una ciudad; entonces piensan que nosotros somos "payasos," yo no sé cómo se habla en inglés, que somos creídos,

¿me entiendes? Pero no es así, es por el modo de vida que llevamos; y en una ciudad tú tienes que aprender a vivir, sino la ciudad te come, ¿me entiendes? Entonces a nosotros mismos no nos quieren, imagínate, dime si no también hay racismo ahí. Hay un dicho que dicen de Guadalajara, dice: "Mata un chilango y harás patria" [*risas*]. Imagínate, mata a un chilango—O sea que te digo también.

SARAH: ¿Y ha visto eso aquí también? Que la gente trata así.

MARTÍN: ¡Oh sí! También. "Ah no, mira, ahí viene un chilango." O sea que entre nosotros mismos también es lo mismo. Pero yo pienso que hay que llevar las cosas así bien, ni creerte tanto de esos dichos, hablarle a la gente; aquí en mi vecindario toda la gente nos saludan.

(MARTÍN: And so I'm telling you amongst us there's also that [racism], because of our races. And not from—let's also talk about Mexico. They don't like us, Sarah, they call us *chilangos*, those of us from Mexico City. They call us *chilangos*. Realize that they do not like us. It's that—look, we have another standard of living, we come from a city. You understand me? We didn't come from a town. And unfortunately things are very different in a town than in a city. And so they think that we're "clowns," and I don't know how you say it in English, that we're arrogant, you understand me? But it's not like that, it's because of our way of life. You have to learn how to live in a city, if not the city will devour you, you understand me? And so they don't like us, imagine that, tell me that there also isn't racism there. There's a saying in Guadalajara, it says: "Be a patriot and kill a *chilango*" [*laughs*]. Imagine that, kill a *chilango*. What else can I say.

SARAH: And have you seen that here? That people treat you that way?

MARTÍN: Oh, yes! "Oh no, look, there comes a *chilango*." Between us it's the same [racism]. But I think you need to take those types of things well, not believe in these kinds of things, talk to people; here in my neighborhood everybody greets us.)

Based on his comments, Martín believes "racism" (he uses the term in the same prejudice-based way Marta and Diana do) among Latino/as exists and has shaped his experience in both Mexico and the United States. At the end of his comments, however, he states that one should not believe in racist characterizations of others and that it is important to talk to people. He then asserts how everybody greets him and his family in Creekridge Park. This last statement is particularly noteworthy since Martín had just spent a considerable amount of time speaking about intra-Latino/a prejudice. Since he views his neighborhood as predominantly White/American, his final statement may be an attempt to fit in with the *tranquilo* neighborhood he has described.

The experiences of my respondents with other Latino/as are particularly relevant when we take into account the social network data of Latino/as. All of my Latino/a respondents indicated that they spent the most time with other Latino/as, generally other compatriots and family members. The importance and strength of ethnic community networks, especially for first-generation immigrants, is a well-established finding in the immigration literature.[23] The behaviors of immigrants, however, do not take place in a vacuum. Language is an important part of this pattern, and documentation issues are also relevant for Durham's Latino/a population.[24] As I discussed earlier, concerns over neighbor reactions kept Latino/as from complaining about neighborhood issues. According to the interview data, the move to Creekridge Park was generally positive for my respondents, as the neighborhood environment was more *tranquilo*. Some respondents also saw their position as Latino/as as an impediment to incorporation in the United States.

Latino/a residents did not speak about diversity or ever use it as a descriptor in the way White residents did. In fact, Latino/a residents did not frame Creekridge Park as a neighborhood per se but, rather, shared what they enjoyed about their particular home or the immediate surrounding area. As mentioned in the previous sections, most Latino/a residents moved to their current home to escape former subpar housing. As a result, they were likely to include a comparison to their former location in their description of their current street. They also did not describe Creekridge Park as a Latino/a neighborhood. For example, Juliana describes the neighborhood as a good place:

> Yo describiría que es buen lugar, un buen lugar. De hispanos no hay muchos, solo nosotros, los que viven aquí, allá en frente, solo mi tía y mi tío, y—ah, sí, ya me acordé, que apenas ahorita cuando termine acaba de llegar una familia que es un salvadoreño con una cubana que viven también a la par de esta casa que sigue, a la otra casa, a la par viven ellos; apenas acaban de venirse a vivir ahí. . . . Y ellos también nos preguntan que cómo es aquí la calle, pues nosotros le decimos que es buena—un buen lugar, estamos en buen lugar.

(I would describe it as a nice place, a nice place. There are not a lot of Hispanics, only us, the ones that live here. Across the street, only my aunt and uncle and—oh yeah, I just remembered that very recently a Salvadoran man with a Cuban woman moved in next door to that house over there. They just recently came to live here. . . . And they also asked us what this street is like, and we told them it was nice, a nice place, we're in a nice place.)

For Juliana, the two main descriptors of the neighborhood are that it is nice and that there are not many other Latino/as in the area. She lives in a single-family home in subregion five. Martín, who lives in subregion one, also describes it as a predominantly White neighborhood:

Aquí lo que más viven son americanos, o sea gente blanca. Hay como unas cuatro familias me imagino, más o menos, no sé, de afroamericanos, pero son gente que también son muy tranquilas, o sea no son escandalosos. Yo he tomado el bus, Sarah, a veces, el bus; mi esposa diario lo toma para su trabajo; y en el bus sube y ellos son bien escandalosos, hablan mucho, como que gritan al hablar, o sea no tienen una voz educada. Y aquí no, la gente que vive aquí es gente muy educada, muy, sí, muy educada, no hace ruido ni nada, pero es muy buena gente; no molestan, ni tampoco nosotros los molestamos.

(Mostly Americans live here, or rather White people. I imagine that there are like four African American families, give or take, I don't know, but they are also very quiet, they aren't scandalous. I have taken the bus, Sarah, and sometimes the bus—my wife takes it every day because of her job and in the bus they [Blacks] get on and off and they are very scandalous, they talk too much, it's as if they yell to speak, they don't have a polite voice. And here, the people that live here are very polite people, very, yes, very polite. They don't make noise or anything, but they are good people. They don't bother and we don't bother them either.)

Martín is clearly using behaviors and contexts (e.g., city bus versus *perfecto* neighborhood) to make class distinctions that positively classify his Black neighbors and, by extension, himself. By distinguishing between the *escandalosos* (scandalous people) he sees on the bus and the quiet, *buena gente* (good people) that live in Creekridge Park, he uses racist and classist ideas to make his argument; note how his White neighbors do not need any qualifiers. They, like the neighborhood, are presumed to be *perfecto*. Through his comments Martín is trying to highlight that he no longer has to live with *escandalosos* now that he's moved to Creekridge Park. All of these descriptions help him construct his desired narrative of upward mobility and assimilation.

INTERRACIAL INTERACTIONS

Interracial neighbor-to-neighbor interactions were an important window into the life of Black and Latino/a residents in Creekridge Park. Let us first start with Cheryl. Earlier in this chapter we heard about Cheryl's desire for in-depth and extensive neighborhood interactions. She described herself as nostalgic for the types of relationships she had while growing up in predominantly Black neighborhoods. When she moved to Creekridge Park, she attempted to reach out to an elderly White neighbor, and the woman ignored her. She assumed that there was some type of racial animus but eventually concluded that it was actually a hearing problem:

> First of all, I was so excited, remember, to move into a neighborhood so I could recapture something from my childhood. So when I was sitting out on the porch, I was babysitting somebody's child, and I saw my neighbor across the street, who was a white-haired, older woman, and I spoke to her and she literally ignored me. She, I assumed, heard me, turned her back and went back in her house. Now, what I did not discover until probably years later, maybe—well, you know what, it wasn't even years later, it may have been a couple of months. That woman's address is 1550 Colony Street. My address is 1550 Pine Avenue. So she would get my mail and I would get her mail. And so we were thrust into each other's lives, taking each other mail. I didn't know until I took her her mail the first time it came here that she doesn't hear well. So the reason she didn't speak had nothing to do with my race or my newness to the neighborhood, but had everything to do with the fact that she was eighty some years old and she didn't hear me, which blew me away because I really thought that she was resentful of the fact that somebody Black had bought her friend's house. And it had nothing to do with that.

Cheryl's encounter with her elderly White neighbor reveals that residents do not move into their neighborhoods as blank slates. Previous experiences impact how individuals approach and interpret future interactions. As such, Cheryl, a North Carolina native, had a particular schema in which she interpreted the lack of engagement from her elderly White neighbor. At the same time, because of their particular circumstances, Cheryl and her neighbor interacted, and their interactions became more positive. Cheryl even shared that when her elderly neighbor passed away, her children came and thanked Cheryl for her care of their mother. They said her mother was very fond of her and that they appreciated Cheryl checking on her after severe weather. This is an example of how intentional acts to get to know neighbors can produce positive neighbor relations and how those from dominant groups who are in vulnerable positions, such as Esther in Chapter 3, are more likely to have relationships marked by low interracial social distance than the average White homeowner.

Cheryl also shared a story about her interactions with her Latino neighbor Óscar. She recounted that their rapport was initially positive; when he and his family moved in, they invited Cheryl to their son's birthday party. She then recapped how their relationship shifted when another neighbor reported Óscar to Neighborhood Improvement Services:

And I thought we were going to have a great relationship. And actually, we always spoke. Something happened and I speculated about what in the world could have happened that all of a sudden the mother is still speaking but the husband don't speak, even when I speak and it's apparent I've spoken. And one of the things that happened was they used to keep a lot of junk in the front yard and at some point I saw a city truck over there and shortly thereafter that junk was gone. I suspected somebody complained and I wondered if he assumed I was the one who complained. And one day, our neighbor down the street, a White guy, happened to be going by, complimenting me about some of the stuff I was doing in my yard and somehow or another, he ends up saying to me he was the person who complained and had that stuff cleaned up 'cause he said something like, "You know, it's wonderful that you are doing these things to your yard. It looks great." And he said, "And of course, the house across the street doesn't look that great, but at least it looks better." And I said, "Yeah, I know that they moved a lot of that stuff." He said, "Actually, I was the person who complained they got it done." So I had been trying to get up the courage to ask my neighbor had I done something to be offensive or disrespectful 'cause I wanted to apologize 'cause I didn't know why he had stopped speaking. So after he had said that to me, the next day I approached my neighbor and I asked him and he said, "Oh, no, no, no." He said, "Nothing." And I said, "Well, I just wanted you to know that I won't share who did it, but I know that somebody talked about the things you had in your front yard and they complained to the city and that's why it's gone." I said, "The reason I'm telling you is not 'cause I want you to confront that person, which is why I won't tell you who it is." I said, "The reason I'm telling you is I need you to know that if I had a problem with something in your yard," I said, "first of all, I respect the fact that this is your yard. You can keep in it whatever you want." I said, "But the other issue is, I want you to know that if I had a issue with something in your yard, I would talk to you before I would call the city." He seemed to be fine with that. He still doesn't speak. I can't do anything about that. So I feel bad about it. But—and I especially feel about it because I'm sure that they don't get that I'm one of the strongest advocates around immigrant rights in this community, much less in this neighborhood. And that if ever they were in crisis, if they wanted to go somewhere, this would be the place to go. And so I feel terrible about that, especially because not only would this be a place his family could go, anybody that they know could come here. And I would work with the network of allies that I have in the Latino and African American community to get whatever support they needed. So, you know, I can't do nothing about that, but it's unfortunate because there's also a language barrier. He speaks better English than his wife does, but it is one of those things that's going to mitigate against relationship building with neighbors.

Unlike the White homeowners who actively participated in social control practices, including the White neighbor who told Cheryl he reported Óscar to Neighborhood Improvement Services, Cheryl was not interested in policing her neighbor's lawn. Her priority was maintaining a positive relationship with her Latino/a neighbors and, in the case of a conflict, communicating directly with them.

Later in the interview when I specifically asked her about interracial interactions in the neighborhood, Cheryl stated that she did not see them often. She continued, saying that when they did happen, these interactions generally resulted from "efforts that people intentionally make." She then recognized that people have different values:

I think the exchange with my next-door neighbor and the impact of this White guy—you know, I guess that's one of the things I want to speak to is just the value differences. There are, I mean, it's a value difference to expect that your yard looks a certain way. And you're placing value on somebody having the right to store their work property on their, where they live. And so the idea that part of what's going to happen in this neighborhood is going to be impacted by young, White, upwardly mobile residents who come into this neighborhood and want to impose on whoever is here their standard of what's right about living in this neighborhood. And I think that what will mitigate that, their approach to neighborhood living, would be having closer relationships and understanding why people have different views about how they keep their property or how they use their property. 'Cause see, for me, it's a utilitarian issue of this man placing the stuff from his work on this lot. Now, the interesting thing is this guy did at least acknowledge that there's tons of space behind the house where he could have put this stuff and it didn't have to be out front. But again, he didn't have the relationship, he didn't have a conversation, he just called the authorities and said there are laws that stop this, get this man to clean his property up. And so, I just think it's a interesting dynamic to have White, upwardly mobile professionals moving in to a neighborhood and creating or having an expectation that the standards that get met are those that they set when they new to the neighborhood, you know. And so I think it's a basis for potential conflict down the road.

Cheryl's argument presents a clear critique of the patrolling and patronizing practices I discussed in Chapter 3. She also argued that more intimate relationships between neighbors, particularly Whites and non-Whites, would help curtail some of these white codes. Research on friendship, however, indicates that these micro-interactions are limited in their ability to challenge structural inequality. As sociologist Jesse Rude finds in his research: "Interracial friendships are not a panacea for race relations because their direct impact on the structural inequalities associated with race may be negligible. However, insofar as they provide a space for problematizing racial concepts such as whiteness and blackness, interracial friendships may serve to bring the realities of racial inequality and privilege into the light of consciousness where they can be addressed."[25] Interracial friendships, therefore, in and of themselves are not the end-all for racial issues, but they are an important arena in which to openly and honestly discuss inequality and privilege.

When I specifically asked Jerry about diversity in Creekridge Park, he said that there was diversity in the neighborhood and that he had no problem interacting with his neighbors of different racial-ethnic backgrounds. He did, however, indicate that there was not a lot of sustained interracial interaction:

> Well, as far as diversity, we have [inaudible]. Hispanic, Black, Caucasian, uh, people coming from the Caribbean. It's—it's like that. But most times, well, Hispanic, I speak to them. Sometimes, we have a—a barbeque or something like that. But we have different cultures. And most of the times, people stay and do what they do together. But we speak to each other. We civil. My neighbor right next door, he's Caucasian. I've seen his kids grow up. I buy Girl Scout cookies and stuff from his—from his daughter. They know me. Visit? No. But yeah, he's been here. If I would ask him to come over and speak and—and talk and—and it's all right. It's all right. But it's just that maybe I'm just different because maybe I was in the military, and I've been around a different—and experienced a lot. And—and maybe I think different as to, you know, I know what I want in life. I'm not—I'm not angry at anybody.

If you recall from Chapter 3, Jerry also described his feelings of apprehension at the all-White events he attended at his neighbor's house, which provided more insight into the experience of non-Whites in Creekridge Park. As an additional point, Jerry brings up his military experience to explain his ability to communicate and interact with different types of people—a detail also identified by White renter Lois, who lives in Pine Grove Apartments. She had relationships with her non-White neighbors and explained that she and her family were not prejudiced people because her husband was in the military.

Cristina, a Latina newcomer who rents in the Pine Grove Apartments, shared her interpretation of the normative behaviors in her apartment complex. Living in an area that is predominantly Black and Latino/a, she noticed that Black renters were much more social and friendly than Latino/a renters. She drew on her experience as a social worker and as the wife of a Black American civil servant to create what she called her *teoría muy, muy, muy humilde* (very, very, very humble theory). She suspected that although both groups relied heavily on social exchange in their communities, immigration fears pushed Latino/as to be more reclusive. As she put it, Blacks lived in their comfort zones in the United States, while many Latino/as worried about being undocumented or driving without a license. Cristina's insightful observation about the social isolation of Latino/a migrants in Durham echoes the experiences some Latino/a respondents shared with me.

When I first spoke with Héctor, a mechanic in his early fifties, he suggested we meet at one of the neighborhood's new Mexican restaurants, Restaurante Aztlán. During our interview it became clear that he spent a lot of time in this space. He even had a special arrangement with the owners: they provided him multiple meals a week for a negotiated payment. I asked him what kind of customers came to this restaurant, and he said,

> Viene de todo. Aquí vienen, bueno, unos señores de la cruz roja que vienen aquí, unas señoras americanas blancas, unos morenos que son bien alegres, bien amigos, y ve los [empleados de la estación de servicios de emergencia] hay—ya le digo cuatro—cinco morenos y hay como seis blancos. Las señoras, unas señoras que vienen ahí, unas gorditas les digo yo que se pongan a dieta. No, vienen a comer aquí, bien viera que bien. Sí, aquí a las doce es que hay comida, vienen alegres. Sí, es bien, es bien—la gente es bien tranquila aquí.

> (All types of people come. Some men from the Red Cross come here, some White American ladies, some Blacks who are very happy, good friends, and the [employees from the emergency services station] are, I'll tell you right now four—five Blacks and there are like six Whites. The ladies, there are also some ladies that come here, some chubby women whom I tell need to go on a diet. No, they come to eat well here, you should see how well. Yes, here at twelve [o'clock], when there's food, they come happy. Yes, it's very, it's very—the people are very easygoing here.)

Héctor saw the restaurant as a multiethnic space—which is a contrast to other neighborhood restaurants, including Stella's Café. From his comments, it seems he also interacts with some of the customers, including telling a group of women (who are presumably regular customers) that they need to go on a diet. Although he mentions this as a joke during our interview, it is entirely possible that he also says this "joke" to the women in question. When we met on a weekday, Héctor and I were the only customers in the restaurant. A television in the back of the restaurant was playing Spanish-language programming at a high volume, and it did not seem like Restaurante Aztlán would get very much movement that night.

Neighborhood Association

The Creekridge Park Neighborhood Association (CPNA) and smaller, independent, block-level neighborhood watch efforts served as organizational elements in Creekridge Park. As other studies on neighborhoods have shown, these formal organizations often are springboards for more informal conversations before and after their events.[26] None of the non-White residents I interviewed currently participated in the CPNA. Although some of them had attended neighborhood events in the past (for example, I met Connie and Juliana at two distinct neighborhood events), they did not participate in the CPNA as general or board members. Some of them, such as Mary, had no interest in it:

MARY: No, I haven't joined yet. I haven't even been to one of their meetings. They invited me to a couple of them. I know I ain't goin' to none now 'cause I'm having to deal with this fatigue.
SARAH: Right, okay, so you've never been to any of their events?
MARY: No.
SARAH: So you're just—not really an interest?
MARY: [laughs] You're right, not really, you know. I know they nice and friendly . . . if I'm being honest, you know.

Mary laughed, admitting that although she knew the folks of the CPNA were "nice and friendly," she did not have an interest in joining or attending their events. Cheryl, who more actively involved herself in citywide political matters, said that she did not want to join because it was too much like work to try and recruit non-White participants:

I know that we have a active neighborhood association and I've always paid my dues. And I've been to a few meetings early on, but there are a number of reasons from the fact that I travel a lot and I think, you know, there's a whole lot about what happens at neighborhood association meetings that I can get from the newsletter and, you know, just traveling a lot, being busy and not feeling necessarily motivated to be at those meetings, except when we have a crisis and they need support, extra money, signing on to things, that kind of thing. So I've not been very active in it, but I always pay my dues. And like I said, I don't know, I mean, I don't remember now, you know, why I didn't go, but I know I like to keep abreast of what's going on. And unfortunately, I haven't even been able to go to the cookouts that they have. . . . But I must say that my experience early on, I don't know what it's like now, was that it was mostly just Whites and I might be the only Black, which I'm sure contributed in part to my not wanting to go on a regular basis. But I often remember thinking that I was going to start knocking doors to other African Americans to encourage their participation, but because that's the nature of what I do anyway, it just was like another job in my off time and so I was like "nah."

Cheryl provides great insight into the complexity of being the only non-White participant at these neighborhood events. While Cheryl wants to see better representation, she does not necessarily have the energy to be the sole recruiter of Black and Latino/a residents. Her remarks also serve as a challenge to the universality and inclusivity of the CPNA presented by some White residents.

Connie, whom I met at a CPNA event, indicated that she appreciated the quarterly newsletter but steered clear of the online listserv: "I'm not even on that list but I just get tired of emails. I like the little newsletter that comes out because that's very informative and that's gotten me out to do things and that enough for me. I like having that piece of paper that I can lay back and read." As I discussed in Chapter 3, the newsletter was written exclusively in English. Most Latino/a residents were either not familiar with the newsletter or did not read it. For example, as stated in Chapter 1, Martín explained that since it came entirely in English and it did not matter to him and his wife, he threw it out.

A couple of blocks in the Creekridge Park area also had active neighborhood watches. Neighborhood watches cover a much smaller section than most neighborhood associations. One of the goals is to have the contact information for every member of the watch, so the ideal coverage area is a block or two. Jerry decided to head up his block association when he first started to have issues with the neighbors behind him: "Well, when we first moved here, it was real quiet, real nice. Then it was a period about maybe two or three years ago, these apartment buildings in the back, it was a big change in who they were letting move back there. And then that's when a lot of problems started. And then I even decided to head the, um, block association for my block because I just can't—I can't stand what was going on, and I'm not the type of person to just sit around." He concluded by saying that he thought his fellow block association participants saw him as an "angry man." When I asked him if they really did, he clarified: "Well, you know, like—yeah, in a way. Because you know, there's a lot of people sit and they want to talk about tree planting and—and, you know, things that to me, good idea, but I'm worried about bullets. You follow where I'm coming from? That's some real stuff there, you know. But I got to listen to other people, too, but I got—what's important? You know, we plant trees around here. They—I think the city do—was in partnership that we do, um, the trees. We got together and planted trees and stuff. At each house and everything." Jerry's interest in the neighborhood watch was primarily related to safety, particularly because he had been threatened by some of his neighbors from the rental property behind his home. He did acknowledge that some neighborhood watch participants were interested in other issues, such as greening the neighborhood, a practice I discuss in Chapter 3. His comments above also elucidate that the city was involved in the planting of trees on Tyler Street, where he lives; this may explain why he was so frustrated with the lack of police response to his safety concerns.

Angela, who lives in an adjacent neighborhood, participated in her neighborhood watch, but she also believed it had some shortcomings regarding renter incorporation:

ANGELA: So I think trying to befriend people who might just be passing through may cause them to stay longer. You know, you have, um— and I think, for instance, they will do their, um, their neighborhood meetings and what have you, but they won't invite—for instance they've never extended an invite I think to the Acostas, the family from Honduras right, right next door. Now they own their little house and they're—they're—they're nice people and, you know, their daughter and my daughter, they play and they go, you know, different, you know, activities or what have you, but they won't do that. Or even, um, I've never seen—to me—okay, Mr. Hunt's not somebody who's on the computer, per se. But Mr. Hunt lives in this gray house over here [and] has been in this neighborhood for over 30 years. . . . And if they were to do that, um, I think they would be, um, it would be better. In my opinion. Um, but—

SARAH: And why do you—why do you think that is, that they haven't extended those invitations?

ANGELA: I think because they're renting. I really do, I think because they feel they don't own their homes, you don't, you know, we don't need to consider them. That's my honest opinion there. Because to me you'd be surprised—I mean somebody like Mr. Hunt, his daughters who are in and out there with him, or the people who rent in this, um, the brick house. There's one very stable family who's been there for—I don't know—God only knows how many years—I came and met them here. And they're still here, so, uh,—but you know people—people like that, you'd be surprised how anybody can come to your rescue if they know you, if they feel a connection to you, so, you know, as you pass although they may say, "Oh, the people in the brick house cause trouble," I've never seen any trouble that they've caused, you know what I'm saying? So, and—but again if you're walking down the street and somebody is trying to bother you, I can assure you Ray's on the corner, you know, sitting on his porch—he's not going to allow that to happen, because he knows me. You know, he knows my daughter, he knows my bad dog, you know [*laughter*]. You know what I'm saying? So he'll come out because he knows—he knows us, or the guy across the street. So you've kind of extended that hand of friendship. Look, we're here, you're part of this neighborhood also. And I think if they did a little bit more of that, it would be beneficial to everybody concerned.

As Angela pointed out, some Black residents are aware of and participated in larger neighborhood events, but they are generally homeowners. A majority of Black and Latino/a residents in Creekridge Park, however, are renters and are the least likely to be incorporated into these associations. These associations conducted business in English only, hindering the participation of more recent Latino/a migrants. The CPNA is one of the avenues through which White homeowners and some renters socialized and built friendships, but its current practices exacerbated the social isolation of Black and Latino/a Creekridge Park residents.

In terms of political participation, non-Whites did engage outside the neighborhood. As Cheryl mentioned, she participated in local government both as an elected official and as a nonprofit employee. She also called herself "one of the strongest advocates around immigrant rights in this community." Héctor, who hails from Honduras, also mentioned attending a meeting at a Latino/a nonprofit in support of using Mexico's Matricula Consular (consular documents) as valid identification in North Carolina.[27] Lastly, Cristina works at a Latino/a nonprofit organization in Durham, advocating and working with Durham's immigrant population.

She also expressed a sensitivity to the issue of Black-Latino/a relations, which she deals with as a social worker. Although political participation may not necessarily take place within the CPNA, Black and Latino/a residents do take part in efforts to improve the standing of their respective communities and their relationships with each other through other outlets.

CONCLUSION

Black and Latino/a residents shared some similarities with their White neighbors. For example, some Black residents appreciated the proximity of their homes to downtown and the multiethnic nature of the neighborhood, while both Black and Latino/a residents highlighted the quiet/ *tranquilo* aspects of life in Creekridge Park. At the same time, there were some marked differences between all three groups. Many non-White residents described the social costs they associated with their moves to Creekridge Park. In order to maintain their home values or live in a less *escandaloso* (scandalous) neighborhood, they moved into an area where they experienced more social isolation. While Black residents were more likely to identify their social isolation as a cost of living in Creekridge Park, Latino/a residents generally characterized their neighbors as friendly. These distinct experiences of the same space are intricately tied to the divergent social locations and contexts of Blacks and Latino/as. On the one hand, the satisfaction of Latino/a residents with greetings from their neighbors is likely related to the otherwise unreceptive context of the United States. Black residents, on the other hand, are less likely to receive hellos due to racialized and class assumptions about them. In addition, a few Black residents who did have greeting relationships with their neighbors were looking for deeper interactions with their White neighbors but did not find them. Therefore, the "friendliness" of this neighborhood, as described by White residents in Chapter 2, is not experienced by all residents. Contrary to sociological theory, non-Whites did not experience the benefits of bridging social capital because they generally did not have reciprocal and close relationships with their White neighbors.

The experiences of both Blacks and Latino/as provide more evidence for the ideological whiteness of this space, where White residents are able to dictate the norms and values of the neighborhood for their benefit. White residents' privileged social positions shape the positive experiences they have in Creekridge Park. This pattern becomes all the more clear when compared with the narratives shared by my Black and Latino/a respondents. While Black and Latino/a residents experience social isolation, White residents have multiple welcoming avenues to make friends. While Jerry's pleas with the police fall on deaf ears, White residents have meetings with the local police captain to ask questions and have their concerns addressed.[28] White residents can enjoy neighborhood spaces and events surrounded by people who look like them. In contrast, Cheryl's efforts to participate in the CPNA are spoiled because she does not want to be the only person of color in attendance, and Jerry is accused of being a panhandler at Stella's Café. These inequitable outcomes illustrate the power of whiteness and Creekridge Park's white, urban, middle-class habitus. In the final chapter, I discuss the implications of these findings for future research.

CHAPTER 5 Solving the Wrong Problem

> *If the end goal of integration strategies is to reduce racism, then as the analysis presented here suggests, we have not made much progress and will not until we deal head-on with structural racism and policies that privilege the white position.*
>
> —JANE L. SMITH, "Integration: Solving the Wrong Problem," 242

In an insightful chapter about integrative housing efforts, urban scholar Janet L. Smith asks "Are we trying to solve the wrong problem?" in response to the unconvincing evidence regarding poverty deconcentration programs such as Moving to Opportunity.[1] Based on data shared by the White, Black, and Latino/a residents of Creekridge Park, I similarly argue that scholars and policy makers focusing on proximity between racial-ethnic groups are fixating on the wrong problem. Studying segregation helps us understand an important process by which racial inequality is reproduced contemporarily, but that does not mean statistically integrated multiethnic spaces are equitable. As we saw in the previous chapters, if we do not fully consider power and the limitations of good intentions in interracial interactions, we cannot challenge the inequitable racial contract.

Neighborhoods have always been an important part of the scholarly conversation on racial and ethnic stratification. Decades of research on segregation in housing and discriminatory housing policies and more recently on "integrated" neighborhoods have put residential matters at the center of discussions of racial inequality. While the evidence that residential segregation helps facilitate stratification is well established, I illustrate with data from Creekridge Park how the relationship between proximity and equity is not fixed. Similarly, I elucidate how diversity, in its current forms, is about neither equity nor justice but, rather, reinforces white privilege.

White residents of Creekridge Park, much like gentrifiers in previous studies on urban change, emphasize the positive aspects of multiethnic spaces. White Creekridge Park residents highlight their desire to live near people who are different from them, yet their social networks tend to be homophilous. Why does this happen? Diversity in its current form focuses on the acceptance of difference while simultaneously reinforcing the racial status quo. In practice, diversity ideology maintains an inequitable racial system because it is an accommodationist framework that focuses on the intentions of privileged persons as opposed to the racialized outcomes of their actions.

Desire and good intentions alone do not challenge structural inequality. Taking action and interrogating the results of our practices is necessary to impede the reproduction of privilege and disadvantage. I argue that similar to decades of social science research on prejudice, diversity ideology focuses on attitudes rather than social systems. By expressing a desire for diversity, White residents act in accordance with diversity ideology. That desire and good intention is the endpoint. Diversity ideology and the white, urban, middle-class habitus of Creekridge Park allow Whites to positively classify themselves in relation to other White homeowners without acknowledging and questioning their own privileged social position.

Diversity ideology dictates that by moving into a multiethnic community, White residents should and will be rewarded. White residents get to view themselves positively in comparison to other White homeowners while simultaneously maintaining their race and class privilege in this multiethnic and mixed-income environment by enacting white codes. They shape the way the neighborhood develops, as well as how and why residents are sanctioned, and receive the benefits of police cooperation and city-level consideration. Creekridge Park, like many other multiethnic spaces, is a white-controlled space.[2] Even though various racial-ethnic communities live in the neighborhood, it is still a space that is primarily framed by the needs and desires of White residents, particularly White homeowners.

In this book, I have emphasized the importance of Creekridge Park's white, urban, middle-class habitus in maintaining the racial contract. This habitus, embodied by many White homeowners, helps us better understand how dispositions are shared by individuals in similar social positions. It also allows us to identify how whiteness (a set of power relations that benefits Whites) influences the actions of Whites across the attitudinal spectrum. While White residents in Creekridge Park score more liberally on racial attitude measures, they still reproduce whiteness. We also see that multiple ideologies, including diversity ideology, can successfully be incorporated into this system of whiteness, ultimately supporting white privilege. In addition, the experiences shared by residents in Creekridge Park illustrate how the reproduction of whiteness happens without much fanfare. It is maintained by everyday actions that are often seen as harmless and sometimes even universally beneficial by the White individuals enacting them. In contrast to White perceptions, we saw in Chapter 4 that Black and Latino/a residents do not experience these actions in the same way. This is the power of whiteness. The narratives of white universality and neutrality enable inequitable relations to continue, while the framework of "good intentions" allows White residents to avoid grappling with their role in producing disparate outcomes. Although I only studied interracial interactions in a multiethnic neighborhood, because of the structural and systemic bases of these processes, it is likely that similar patterns of behavior that emphasize non-White social control and high interracial social distance mark other multiethnic settings. This is an area ripe for research; more social scientists need to continue to explore the racial particularities of multiethnic spaces.

Despite being framed in the academic literature as the ones who will most benefit from living in a multiethnic neighborhood, non-Whites are sometimes the losers in these situations. As other studies on mixed-income developments such as Moving to Opportunity and HOPE VI have found, current conceptualizations of "integration" have not produced the ideal social scientists hoped for.[3] Sociologist Stephen Steinberg astutely commented that programs that focus on poverty deconcentration through housing are "based on a faulty theoretical premise—namely, that concentrated poverty can be severed from its root causes and projected as the focal point of social policy."[4] Similarly, studies that focus on proximity in housing and statistical integration without a larger structural racial framework fail to see how power, privilege, and whiteness are inextricably tied to contemporary racial matters.

For the Black and Latino/a residents I interviewed, living in a multiethnic neighborhood was a decision marked by material benefits and social costs. Non-White residents dealt with a variety of scenarios Whites rarely encountered. White residents described how they labeled renters as disinvested, while Black residents explained how they were ignored by their neighbors because of their skin color and (presumed or real) housing tenure. At the same time, if a Black resident joined a neighborhoodwide effort, he or she was commonly the only person of color in a room. Similarly, Latino/a residents were seen as *other* and were commodified in this multiethnic space. Latino/as in Creekridge Park, however, were less likely to identify these practices as negative, since their relocation to this neighborhood was often an upwardly mobile move. Their interpretations of Creekridge Park were largely influenced by their social positions as Latin American migrants in the United States, an otherwise unreceptive experience. As a result, many of the Latino/a respondents indicated that they were satisfied with a simple *hola* or *¿cómo estás?* from their non-Latino/a neighbors. The bottom line remains that Black and Latino/a residents do not experience multiethnic spaces in the same way as Whites, which is inextricably tied to the realities of racial inequality, power, and whiteness in the United States.

The problem with diversity ideology—and one of the central findings of this project—is that living in the same neighborhood is not enough. Common lay and scholarly understandings of racial inequality, which ignore power differentials, fail to see how multiethnic spaces can be white spaces. As we know from studies of the Jim Crow South, however, the proximity of non-Whites to Whites has never been in and of itself a challenge to racial inequality.[5] If proximity were enough to eradicate inequity, for example, reciprocity rather than paternalism and high social distance would characterize interracial interactions and relationships in Creekridge Park.

Immigration and processes of neighborhood change (e.g., gentrification, white flight, and aging population) have made multiethnic neighborhoods much more common than they used to be. That is the story of Creekridge Park. At the same time, our analysis of these spaces must be based on a more sophisticated and nuanced understanding than the presumption that statistical integration mandates equity across groups. As scholars, we need to conduct more microlevel research on neighborhoods to fully understand the processes that affect life in multiethnic America— to understand how whiteness, power, and contemporary conceptualizations of race play a role in the maintenance and dismantling of racial inequality. Although not an easy task, studying residential spaces where more than one or even two groups live gives us insight into what dissimilarity indices mean on the ground and whether we are, in fact, studying the wrong problem. My multimethod approach, which emphasizes microlevel processes, is just one example of how to conduct this type of research.

Many researchers of racial inequality, particularly those who use a structural and critical race perspective, are met with negative and even sometimes angry responses when they publish their work. For example, sociologist Eduardo Bonilla-Silva, whose work focuses on contemporary racial ideologies in the United States, has on multiple occasions acknowledged the anger with which some of his work is received. In fact, in later editions of his influential book *Racism without Racists: Color-Blind Racism and the Persistence of Racial Inequality in the United States*, he directly acknowledges these types of responses in a chapter titled "Queries: Answers to Questions from Concerned Readers." In a similar vein, I anticipate that some readers will feel my narrative is far too critical. Some people may feel I should give the White residents of Creekridge Park a break because of how far we have come since the days of de jure segregation. Let me be clear: I am not judging any of my respondents as good or bad people. My job as a researcher and as a sociologist is to chronicle the experiences of White, Black, and Latino/a residents in Creekridge Park. As part of my scholarly work, I discuss the shortcomings of diversity ideology and the exclusionary practices of the white, urban, middle-class habitus. While these were both enacted by individuals, they are also rooted in larger structures of inequality. To interpret inequality as a result of the failings of individual "bad eggs" is inaccurate, shows poor analysis, and serves to strengthen inequity. If we never identify the full extent of the processes and systems that reproduce injustice and how even well-intentioned people are implicated in these processes, we will never be able to dismantle them. Based on our conversations, I know some White Creekridge residents care about issues of justice and inclusion; some do not. I am not here to judge their hearts or intentions. As I stated before, racial inequality and discussions of power are beyond good and evil. Let us take this opportunity to reframe the conversation on racial inequality from one about good and bad individuals to one about power, privilege, and outcomes.

Similarly, some readers may be wondering who my respondents are and which Durham neighborhood I studied. Although location always matters and we should not undervalue the role of space in framing interactions (which is why I included multiple maps of Creekridge Park), in many ways that conversation is a distraction from the one that I think is more important. We often discuss racial inequality in the United States as an individual problem or an aberration, rather than as a constitutive element of our society. As a result, trying to identify the neighborhood and the individuals quoted in these chapters can be a way to avoid identifying how we may be complicit in some of the same inequitable practices. It may not be easy to silence the curiosity about identities, but it is an opportunity to engage more deeply with the arguments I have presented, to ask how we can enact power-based interpretations of diversity, to be more mindful of our own privilege and areas for growth, and to build coalitions to combat systemic inequality. We live in an imperfect world with no magic bullet to eradicate inequality. There is no universal prescription, no checklist that, once completed, designates any one of us as just or equitable and free of responsibility. There is no perfect neighborhood that, if created, would automatically end racial inequality. Segregated neighborhoods are but one way that racial inequality is reproduced, but they are not the cause of inequity. At the same time, we now know that multiethnic and statistically integrated neighborhoods also have their own codes of conduct that reinforce whiteness and high social distance. This finding underlines the importance of a structural approach to inequality for a more complete understanding of racial matters.

So where do we go from here? What is my desired outcome from this book? I hope that lay folks—particularly those in privileged social positions—reading this book will begin to more critically engage white spaces. Rather than enter an all-White neighborhood association meeting and say, "Well, everyone is welcome," interrogate whether that is accurate. Are there practices that mark your organization as a politically white one, one that benefits and privileges the interests of Whites over the interests of your Black, Asian, or Latino/a neighbors? In addition, I hope to decentralize homeownership, challenging the dominance of homeowner interests over those of renters as a universal good. Rather than viewing renters as an impediment to their financial bottom line, what if homeowners joined renters rights groups and served as allies? There is a very strong antirenter bias that prevails in our national conversations on housing, particularly in regard to lower-income renters and renters of color. Decentralizing homeownership can help us frame rentership as a dignified housing option instead of one that reflects a behavioral deficiency and necessitates social control and high social distance—an important shift for more just and inclusive neighborhoods.

Is the proximity of Whites to communities of color really the crux of racial inequality, as proponents of statistical integration argue? Based on my study of Creekridge Park, the answer is no. Although residential segregation is a process that facilitates racial inequality, statistical integration cannot be the end goal. By focusing on diversity as acceptance rather than as reciprocal engagement and equity, we limit the scope of the conversation and, in turn, our actions. Scholars must take into account measures of power and the distribution of resources across different groups when discussing integration. They must also consider social interactions, including measures of reciprocity and closeness. Lastly, we need to challenge the ideological assumptions of current research to make sure we as social scientists are asking the right questions and solving the right problem. We must consider not only material outcomes but also the social, political, and psychological effects of living in a multiethnic space for all racial-ethnic communities, particularly marginalized ones. Scholars need to conduct more studies that look at neighbor-to-neighbor interactions to complement census data on neighborhoods. Large-scale demographic studies offer important insights, but they do not complete the whole sociological picture. Microlevel data that speak to the experiences of multiple groups are indispensable to understanding racial matters in multiethnic America.

After I asked Mary, a Black longtime renter, if she would describe the neighborhood as diverse, as the neighborhood association has, she responded with her own query: What did I mean by diverse? What an important question! Diversity and integration are used so frequently by White homeowners as well as scholars and policy makers, but what do those terms really mean? Mary's inquiry also draws attention to the current limitations of these concepts and how little they have to do with racial justice. As researchers, policy makers, and individuals who care about equity, we need to answer Mary's critical question before we use diversity and integration as a rallying cry.

APPENDIX A Researcher in the Field

GETTING IN

Field Presentation

My introduction to Creekridge Park and its residents came through a university connection. As I researched the neighborhood, which I identified using census data, I stumbled upon a familiar name on their neighborhood association webpage. I contacted Charles, a White, thirty-something homeowner and eventual key neighborhood informant. I asked him if he would be willing to meet with me about my project, and he agreed. We discussed his experiences in Durham, including his and his wife's struggles to find a home, and he agreed to give me a guided tour of Creekridge Park. He also put me in touch with Deborah, a member of the Creekridge Park Neighborhood Association (CPNA). Deborah, a White, middle-class, fifty-something homeowner who was actively involved in CPNA and Durham neighborhood issues, served as a gatekeeper. After I had a preliminary interview with her, she agreed to let me send my solicitation for interviews around the CPNA listserv. After I sent my email detailing who I was and that I was interested in speaking with neighborhood residents, Deborah sent an email vouching for me and saying that her interview with me was enjoyable.

Before entering the field, I considered the impact my appearance and social location as a mid-twenties, light-skinned, Latina graduate student enrolled at Duke University would have on my interactions with residents. I decided, after reading several accounts of female researchers in the field and discussing the issue with colleagues, that I would mildly alter my otherwise traditionally feminine presentation.[1] This decision was meant to minimize both sexual advances to me in the field and perceptions of me as a "threat" to established relationships. To accomplish this end, I proceeded to

a. wear minimal makeup (e.g., concealer and light blush, but no eyeliner or mascara);

b. wear no jewelry, except a ring on my right ring finger to indicate my status as "not single"; and

c. dress professionally but casually so as to appear competent and approachable. I generally paired collared shirts or blouses with jeans or shorts (just above the knee), depending on the weather. I never wore skirts, dresses, or heels.

In my daily life, I am often told that I appear younger than I am, and I believe my presentation as "young" helped shape residents' perceptions of me as nonthreatening. Similarly, taking into consideration Katheryn Russell-Brown's work *The Color of Crime* and the "criminalblackman" trope, race and gender certainly played roles in my construction as safe and nonthreatening, particularly with my White respondents.

Field Roles

My self-presentation as a young student and "acceptable incompetent" helped defuse power during my interviews and maintain my approachability.[2] I introduced myself to all of my respondents as a student at Duke University. I think most people initially assumed that I was an undergraduate because of my appearance and demeanor. Some participants asked if my data collection was for my thesis; I always responded, "Yes, for my dissertation." Referring to my graduate student status was somewhat dependent on who I was speaking with. If I was trying to assert my expertise, I was more likely to mention my status as a Ph.D. student. If I was meeting with someone older and with significantly less education than I had (e.g., less than a college degree), I deemphasized my schooling and credentials. Upon further reflection, this move was as much an attempt to build rapport and maintain my approachability as it was a reflexive response to deemphasize my own success. This is certainly tied to my own gender and religious socialization on the importance of self-effacement. Due to my socialization as a Catholic Latina, humility and serving others are deeply embedded gender, religious, and cultural practices, and these values dictated my interactions with Creekridge Park residents. I was visiting the homes of people I did not know well and tried to be as inoffensive and unobtrusive as possible. Similarly, my status as a graduate student at Duke would occasionally cause me discomfort when I asked residents for their demographic information at the end of our conversation. I would question respondents about their age, racial and ethnic identification, occupation, and the highest level of education they completed after we were done with the interview guide. As someone who was earning their Ph.D. from an elite institution and looked more like an undergraduate, I often felt uncomfortable with the education question. In an attempt to shift the power back to respondents, I repeated before the demographic questions that they did not have to answer any questions if they did not want to.

Central to my success in Creekridge Park was my skin color privilege, among other characteristics (e.g., Duke affiliation). Although these characteristics mean different things to different people, they generally helped construct me as a credible and approachable person because we live in a racialized system that values and rewards whiteness. Occasionally White residents would ask me questions about my background—where I was from, where my last name was from, where in Durham I lived. Answers about my personal history and family depended on the respondent's specific question. If residents asked where my family was from, I said Nicaragua. If they asked where my last name came from, I responded that I was not sure, but maybe from Spain at some point. If they asked where I was from, I said I grew up in Miami, Florida.[3] In a revealing exchange, Matt, a White homeowner, commented that my last name was special[4] and that he loved it, finally asking if my family had changed it when they came through Ellis Island. Unlike the millions of European immigrants who passed through that gateway in the late nineteenth and early twentieth centuries, my parents moved to Miami in the 1980s. By presuming I am a European-descended White person, Matt's question includes an inaccurate and racialized assumption about my family's immigration experience. His fascination with last names did not end with mine. Matt also stated that my advisor had an "interesting" name; his name (Eduardo Bonilla-Silva) was on the informed consent form all interview participants had to sign. He then asked, "Is he a little bit Hispanic?" When I mentioned that he is Puerto Rican, Matt responded, "Oh, that's good. He'll provide you [with an] interesting perspective on other ethnicities." This statement further confirms that he was reading me as White and "Hispanics" as a distinct group that I was not a part of. Similarly, a few Black and Latino/a participants asked me explicitly if I was White or made allusions to my presumed White identity when they were referencing Whites during our conversations. If they asked me a direct question about my racial identity, I responded that I was Latina. Most Latino/a respondents, however, knew that I identified as Latina and that my parents were from Nicaragua, as I discuss below.

GETTING ALONG

Interview Approach

When approaching White residents of Creekridge Park and the surrounding areas, I told them that I was interested in people's neighborhood experiences and the social interactions that take place around the neighborhood. By focusing on the term "social interactions," I was able to encompass a wide range of issues without specifically naming race, ethnicity, immigration, and class as central to my work. The only times I explicitly stated that I was interested in studying issues of race and ethnicity were when I spoke with Black and Latino/a residents. This strategy was specifically invoked to establish a sense of rapport and camaraderie with residents of color who, understandably, were somewhat hesitant to share their lives with a White-looking researcher from Duke University. Feminist sociologist Joey Sprague states in her work that "the best way to build rapport is to be a good listener who is sensitive to the dynamics of power and privilege."[5] My acknowledgment of the presence and importance of race as a mitigating factor in how Black and Latino/a residents may experience life in Creekridge Park was an attempt to indicate my sensitivity to residents of color and construct my approachability and credibility within a racialized system.

Interview Hiccups

Since I conducted my interviews with Latino/a residents in Spanish, those interviews and meetings often began with the respondents inquiring where I was from and how I knew Spanish. Here I would indicate that my parents were from Nicaragua and I was born in Puerto Rico. Although I am a native Spanish speaker, my Spanish is not as good as it used to be. I did occasionally stumble on words and was not familiar with some colloquialisms used by my Mexican respondents. These hiccups, however, helped construct my approachability and defused power, if only temporarily, between myself and my Latino/a participants. I found this particularly useful in my encounters with Latina migrants, who seemed least comfortable speaking with me. This discomfort, I believe, is in part because of their incredibly vulnerable structural position in Durham. Not all of the Latinas that I spoke with were undocumented, although the female migrants who were least comfortable speaking with me were. Maintaining a certain level of distance is probably a good strategy for undocumented women because they do not know me; I could have been a threat. In these encounters, however, my making a mistake was one way I was constructed as nonthreatening. My mistakes reified my position as a student and someone who was eager to learn from them.

This highlights an important point: although I stand in solidarity with contemporary undocumented and marginalized Latino/a migrants in North Carolina, our structural positions are far from equivalent. In line with Sprague's work on field research, "Being in the same racial/ethnic group is no guarantee of achieving an insider understanding on the part of even the most sympathetic researcher."[6] Even as a self-identified Latina, I still had to grapple with my own skin color, citizenship, class, and English-language privilege when meeting with Creekridge Park residents from Latin America. In one instance during his interview, Martín, a Mexican migrant, asked me if I was White. I responded by saying, "No, I'm Latina." Later in the conversation, however, he made a statement about "you Whites/Americans," then corrected himself to say "them Whites/Americans." Reflecting on this encounter, I realize identifying myself with the panethnic "Latina" label in response to his question further marked me as American, perhaps explaining his use of the term *americanos* to originally include me.[7] As research has shown, national identities are much more relevant than panethnic labels in Latin America and for recent Latin American migrants in the United States.[8] This encounter also underscores a central point: although my approachability and credibility always hinge on my race, class, gender, and other characteristics, these are perceived in complex ways by respondents. For example, a strict insider-outsider framework would assume that Martín would share his story with me because we are both Latinos. My interactions, however, indicate that because of my standpoint, Martín framed me as *americana*, a group distinct from *mexicanos* like himself. Martín, however, still spoke with me and felt comfortable enough to share his migration story. Therefore, his construction of my approachability and credibility was based on other factors (e.g., my credibility as an American student who could tell his story). This more accurate portrayal of my field experience not only illuminates field dynamics but allows me to better present and understand the data that I accessed from our interview. For example, because of his identification of me as *americana*, I can contextualize his insistence on how life in Creekridge Park was *perfecto* and that he had no complaints.

As a rule of practice, I never corrected respondents unless it related to information that I had shared with them about my study. If they misidentified a street name or could not come up with a neighbor's last name, I never chimed in. Sociologists John Lofland, David Snow, Leon Anderson, and Lyn Lofland advise that this is also part of being nonthreatening. They call for researchers to refrain from threats "to the beliefs, practices, existing social arrangements, and even self-esteem, that are communicated by argument, ridicule, sarcasm, gestures of disinterest, and so forth."[9] This practice of silence, however, also had racial implications at times. As demonstrated above, my passing as White and non-Hispanic in Creekridge Park was not made apparent through declarative statements of my identity but through underlying assumptions. Whiteness, like other categories of dominance, maintains its power by constructing its normativity. As such, it can often go unspoken, although it is always being performed.[10]

As has been documented by others, this disconnection between unspoken assumptions about myself and my own identity caused me distress.[11] Similar experiences are discussed by LGBTQ researchers regarding their decisions to disclose (or not) their sexual identity in the field.[12] Sometimes these silences felt innocuous, and sometimes they were much harder to perform. For example, before my interview with Roy and Valerie, a married, White, upper-class couple, they discussed the types of tea they had available. One was manzanilla, which Roy identified as apple, and the other was chai. They then turned to me and asked what kind of tea I would like. Apple, I responded. Although the distinction is irrelevant to my study, manzanilla is actually Spanish for chamomile, not apple, which is manzana. As usual, I stayed quiet about the misnomer.

Another, more stressful example occurred during my interview with Jamie, a fifty-something White homeowner. During our conversation Jamie explained her work, which addresses the underlying genetic and historical causes of behavior through physical therapy. She explains:

> And another thing that, you know, I used to get really upset over when I was growing up in Columbia [South Carolina], because my family was, my mother and father were quite prejudiced against black people is, there was always jokes in school about how a black person lived in a very poor house but had a great big Cadillac, new Cadil-

lac sitting outside the door. And we were talking about that the other night. And that also goes back to African culture because in, uh, the African communities, the chief and the medicine man, they always dressed outrageously, um, flamboyantly and richly compared to the other villagers because it was status, right? Status held a big, big place in African villages. And, now it's shown up differently in America. The status is having that great car to set you apart that you're somebody, right? And in European culture, that isn't where we put our eggs. That isn't the basket that we put out eggs in. You know, for us, we're, you know, we come out of a different kind of a, uh, genetic culture from European culture and it's all about working hard and providing for your family and having a good roof over your head and it's not about status symbols so much. Although, you wouldn't, I mean, some people have that, but it's, it's just very different. So it's always very interesting to look at how all of that works you know and how it manifests itself in different times and different places.

Despite my blanket rule and my confidence in my decisions, both of these interactions caused me distress. Correcting Roy and Valerie could have changed or ended our conversations on relevant issues, such as Latino/a migration and residential politics. Similarly, challenging Jamie's assessment of the differences between Blacks and Whites would have violated norms of fieldwork and potentially shut the conversation down. While I disagree with Jamie's comments, my job is not to argue with her. I must document her experience and make sense of how her work and beliefs relate to her championing of the "liberal," "accepting," and "diverse" neighborhood she lives in. In this interaction, silence facilitated the data collection process by maintaining my approachability and marking me as safe and nonthreatening. In addition, my light-skin privilege made me privy to information that my respondents may not have shared with non-Whites. Jamie's use of "us" and "we" when referencing Europeans and Whites can be interpreted as her inclusion of me in that category.

STUDY DESIGN

The data for this book were collected via three methods: (1) semistructured interviews, (2) participant observation, and (3) a neighborhood survey. Semistructured in-depth interviews are the centerpiece of my data collection process. Interviews uncover the rich data of individual accounts, directly addressing the research questions concerned with neighbor-to-neighbor relationships, including how residents approach and characterize these relationships. The initial questions were developed after preliminary interviews, including a neighborhood tour, with three key informants. These questions were continually refined as different conceptualizations and themes were uncovered. Interviews took place in both English and Spanish, depending on the language preference of the respondent. I conducted all the interviews myself and am fluent in both languages. The interviews generally took place at the respondent's home or a neighborhood space, such as a coffee shop. The locations of these interviews generally depended on respondent preference. If I met them at their home, I always brought respondents some type of food item from a local bakery. If we met at a restaurant, I always offered to purchase coffee or a meal. This gesture, although minimal, was meant to achieve some semblance of reciprocity, especially since I could not afford to pay respondents for their time.[13] As a young, petite woman, I also took some precautionary measures to ensure my safety when I met respondents. For example, I met most male respondents in public spaces, such as restaurants. Of the men I met in their own homes, almost all were interviewed with their partners present or were elderly.

I employed sociologist Mario Small's sequential interviewing method as I conducted my interviews. Small affirms that "case study logic can be effectively applied to in-depth interview-based studies" and is better suited for qualitative work than the sample-based logic of quantitative methods.[14] Rather than attempting to import the logic of statistics into qualitative research in vain, Small argues that researchers should change the criteria for their interview data and attempt to attain saturation through the literal and theoretical replication of cases/interviews. Instead of focusing on the representativeness of the sample, the researcher should purposefully choose respondents based on her or his "increasingly refined and continuously reevaluated understanding of the underlying phenomenon."[15] The evidence-based recruitment criteria for this study included housing tenure (e.g., renter/owner); time in neighborhood (e.g., newcomer, longtime resident); racial-ethnic background (e.g., Black, White, Latino/a); gender (e.g., male, female); and socioeconomic status (e.g., professional, self-employed, fixed income). I sampled across these categories to maximize understanding of the social processes in play and illustrate the different ways residents understand and experience life in a multiethnic neighborhood. I interviewed 63 total respondents, including

21 White males, 28 White females, 3 Black males, 4 Black females, 4 Latinas, 2 Latinos, and 1 other female.[16] Ultimately, the central concern of the sequential interviewing method is on understanding the *how* and *why* of social phenomena rather than identifying the *what* and its rate of occurrence in the general population. This approach is more insightful than an attempt at random sampling because I can make inferences about the mechanisms of social control and social distance in a multiethnic context and the meanings and values attached to these processes by residents. Each interview served as a new case, providing information about the variation within the neighborhood. Using each interview as an independent case facilitated the construction of data-driven theories and hypotheses that were tested and modified throughout the interviews.

The participant observation component addressed research questions about neighbor-to-neighbor relationships and the events that structure these relationships. Often reports on interracial social interactions and friendships are exaggerated by survey respondents.[17] By personally observing potential sites of interracial interaction, I cross-examined self-reported data from interviews and the survey on interracial interaction in public spaces and at neighborhoodwide events.

The final component was the neighborhood survey. The survey distribution was divided into two phases. The first phase was dissemination through an online format. The online survey was advertised via the neighborhood association listserv, neighborhood association quarterly newsletter, and hand-delivered bilingual fliers to each home, including each individual apartment in the complexes. The fliers included the survey link and also indicated that paper versions of the survey were available.[18] The survey was available in both English and Spanish. The second phase included a targeted mailing of the survey advertisement to streets with low response rates (less than 10 percent), which primarily focused on Pine Grove Apartments. Survey participants who provided their contact information on a separate form were entered into a raffle with a one-in-twenty-five chance of winning. The prizes were gift cards to their preferred supermarket.

With the household survey, data on residents' racial attitudes were collected in addition to data on neighbor-to-neighbor relationships. Demographic and behavioral questions (e.g., Where do you do your grocery shopping?) were also included. The questions for these surveys were based on field observations and in-depth interviews, as well as national survey instruments related to interracial relations, attitudes, and behaviors. The survey supports the unique opportunity to analyze neighbor-hood racial attitudes and social networks, serving as a comparison to other nationally collected data on these subjects. Although causality can-not be inferred from a cross-sectional comparison, the data are still im-portant to understanding how residents of multiethnic neighborhoods differ from the national and regional means.

DATA ANALYSIS

The case study logic of the interview process demands the continual re-finement of interview questions. Therefore, the preliminary analyses of interviews began immediately following the first interview. Analyses of data collected through participant observation were also important to the construction of interview questions and the survey instrument. Organiz-ing and analyzing the survey data followed all data collection phases. The method of data analysis I used was modified grounded theory.

Modified grounded theory is an iterative process of data analysis that uses data and existing theories to inform each other, producing new con-ceptual models. Multiple phases of data analysis are necessary to reach a cohesive understanding of the relationship between various concepts. These individual events, interpretations, and accounts are grouped by themes named in the literature and by the respondents. Using respon-dents as sources of both data and theoretical conceptualizations is one of the strengths of qualitative research. As major themes were identified, codes were then established to group them. Another round of data analy-ses followed to facilitate a better understanding of the relationships be-tween these different concepts. Highlighting contradictions is a major asset of qualitative research as well, since contradictions often expose unspoken ideological assumptions. After these concepts, categories, and contradictions were processed in multiple iterations, a cohesive theory was produced.[19] The results of these analyses are presented in Chapters 2, 3, and 4.

APPENDIX B *Guide for In-depth Interviews*

How long have you lived in the neighborhood? Have you lived in other neighborhoods/areas in Durham before? Were there other areas you were looking at closely when you chose to live in Creekridge Park?

Do you know anything about the history of this neighborhood?

Why did you move here? What were you looking for in terms of house/apartment complex/neighborhood?

Do you rent or own? If own, how long have you owned your home? If rent, who is your landlord? Do you know if they own other property across the neighborhood?

What do you know about landlords in this neighborhood? Do you have any kind of relationship with them?

Do you live with anyone? (If children, probe about age and schooling.)

Who are your neighbors? Are they renters or owners?

Do you have any friends that live in the neighborhood? Where do they live? How did you meet them? What kinds of things do you do together?

If they don't have friends in the neighborhood: Who do you spend the most time with that lives in the neighborhood? How did you meet them? What kind of things do you do together?

What kind of people would you say live in the neighborhood? How would you describe the residents to someone who doesn't live there? (probe: demographics, class, occupations, household/family type)

What kind of people live on your street/in your building?

Would you say the neighborhood has any leaders? Who would you consider a leader? Why?

Are you involved with any neighborhood-specific organizations (e.g., CPNA)? If yes, why did you choose to join? Do you attend meetings regularly or whenever there is a specific issue of interest? If not, have you been asked to join any?

Are you familiar with the neighborhood association? Do you receive the CPNA newsletter? Do you read it? Are you on the neighborhood listserv?

Are you a member of any other clubs or groups that meet regularly? It can be informally or formally.

How do you spend your free time? Are there areas not directly in the neighborhood that you spend a lot of time in?

Have you ever been involved in any neighborhoodwide efforts to address issues, like the expansion of The Bakery or others? (prompt: recent traffic concerns, new development)

What areas do you consider to be a part of the neighborhood (specific streets, businesses)? Where would you draw the neighborhood boundaries?

What areas in the neighborhood do you frequent the most?

What do you know about The Center? What do you think about their presence in the neighborhood? Have you ever used their services?

Have you ever participated in neighborhoodwide events, such as National Night Out, the Annual Picnic, or the Pine Grove Open House?

Other than these large events, do you think neighbors spend a lot of time interacting socially? Where do these interactions happen?

If you had a problem with a neighbor or in the neighborhood, how would you handle it? (probe: individually, go to property management, neighborhood association, police) Have you ever had any problems in the past? How have you handled them?

Do you feel safe in your neighborhood? Have you dealt with any crime-related issues?

What do you think makes someone a good neighbor? Do you have good neighbors?

Do you think other neighborhoods in Durham look like this one, or is Creekridge Park different? How?

The CPNA claims on its website that the neighborhood is mixed-income and diverse—do you think that is true? Why or why not?

Do you see interracial interactions in the neighborhood? Like, whites and blacks and Latinos spending time together? Do you have a specific example? Where do you see this? If you don't see it, why do you think that is?

Now to finish up I'd like to ask some question about your personal characteristics. Remember, you don't have to answer these questions if you do not want to.

- How old are you?
- How do you identify racially and ethnically?
- What is your occupation?
- What was the highest level of education you completed?

I am trying to get a sense of who lives in this neighborhood and what the experiences of residents are. Are there people that you think I should talk to or that would be willing to speak with me?

Is there anything I didn't mention that you think I should know to understand life in this neighborhood?

APPENDIX C *Interview Participant Demographics*

ADRIENNE, White female, early thirties, newcomer, homeowner, Emerson Court

ALAN, White male, fifties, longtime resident, homeowner, Emerson Court

ANGELA, Black female, late forties, established resident, homeowner, Creekridge Road

ANN, White female, late thirties, newcomer, homeowner, Cardinal Street

BETH, White female, fifties, established resident, homeowner, Emerson Court

BRENDAN, White male, early thirties, newcomer, homeowner, Smith Road

BRYAN, White male, fifties, longtime resident, homeowner, Pine Avenue

CHARLES, White male, early thirties, established resident, homeowner, Peach Avenue

CHERYL, Black female, fifties, established resident, homeowner, Pine Avenue

CONNIE, Black female, fifties, longtime resident, homeowner, Pine Avenue

CRISTINA, Latina Female, newcomer, renter, Pine Grove Apartments

CYNTHIA, White Female, sixties, established resident, homeowner, Harris Street

DANIEL, White male, fifties, established resident, homeowner, Peach Avenue

DAVID, White male, eighties, longtime resident, homeowner, Creekridge Road

DEBBIE, White Female, fifties, established resident, homeowner, Valley Court

DEBORAH, White female, established resident, homeowner, Union Avenue

DENISE, White female, late twenties, newcomer, renter, Central Street

DIANA, Latina female, early forties, newcomer, renter, Cardinal Street (formerly)

ED, White male, fifties, longtime resident, business owner, Cardinal Street

EMMA, White female, late twenties, newcomer, homeowner, Colony Street

ERIC, White male, late twenties, newcomer, homeowner, Central Street

ESTHER, White female, renter, longtime resident, Pine Grove Apartments

GEORGE, Black male, late twenties, newcomer, renter, Valley Court

HÉCTOR, Latino male, fifties, established resident, renter, Cardinal Street

JAMES, White male, late forties, established resident, renter, Harris Street

JAMIE, White female, fifties, established resident, homeowner, Creekridge Road

JERRY, Black male, sixties, established resident, homeowner, Tyler Avenue

JUDY, White female, early forties, established resident, homeowner, Peach Avenue

JULIANA, Latina female, early thirties, newcomer, renter, Pine Avenue

JULIE, White female, early thirties, newcomer, homeowner, Cardinal Street

KEITH, White male, fifties, established resident, homeowner, Central Street

KEN, White male, late thirties, newcomer, homeowner, Cardinal Street

LAWRENCE, Black male, early thirties, newcomer, renter, Valley Court

LIZ, White female, late forties, established resident, homeowner, Cardinal Street

LOIS, White female, sixties, newcomer, renter, Pine Grove Apartments

LORI, White female, late twenties, newcomer, homeowner, Emerson Court

LUKE, White male, early thirties, newcomer, homeowner, Colony Street

MARIE, White female, eighties, longtime resident, homeowner, Creekridge Road

MARTA, Latina female, late twenties, newcomer, renter, Cardinal Street (formerly)

MARTÍN, Latino male, early forties, newcomer, renter, Orchid Place

MARY, Black female, fifties, longtime resident, renter, Colony Street

MATT, White male, fifties, longtime resident, homeowner, Peach Avenue

MICHELLE, White female, late twenties, newcomer, homeowner, Central Street

PATTY, White female, late twenties, newcomer, homeowner, Harris Street

RAY, White male, sixties, established resident, homeowner, Union Avenue

RHONDA, White female, early thirties, established resident, homeowner, Peach Avenue

ROBIN, White female, fifties, established resident, homeowner, Central Street

ROSE, White female, established resident, homeowner, Peach Avenue

ROY, White male, late thirties, established resident, homeowner, Creekridge area

RUSS, White male, fifties, established resident, homeowner, Central Street

RUTH, White female, fifties, established resident, homeowner, Harris Street

SANDRA, White female, late thirties, newcomer, homeowner, Pine Avenue

SCOTT, White male, early thirties, established resident, homeowner, Harris Street

SETH, White male, early forties, established resident, homeowner, Harris Street

SHARON, White female, early thirties, established resident, homeowner, Harris Street

SONIA, female, longtime resident, homeowner, Mason Avenue

STEPHANIE, White female, early thirties, established resident, homeowner, Central Street

TAMMY, White female, fifties, established resident, homeowner, Central Street

TERRY, White male, fifties, established resident, homeowner, Creekridge Road

THOMAS, White male, late twenties, newcomer, renter, Central Street

TIMOTHY, White male, fifties, established resident, homeowner, Harris Street

TINA, White female, early thirties, newcomer, homeowner, Central Street

VALERIE, White female, early thirties, established resident, homeowner, Creekridge area

Notes

1. "Creekridge Park" is a pseudonym I chose in order to protect the identities of my participants. Geographic details have also been slightly modified to obscure the exact location of Creekridge Park. All resident and street names are also pseudonyms.

2. I use the capitalized term "White" to refer to individuals who are White and non-Hispanic. I use the lowercase term "white" to refer to a set of power relations that systemically (i.e., socially, politically, and historically) privilege European descendants and disadvantage racial others. I discuss this distinction a bit more later in the chapter. Throughout the book I also use three terms to designate how long residents have lived in the neighborhood: newcomer—less than five years; established resident—more than five and less than fifteen years; and longtime resident—fifteen or more years.

3. I conducted all interviews with English and Spanish speakers myself. I am a native Spanish speaker and translated all of the quotations in this book myself, with some help from a Spanish-speaking consultant. Rather than use literal translations of the Spanish language comments, I used interpretive translations to improve the readability of the translated quotations. All Spanish-language interviews and about 50 percent of the English-language interviews were transcribed by a transcription service. I transcribed the other 50 percent of the English-language interviews.

4. "Latino/a" is a commonly used identifier for Latinos and Latinas. For those wondering how to pronounce it, I use it here as shorthand for the longer phrase "Latino and Latina." Latino/as is shorthand for the plural "Latinos and Latinas." For an in-depth discussion of this phrase, see Milian's *Latining America*.

5. Glaeser and Vigdor, "End of the Segregated Century."

6. Interracial relationships include friendships, neighborships, and romantic partnerships.

7. Maly, *Beyond Segregation*.

8. Ellen, "Stable Racial Integration," 29.

9. For more on the shortcomings of statistical integration measures, see Hartman and Squires's *Integration Debate*, especially chapter 15 by Stephen Steinberg. Maly's *Beyond Segregation* also provides a critique of the dichotomous numerical measurement of integration.

10. I use equity in line with Frazier, Margai, and Tettey-Fio's work. In their *Race and Place: Equity Issues in Urban America* they define equity as "the fair distribution of risks,

costs, services, and benefits across demographic groups, neighborhoods, counties, states, countries, and even generations" (16).

11. In *Race and Culture*, sociologist Robert Park defines social distance as "the grades and degrees of understanding and intimacy which characterize personal and social relations generally" (256).

12. Anderson, *Durham County*, 203.

13. Ibid., 223.

14. Ibid., 138–39.

15. Du Bois, *Souls of Black Folk*, 260.

16. Ibid., 166.

17. Anderson, *Durham County*, 310.

18. Ibid., 335.

19. Kim, "Racial Triangulation." The majority of the Latino/a migrants in Durham and North Carolina are from Mexico and Central America.

20. For more on Los Angeles, see Bobo, Oliver, Johnson, and Valenzuela, *Prismatic Metropolis*; Charles, *Won't You Be My Neighbor?*; and Horton, *Politics of Diversity*. For studies on New York, see Maly, *Beyond Segregation*; Rosenbaum and Friedman, *Housing Divide*; and Sharman, *Tenants of East Harlem*. For more on Chicago, see Maly, *Beyond Segregation*, and Wilson and Taub, *There Goes the Neighborhood*.

21. Hirschman and Massey, "Places and People," 3.

22. Census 2010 Summary File 1 North Carolina/prepared by the U.S. Census Bureau, 2011; Census 2000 Summary File 1 North Carolina/prepared by the U.S. Census Bureau, 2001. Accessed July 1, 2013 (www.census.gov).

23. Winders, "Placing Latino Migration" and "Nashville's New 'Sonido.'"

24. In 2012, about 53 percent of Durham's Latino/a population was foreign born. Previous estimates indicate that up to 90 percent of Durham's foreign-born Latino/a population is undocumented. See Parrado and Flippen, "Migration and Gender among Mexican Women."

25. *Ex-Officer Pleads Guilty to Stealing from Hispanic Drivers*.

26. To further protect the identity of my respondents, I have slightly modified the census-based numbers for Creekridge Park demographics. The percentages, however, are comparable so readers can understand and analyze population trends.

27. Leip, *Atlas of U.S. Presidential Elections*.

28. Smith, Marsden, Hout, and Kim, *General Social Surveys*.

29. NYT/CBS News, "Poll: April 28–May 2, 2010."

30. For more on traditional gentrification processes, see Freeman, "Neighbourhood Diversity, Metropolitan Segregation and Gentrification"; Ley, "Artists and Gentrification"; and Zukin, "Gentrification."

31. Southern Redlining Coalition, "Sustainable Archives and Leveraging Technologies."

32. A block group is a collection of census blocks.

33. Census 2010 Summary File 1 North Carolina/prepared by the U.S. Census Bureau, 2011. Accessed July 1, 2013 (www.census.gov).

34. Southern Redlining Coalition, "Sustainable Archives and Leveraging Technologies."

35. Zukin, "Gentrification"; Hallman, *Neighborhoods*; Nager, "Continuities of Urban Policy"; Rabrenovic, *Community Builders*.

36. Durham County Register of Deeds, "Index to Corporations."

37. Southern Redlining Coalition, "Sustainable Archives and Leveraging Technologies."

38. In order to protect the identity of the neighborhood, I will not specify whether Creekridge Park is home to a fire, police, or emergency medical station.

39. Giddens, *Constitution of Society*, 257–58.

40. Ibid., 24.

41. Bourdieu, *Theory of Practice*, 214.

42. Ibid.

43. Ibid., 78.

44. Frankenberg, *White Women, Race Matters*; Hartigan, *Racial Situations*; Lewis, "What Group?"; McDermott and Samson, "White Racial and Ethnic Identity"; Roediger, *Wages of Whiteness*; Wellman, *Portraits of White Racism*; Hartmann, Gerteis, and Croll, "Assessment of Whiteness Theory."

45. Mills, *Racial Contract*, 127.

46. Twine and Gallagher, "Future of Whiteness."

47. Mills, *Racial Contract*, 3.

48. Ibid., 11. For example, see Hartigan's *Racial Situations* for a discussion on class and whiteness.

49. Sullivan, *Revealing Whiteness*, 10. For more on whiteness and its consequences, see Lipsitz's *Possessive Investment in Whiteness*.

50. Bourdieu, "Social Space and Symbolic Power," 21.

51. I identify as Latina and, more specifically, as Nicaraguan.

52. For another example of this type of research, see Royster's *Race and the Invisible Hand*.

53. Shaw, *Cities of Whiteness*, 5. See also Andersen, "Whitewashing Race," and Hurtado and Stewart, "Through the Looking Glass."

54. During my time in the field I was enrolled as a doctoral candidate in the Sociology Department at Duke University and had a master's degree from the same department.

55. Glenn, *Unequal Freedom*, 17.

CHAPTER 2

1. Bourdieu, "Social Space and Symbolic Power," 19; Bourdieu, *Distinction*, 170.

2. Bourdieu, *Distinction*, 6.

3. I have been told on multiple occasions that I need to study X neighborhood in Y city because it sounds just like Creekridge Park. Some of my respondents even mentioned during their interviews that Creekridge Park was similar to neighborhoods in which they had lived previously in other cities, such as Washington, D.C. While readers may identify similarities between the white, urban, middle-class habitus of Creekridge Park and neighborhoods in their own cities (Creekridge Park residents are not the only individuals who participate in these practices and ways of being in the United States or globally), this is but one possibility for a white, urban, middle-class habitus. Not all White, urban-based, middle-class individuals express the same values that my respondents did or embody this particular habitus.

4. I borrow sociologist David G. Embrick's concept of diversity ideology for my analysis, although I focus on the set of beliefs that Creekridge Park residents shared that reconcile racial inequality and desired egalitarianism.

5. Hall, "Race, Articulation, and Societies," 334.

6. Bonilla-Silva, *Racism without Racists*.

7. For more on the historical roots of diversity ideology in corporate America, see Embrick's "Making and Selling of an Illusion."

8. I am interested in the narratives shared by residents, since I can only retrospectively interpret why they moved to Creekridge Park. The "truth" of why they moved to Creekridge Park is less important for the purposes of my study than how they understand and make sense of their decisions.

9. This average is based on 243 home sales.

10. This average is based on 2 home sales.

11. This average is based on 2 home sales.

12. Hummon, *Commonplaces*, 86.

13. Ibid.; Ley, *New Middle Class*.

14. Ley, *New Middle Class*, 205–6.

15. Homes that receive historic designations generally are seen as having "special significance" in regard to history, culture, or architecture. Some guidelines dictate a minimum age requirement (e.g., at least fifty years old). The official guidelines depend on the designating organization. For more on Preservation Durham's different designations, see http://preservationdurham.org/education/historic-designation/.

16. I computed dissimilarity indices for Creekridge Park, which range from 0 to 1, using 2010 census data. The 2010 Latino/a index is .12, indicating that 12 percent of the Latino/as in Creekridge Park would have move to different blocks to create an even distribution across the neighborhood. The dissimilarity index for Blacks in 2010 was .31, indicating that 31 percent of Black residents would have to move from one block to another. Lastly, Whites experienced a small increase in their dissimilarity index to .34 in 2010, which means that 34 percent of White residents would have to move for Whites to be proportionally represented across Creekridge Park. Using Massey and Denton's .3 cutoff, .34 still indicates relatively low segregation across these blocks; see Massey and Denton, *American Apartheid*.

17. Hall, "Race, Articulation, and Societies," 342.

18. Embrick, "Making and Selling of an Illusion."

19. Ibid.

20. Bourdieu, "Social Space and Symbolic Power," 19.

21. Sullivan, *Revealing Whiteness*, 126.

22. For more on the financial benefits of homeownership in gentrifying neighborhoods, see Zukin's "Gentrification."

23. Hallman, *Neighborhoods*, 210.

24. Black, Gates, Sanders, and Taylor, "Why Do Gay Men Live in San Francisco?"

25. Hooks, "Eating the Other," 354.

26. For more on neighborhood preferences, see Swaroop and Krysan's "Determinants of Neighborhood Satisfaction" and Adelman's "Roles of Race, Class, and Residential Preferences."

27. While Brendan technically lived outside the boundaries of Creekridge Park, he participated in Creekridge Park activities, was on the neighborhood association listserv, and was friends with individuals in Creekridge Park. As part of the study, I interviewed folks from a few adjacent neighborhoods. Throughout the book I refer to them as living in the Creekridge Park area, and not as Creekridge Park residents.

28. Bourdieu, *Distinction*, 2.

29. For more on the multiplicity of ideologies, see Hall, "Gramsci's Relevance," 22.

30. For more on the Black-White wealth gap, see Oliver and Shapiro's *Black Wealth/White Wealth* and Shapiro's *Hidden Cost of Being African American*.

31. Bourdieu, "Social Space and Symbolic Power," 20.

CHAPTER 3

1. Black codes were enacted in the South after the Civil War and the implementation of the Thirteenth Amendment: "Several of the codes undertook to limit the areas in which blacks could purchase or rent property. Vagrancy laws imposed heavy penalties that were designed to force all blacks to work whether they wanted to or not. The control of blacks by white employers was about as great as the control that slaveholders had exercised" (Franklin and Moss, *From Slavery to Freedom*, 250). See also Zinn, *People's History*, 199.

2. The letter welcomed the students to the neighborhood and included a list of practices to establish and maintain open communication between residents, such as sharing contact information. This was one of the strategies employed by the neighborhood association and concerned neighbors after a particularly contentious relationship with the previous class of fraternity members in regard to noise and trash.

3. For more on the inequitable outcome of race-neutral policies, see Saito's *Politics of Exclusion*.

4. For an excellent discussion of white spaces and exclusion, see Chalmers's "White Out."

5. Lewis, "What Group?," 629.

6. For more on whiteness in other contexts, see Hordge-Freeman, Mayorga, and Bonilla-Silva, "Exposing Whiteness," and Dalmage, "Protecting Racial Comfort."

7. Cheryl stated during her interview that her neighbors are predominantly White.

8. Blokland, "Gardening with a Little Help."

9. Glenn, *Unequal Freedom*, 13.

10. Ibid., 14.

11. I mention these practices specifically because the board stated them as future goals and/or ways to increase Latino/a involvement.

12. Latino Outreach, "Latino Community Outreach."

13. Delcher, Johnson, and Maldonado-Molina, "Driving after Drinking."

14. Blouin, "Understanding Relations between People and Their Pets."

15. The board member mentioned this email exchange at a CPNA meeting.

16. I use Allan's definition of friendship, which highlights "the quality and character of the relationship involved" and the importance of equality in the relationship (*Friendship*, 16). Rude and Herda, in "Best Friends Forever?," also highlight the importance of closeness and reciprocity in their definition.

17. This number may be an underestimate. We know from the interview data that those residents who live on boundary streets, such as Cardinal Street and Harris Street, are likely to have friends on adjacent streets that are technically in other neighborhoods.

18. Allan differentiates between friendship and mateship, emphasizing the importance of social context for mateship. He writes, "This form of social relationship allows those involved to have a greater control of the 'content' of their tie, as it is focused more explicitly on the setting in which they meet" (*Friendship*, 26). I argue that neighborship, like Allan's mateship, is constructed around and defined by the neighborhood environment. Once a resident moves out of Creekridge Park, his or her relationships and socializing with neighbors are likely to end, unless they are friends.

19. Butler, "Social Capital," 225.

20. Merry, *Urban Danger*, 14–15.

21. Rosenbaum, "Community Crime Prevention," 348.

22. For more on race, the body, and policing, see Russell-Brown, *Color of Crime*; Weitzer, "Racialized Policing"; and Weitzer and Tuch, "Racially Biased Policing."

23. For more on friendships, see Allan, *Friendship*, and Rude and Herda, "Best Friends Forever?"

24. These two federally funded programs focus on the creation of mixed-income neighborhoods through the relocation of poor minority residents to more affluent areas.

25. Jackman, *Velvet Glove*, 14.

26. Rabrenovic finds similar tensions in her study of a gentrifying neighborhood in *Community Builders*.

27. Esther has since passed away.

28. Smith, "Measuring Inter-Racial Friendships."

CHAPTER 4

1. Omi and Winant, *Racial Formation*, 118.

2. See Eric Fischer's digital map gallery at http://www.flickr.com/photos/walkingsf/sets/72157626354149574/.

3. Charles, "Dynamics of Racial Residential Segregation," 189. Maria Krysan presents similar findings in "Community Undesirability."

4. Giddens, *Constitution of Society*, 257.

5. Marta and her friend Diana no longer lived in Creekridge Park at the time of our interview, but in an adjacent area. I interviewed them together.

6. McClain et al., "Racial Distancing."

7. Rodriguez, *Changing Race*; Wade, *Race and Ethnicity*.

8. Jones-Correa, "Commonalities, Competition, and Linked Fate," 84, 90.

9. For more on immigrant networks, see Portes and Rumbaut's *Immigrant America*.

10. Adams and Allan, "Contextualising Friendship," 12.

11. Thank you to Elizabeth Hordge-Freeman for this point.

12. Pitts, "Four Decades Later."

13. Schrock and Schwalbe, "Men, Masculinity, and Manhood Acts."

14. Ibid., 238.

15. *Mollo* is an anti-Black racial epithet, comparable to the n-word in the United States.

16. McClain et al., "Racial Distancing."

17. Charles, "Dynamics of Racial Residential Segregation," 179.

18. Shapiro, *Hidden Cost of Being African American*, 121.

19. For example, when I set up an interview with a White resident who I did not know lived on a fixed income, I suggested we meet at Stella's since it was relatively close to his home. He responded that he could not afford to meet there for lunch. After I told him "lunch is on me," he was happy to meet there. For more on how I negotiated race, class, and gender in my interview locations, see Appendix A.

20. Feagin, Vera, and Imani, *Agony of Education*, 65.

21. Connie said her encounter with her neighbor happened when she first moved in and Creekridge Park was a predominantly White neighborhood.

22. Marta and Diana's definition of racism does not take into consideration issues of power, an important part of scholarly definitions of racism, and is more similar to sociological definitions of prejudice.

23. Portes and Rumbaut, *Immigrant America*, 64.

24. For more on Durham's migrant community, see Parrado, McQuiston, and Flippen, "Participatory Survey Research."

25. Rude, "Interracial Friendships in Context," 4.

26. For examples, see Brown-Saracino, *Neighborhood That Never Changes*.

27. North Carolina's House Bill 33, which passed in March 2011, proposes that the state not accept consulate or embassy documents as a valid form of identification. HB33 did not make it out of the Senate Committee on Rules and Operations. The bill,

reproposed in February 2013 as HB118, has since been under review by the House Judiciary Subcommittee C.

28. In addition to the CPNA meeting where Captain Hanks and two officers were in attendance, Captain Hanks attended at least one other meeting organized by a White Creekridge Park resident to address a series of neighborhood car accidents.

CHAPTER 5

1. The title of this chapter is a reference to Smith's insightful chapter, "Integration: Solving the Wrong Problem," in Hartman and Squires's *Integration Debate*.

2. For more on white-controlled spaces, see Dalmage's "Protecting Racial Comfort."

3. Joseph, "Reinventing Older Communities"; Joseph and Chaskin, "Living in a Mixed-Income Development"; Smith, "Integration"; Steinberg, "Myth of Concentrated Poverty."

4. Steinberg, "Myth of Concentrated Poverty," 219.

5. Johnson, *Patterns of Negro Segregation*; Park, "Concept of Social Distance."

APPENDIX A

1. For a discussion of these issues, see Pascoe, *Dude, You're Fag*; Bettie, *Women without Class*; Royster, *Race and the Invisible Hand*; and Warren and Hackney, *Gender Issues in Ethnography*.

2. Lofland, Snow, Anderson, and Lofland, *Analyzing Social Settings*, 69; Conti and O'Neil, "Studying Power," 73.

3. I tried to present a version of myself that was still reflective of "the real me," as Lofland, Snow, Anderson, and Lofland recommend in *Analyzing Social Settings*. The answers I gave in Creekridge Park are the same answers I give when people ask me these questions outside of field work.

4. At the time of my fieldwork my last name was Mayorga.

5. Sprague, *Feminist Methodologies for Critical Researchers*, 140.

6. Ibid., 65.

7. The term *americanos* can mean Americans generally, although it is often used to specifically refer to White, non-Hispanic Americans. In my interview with Martín, for example, he differentiated between *americanos* and *afro-americanos* (African Americans).

8. See Itzigsohn and Dore-Cabral, "Competing Identities?," and Sears, Fu, Henry, and Bui, "The Origins and Persistence of Ethnic Identity."

9. Lofland, Snow, Anderson, and Lofland, *Analyzing Social Settings*, 68.

10. For more on the distinction between silence and invisibility, see Frankenberg, "On Unsteady Ground," and Gallagher, "White Like Me?"

11. See Lamont, "Life of Sad, but Justified, Choices," and Stacey, "Can There Be a Feminist Ethnography?"

12. See Barton, "My Auto/Ethnographic Dilemma."

13. Snow, Benford, and Anderson, "Fieldwork Roles"; Williams, Dunlap, Johnson, and Hamid, "Safety in Dangerous Places."

14. Small, "'How Many Cases Do I Need?,'" 24.

15. Ibid., 26.

16. In order to protect this respondent's identity, I am refraining from identifying her racial-ethnic identity.

17. Smith, "Measuring Inter-Racial Friendships."

18. Several requests for paper versions of the survey were made via telephone.

19. For more on grounded theory, see Burton, Cherlin, Winn, Estacion, and Holder-Taylor, "Role of Trust," and Charmaz, *Constructing Grounded Theory*.

Bibliography

Adams, Rebecca G., and Graham Allan. "Contextualising Friendship." In *Placing Friendship in Context*, edited by R. G. Adams and G. Allan, 1–17. Cambridge: Cambridge University Press.

Adelman, Robert M. "The Roles of Race, Class, and Residential Preferences in the Neighborhood Racial Composition of Middle-Class Blacks and Whites." *Social Science Quarterly* 86 (2005): 209–28.

Allan, Graham. *Friendship: Developing a Sociological Perspective*. San Francisco: Westview Press, 1989.

Andersen, Margaret L. "Whitewashing Race: A Critical Perspective on Whiteness." In *White Out: The Continuing Significance of Racism*, edited by A. W. Doane and E. Bonilla-Silva, 21–34. New York: Routledge, 2003.

Anderson, Jean Bradley. *Durham County: A History of Durham County, North Carolina*. Durham: Duke University Press, 2011.

Barton, Bernadette. "My Auto/Ethnographic Dilemma: Who Owns the Story?" *Qualitative Sociology* 34 (2011): 431–45.

Bettie, Julie. *Women without Class: Girls, Race, and Identity*. Berkeley: University of California Press, 2003.

Black, Dan, Gary Gates, Seth Sanders, and Lowell Taylor. "Why Do Gay Men Live in San Francisco?" *Journal of Urban Economics* 51 (2002): 54–76.

Blokland, Talja. "Gardening with a Little Help from Your (Middle Class) Friends: Bridging Social Capital across Race and Class in a Mixed Neighbourhood." In *Networked Urbanism: Social Capital in the City*, edited by T. Blokland and M. Savage, 147–70. Burlington, VT: Ashgate, 2008.

Blouin, David D. "Understanding Relations between People and Their Pets." *Sociology Compass* 6 (2012): 856–69.

Bobo, Lawrence D., Melvin L. Oliver, James H. Johnson Jr., and Abel Valenzuela Jr., eds. *Prismatic Metropolis: Inequality in Los Angeles*. New York: Russell Sage Foundation, 2000.

Bonilla-Silva, Eduardo. "'New Racism,' Color-Blind Racism, and the Future of Whiteness in America." In *White Out: The Continuing Significance of Racism*, edited by A. W. Doane and E. Bonilla-Silva. 271–84. New York: Routledge, 2003.

———. *Racism without Racists: Color-Blind Racism and the Persistence of Racial Inequality in the United States*. Lanham, MD: Rowman and Littlefield, 2013.

Bourdieu, Pierre. *Distinction: A Social Critique of the Judgment of Taste*. Cambridge, MA: Harvard University Press, 1984.

———. *Outline of a Theory of Practice*. Cambridge: Cambridge University Press, 1977.

———. "Social Space and Symbolic Power." *Sociological Theory* 7 (1989): 14–25.

Brown-Saracino, Japonica. *A Neighborhood That Never Changes: Gentrification, Social Preservation, and the Search for Authenticity*. Chicago: University of Chicago Press, 2010.

Burton, Linda M., Andrew Cherlin, Donna-Marie Winn, Angela Estacion, and Clara Holder-Taylor. "The Role of Trust in Low-Income Mothers' Intimate Unions." *Journal of Marriage and Family* 71 (2009): 1107–24.

Butler, Tim. "Social Capital and the Formation of London's Middle Classes." In *Networked Urbanism: Social Capital in the City*, edited by T. Blokland and M. Savage, 217–36. Burlington, VT: Ashgate, 2008.

Chalmers, Virginia. "White Out: Multicultural Performances in a Progressive School." In *Off White: Readings on Race, Power, and Society*, edited by M. Fine, L. Weis, L. C. Powell, and L. M. Wong, 66–78. New York: Routledge, 1997.

Charles, Camille Zubrinsky. "The Dynamics of Racial Residential Segregation." *Annual Review of Sociology* 29 (2003): 167–207.

———. *Won't You Be My Neighbor? Race, Class, and Residence in Los Angeles*. New York: Russell Sage Foundation, 2006.

Charmaz, Kathy. *Constructing Grounded Theory: A Practical Guide through Qualitative Research*. London: SAGE Publications, 2006.

Conti, Joseph A., and Moira O'Neil. "Studying Power: Qualitative Methods and the Global Elite." *Qualitative Research* 7 (2007): 63–82.

Dalmage, Heather M. "Protecting Racial Comfort, Protecting White Privilege." In *The Politics of Multiracialism: Challenging Racial Thinking*, edited by H. M. Dalmage, 203–18. Albany: State University of New York Press, 2004.

Delcher, Chris, Rachel Johnson, and Mildred M. Maldonado-Molina. "Driving after Drinking among Young Adults of Different Race/Ethnicities in the United States: Unique Risk Factors in Early Adolescence?" *Journal of Adolescent Health* 52 (2013): 584–91.

Du Bois, W. E. B. *Souls of Black Folks*. New York: Penguin Books, 1903.

Durham County Register of Deeds. "Index to Corporations, Assumed Names and Partners—Durham County, NC," 1881–1983, http://rodweb.co.durham.nc.us/localization/menu.asp. Accessed March 1, 2012.

Ellen, Ingrid Gould. "Stable Racial Integration in the Contemporary United States: An Empirical Overview." *Journal of Urban Affairs* 20 (1998): 27–42.

Embrick, David G. "The Making and Selling of an Illusion: An Examination of Racial and Gender Diversity in Post–Civil Rights U.S. Corporations." Ph.D. diss., Texas A&M University, 2006.

Ex-Officer Pleads Guilty to Stealing from Hispanic Drivers. Capital Broadcasting Company, http://www.wral.com/news/news_briefs/story/2118634/. Accessed August 5, 2013.

Feagin, Joe R., Hernan Vera, and Nikitah Imani. *The Agony of Education: Black Students at White Colleges and Universities*. New York: Routledge, 1996.

Frankenberg, Ruth. "On Unsteady Ground: Crafting and Engaging in the Critical Study of Whiteness." In *Researching Race and Racism*, edited by Martin Bulmer and John Solomos, 104–18. New York: Routledge, 2004.

———. *White Women, Race Matters: The Social Construction of Whiteness*. Minneapolis: University of Minnesota Press, 1993.

Franklin, John Hope, and Alfred A. Moss Jr. *From Slavery to Freedom: A History of African Americans*. New York: Knopf, 2000.

Frazier, John H., Florence M. Margai, and Eugene Tettey-Fio. *Race and Place: Equity Issues in Urban America*. Cambridge, MA: Westview Press, 2003.

Freeman, Lance. "Neighbourhood Diversity, Metropolitan Segregation and Gentrification: What Are the Links in the U.S.?" *Urban Studies* 46 (2009): 2079–2101.

Gallagher, Charles. "White Like Me? Methods, Meaning, and Manipulation in the Field of White Studies." In *Racing Research, Researching Race*, edited by France Winddance Twine and Jonathan Warren, 67–92. New York: New York University Press, 2000.

Giddens, Anthony. *The Constitution of Society: Outline of the Theory of Structuration*. Berkeley: University of California Press, 1984.

Glaeser, Edward, and Jacob Vigdor. "The End of the Segregated Century: Racial Separation in America's Neighborhoods, 1890–2010." Civic Report 66 (2012), Manhattan Institute for Policy Research, http://www.manhattan-institute.org/html/cr_66.htm. Accessed April 11, 2014.

Glenn, Evelyn Nakano. *Unequal Freedom: How Race and Gender Shaped American Citizenship and Labor*. Cambridge, MA: Harvard University Press, 2002.

Hall, Stuart. "Gramsci's Relevance for the Study of Race and Ethnicity." *Journal of Communication* 10 (1986): 5–27.

———. "Race, Articulation, and Societies Structured in Dominance." In *Sociological Theories: Race and Colonialism*, 305–45. Paris: UNESCO, 1980.

Hallman, Howard W. *Neighborhoods: Their Place in Urban Life*. Beverly Hills, CA: SAGE Publications, 1984.

Hartigan, John. *Racial Situations: Class Predicaments of Whiteness in Detroit*. Princeton: Princeton University Press, 1999.

Hartman, Chester, and Gregory D. Squires, eds. *The Integration Debate: Competing Futures for American Cities*. New York: Routledge, 2010.

Hartmann, Douglas, Joseph Gerteis, and Paul R. Croll. "An Empirical Assessment of Whiteness Theory: Hidden from How Many?" *Social Problems* 56 (2009): 403–24.

Hirschman, Charles, and Douglas S. Massey. "Places and People: The New American Mosaic." In *New Faces in New Places*, edited by Douglas S. Massey, 1–22. New York: Russell Sage Foundation, 2008.

hooks, bell. "Eating the Other: Desire and Resistance." In *The Consumer Society Reader*, edited by J. B. Schor and D. B. Holt, 343–59. New York: New Press, 2000.

Hordge-Freeman, Elizabeth, Sarah Mayorga, and Eduardo Bonilla-Silva. "Exposing Whiteness Because We Are Free: Emancipation Methodological Practice in Identifying and Challenging Racial Practices in Sociology Departments." In *Rethinking Race and Ethnicity in Research Methods*, edited by John H. Stanfield II, 123–40. Walnut Creek, CA: Left Coast Press, 2011.

Horton, John. *The Politics of Diversity: Immigration, Resistance, and Change in Monterey Park, California*. Philadelphia: Temple University Press, 1995.

Hummon, David Mark. *Commonplaces: Community Ideology and Identity in American Culture*. Albany: State University of New York Press, 1990.

Hurtado, Aida, and Abigail J. Stewart. "Through the Looking Glass: Implications of Studying Whiteness for Feminist Methods." In *Off White: Readings on Race, Power, and Society*, edited by M. Fine, L. Weis, L. C. Powell, and L. M. Wong, 297–311. New York: Routledge, 1997.

Itzigsohn, Jose, and Carlos Dore-Cabral. "Competing Identities? Race, Ethnicity, and Panethnicity among Dominicans in the United States." *Sociological Forum* 15 (2000): 225–47.

Jackman, Mary R. *The Velvet Glove: Paternalism and Conflict in Gender, Class, and Race Relations*. Berkeley: University of California Press, 1994.

Johnson, Charles S. *Patterns of Negro Segregation*. New York: Harper, 1943.

Jones-Correa, Michael. "Commonalities, Competition, and Linked Fate." In *Just Neighbors? Research on African American and Latino Relations in the United States*, edited by Edward Telles, Mark Sawyer, and Gaspar Rivera-Salgado, 63–95. New York: Russell Sage Foundation, 2011.

Joseph, Mark L. "Reinventing Older Communities through Mixed Income Development: What Are We Learning from Chicago's Public Housing Transformation?" In *Neighborhood and Life Chances: How Place Matters in Modern America*, edited by H. B. Newburger, E. L. Birch, and S. M. Wachter, 122–39. Philadelphia: University of Pennsylvania Press, 2011.

Joseph, Mark, and Robert Chaskin. "Living in a Mixed-Income Development: Resident Perceptions of the Benefits and Disadvantages of Two Developments in Chicago." *Urban Studies* 47 (2010): 2347–66.

Kaufmann, Karen M. "Cracks in the Rainbow: Group Commonality as a Basis for Latino and African American Coalitions." *Political Research Quarterly* 56 (2003): 199–210.

Kim, Claire Jean. "The Racial Triangulation of Asian Americans." *Politics and Society* 27 (1999): 105–38.

Krysan, Maria. "Community Undesirability in Black and White: Examining Racial Residential Preferences through Community Perceptions." *Social Problems* 49 (2002): 521–43.

Lamont, Michèle. "A Life of Sad, but Justified, Choices: Interviewing across (Too) Many Divides." In *Researching Race and Racism*, edited by Martin Bulmer and John Solomos, 162–71. New York: Routledge, 2004.

Latino Outreach. "Latino Community Outreach and Engagement." Durham: Duke University Office of Durham and Regional Affairs, https://community.duke .edu/Duke-Durham%20Relations/latino_outreach/index.php. Accessed August 5, 2013.

Leip, David. *David Leip's Atlas of U.S. Presidential Elections* (2012), http://uselectionatlas .org/. Accessed August 5, 2013.

Lewis, Amanda E. "What Group? Studying Whites and Whiteness in the Era of Color-Blindness." *Sociological Theory* 22 (2004): 623–46.

Ley, David. "Artists, Aestheticisation, and the Field of Gentrification." *Urban Studies* 40 (1996): 2527–44.

———. *The New Middle Class and the Remaking of the Central City*. New York: Oxford University Press, 1996.

Lipsitz, George. *The Possessive Investment in Whiteness: How White People Profit from Identity Politics*. Philadelphia: Temple University Press, 1998.

Lofland, John, David Snow, Leon Anderson, and Lyn Lofland. *Analyzing Social Settings: A Guide to Qualitative Observation and Analysis*. Belmont, CA: Wadsworth/Thomson Learning, 2006.

Maly, Michael T. *Beyond Segregation: Multiracial and Multiethnic Neighborhoods in the United States*. Philadelphia: Temple University Press, 2005.

Massey, Douglas S., and Nancy Denton. *American Apartheid: Segregation and the Making of the Underclass*. Cambridge, MA: Harvard University Press, 1993.

McClain, P. D., Niambi M. Carter, Victoria M. DeFrancesco Soto, Monique L. Lyle, Jeffrey D. Grynaviski, Shayla C. Nunnally, Thomas J. Scotto, J. Alan Kendrick, Gerard F. Lackey, and Kendra Davenport Cotton. "Racial Distancing in a Southern City: Latino Immigrants' Views of Black Americans." *Journal of Politics* 68 (2006): 571–84.

McDermott, Monica, and Frank L. Samson. "White Racial and Ethnic Identity in the United States." *Annual Review of Sociology* 31 (2005): 245–61.

Merry, Sally Engle. *Urban Danger: Life in a Neighborhood of Strangers*. Philadelphia: Temple University Press, 1981.

Milian, Claudia. *Latining America: Black-Brown Passages and the Coloring of Latino/a Studies*. Athens: University of Georgia Press, 2013.

Mills, Charles W. *The Racial Contract*. Ithaca: Cornell University Press, 1997.

Nager, Norma. "Continuities of Urban Policy on the Poor: From Urban Renewal to Reinvestment." In *Back to the City: Issues in Neighborhood Renovation*, edited by S. B. Laska and D. Spain, 239–51. New York: Pergamon Press, 1980.

NYT/CBS News. "Poll: April 28–May 2, 2010." The New York Times/CBS News, http:// s3.amazonaws.com/nytdocs/docs/330/330.pdf. Accessed August 5, 2013.

Oliver, Melvin I., and Thomas M Shapiro. *Black Wealth/White Wealth: New Perspectives on Racial Inequality*. New York: Routledge, 1995.

Omi, Michael, and Howard Winant. *Racial Formation in the United States: From the 1960s to the 1990s*. New York: Routledge, 1994.

Park, Robert Ezra. "The Concept of Social Distance as Applied to the Study of Racial Attitudes and Racial Relations." *Journal of Applied Sociology* 8 (1924): 339–44.

———. *Race and Culture*. Glencoe, IL: Free Press, 1950.

Parrado, Emilio, and Chenoa Flippen. "Migration and Gender among Mexican Women." *American Sociological Review* 70 (2005): 606–32.

Parrado, Emilio A., Chris McQuiston, and Chenoa A. Flippen. "Participatory Survey Research: Integrating Community Collaboration and Quantitative Methods for the Study of Gender and HIV Risks among Hispanic Migrants." *Sociological Methods Research* 34 (2005): 204–39.

Pascoe, C. J. *Dude, You're a Fag: Masculinity and Sexuality in High School*. Berkeley: University of California Press, 2011.

Pitts, Leonard, Jr. "Four Decades Later, Men Recall King's Campaign," http://www.miamiherald.com/multimedia/news/iamaman/pitts.html. Accessed August 22, 2013.

Portes, Alejandro, and Ruben Rumbaut. *Immigrant America: A Portrait*. Berkeley: University of California Press, 2006.

Rabrenovic, Gordana. *Community Builders: A Tale of Neighborhood Mobilization in Two Cities*. Philadelphia: Temple University Press, 1996.

Rodriguez, Clara. *Changing Race: Latinos, the Census, and the History of Ethnicity in the United States*. New York: New York University Press, 2000.

Roediger, David R. *The Wages of Whiteness: Race and the Making of the American Working Class*. New York: Verso, 2007.

Rosenbaum, Dennis P. "Community Crime Prevention: A Review and Synthesis of the Literature." *Justice Quarterly* 5 (1988): 323–95.

Rosenbaum, Emily, and Samantha Friedman. *The Housing Divide: How Generations of Immigrants Fare in New York's Housing Market*. New York: New York University Press, 2007.

Royster, Deirdre. *Race and the Invisible Hand: How White Networks Exclude Black Men from Blue-Collar Jobs*. Berkeley: University of California Press, 2003.

Rude, Jesse Dennison. "Interracial Friendships in Context: Their Formation, Development, and Impact." Ph.D. diss., University of California-Davis, 2009.

Rude, Jesse, and Daniel Herda. "Best Friends Forever? Race and the Stability of Adolescent Friendships." *Social Forces* 89 (2010): 585–607.

Russell-Brown, Katheryn. *The Color of Crime: Racial Hoaxes, White Fear, Black Protectionism, Police Harassment, and Other Macroaggressions*. New York: New York University Press. 2008.

Saito, Leland T. *The Politics of Exclusion: The Failure of Race-Neutral Policies in Urban America*. Stanford: Stanford University Press, 2009.

Schrock, Douglas, and Michael Schwalbe. "Men, Masculinity, and Manhood Acts." *Annual Review of Sociology* 35 (2009): 277–95.

Sears, David O., Mingying Fu, P. J. Henry, and Kerra Bui. "The Origins and Persistence of Ethnic Identity among the 'New Immigrant' Groups." *Social Psychology Quarterly* 66 (2003): 419–37.

Shapiro, Thomas M. *The Hidden Cost of Being African American: How Wealth Perpetuates Inequality.* New York: Oxford University Press, 2004.

Sharman, Russell Leigh. *The Tenants of East Harlem.* Berkeley: University of California Press, 2006.

Shaw, Wendy S. *Cities of Whiteness.* Malden, MA: Blackwell Publishing, 2007.

———. "Heritage and Gentrification: Remembering 'The Good Old Days' in Post-colonial Sydney." In *Gentrification in a Global Context*, edited by R. Atkinson and G. Bridge, 57–71. New York: Routledge, 2005.

Small, Mario L. "'How Many Cases Do I Need?': On Science and the Logic of Case Selection in Field-Based Research." *Ethnography* 10 (2009): 5–38.

Smith, Janet L. "Integration: Solving the Wrong Problem." In *The Integration Debate: Competing Futures for American Cities*, edited by C. Hartman and G. D. Squires, 229–46. New York: Routledge, 2010.

Smith, Tom W. "Measuring Inter-Racial Friendships." *Social Science Research* 31 (2002): 576–93.

Smith, Tom W., Peter Marsden, Michael Hout, and Jibum Kim. *General Social Surveys, 1972–2010.* Chicago: National Opinion Research Center and Storrs, CT: The Roper Center for Public Opinion Research, University of Connecticut, 2011.

Snow, David A., Robert D. Benford, and Leon Anderson. "Fieldwork Roles and Informational Yield: A Comparison of Alternative Settings and Roles." *Urban Life* 14 (1986): 377–408.

Southern Redlining Coalition. "Sustainable Archives and Leveraging Technologies," University of North Carolina, salt.unc.edu. Accessed June 3, 2013.

Sprague, Joey. *Feminist Methodologies for Critical Researchers.* New York: Altamira Press, 2005.

Stacey, Judith. "Can There Be a Feminist Ethnography?" *Women's Studies International Forum* 11 (1998): 21–27.

Steinberg, Stephen. "The Myth of Concentrated Poverty." In *The Integration Debate: Competing Futures for American Cities*, edited by C. Hartman and G. D. Squires, 213–27. New York: Routledge, 2010.

Sullivan, Shannon. *Revealing Whiteness: The Unconscious Habits of Racial Privilege.* Bloomington: Indiana University Press, 2006.

Swaroop, Sapna, and Maria Krysan. "The Determinants of Neighborhood Satisfaction: Racial Proxy Revisited." *Demography* 48 (2011): 1203–29.

Twine, France Winddance, and Charles Gallagher. "The Future of Whiteness: A Map of the 'Third Wave.'" *Ethnic and Racial Studies* 31 (2008): 4–24.

Wade, Peter. *Race and Ethnicity in Latin America.* London: Pluto Press, 1997.

Warren, Carol A. B., and Jennifer Kay Hackney. *Gender Issues in Ethnography.* London: SAGE Publications, 2000.

Weitzer, Ronald. "Racialized Policing: Residents' Perceptions in Three Neighborhoods." *Law & Society Review* 34 (2000): 129–55.

Weitzer, Ronald, and Steven A. Tuch. "Racially Biased Policing: Determinants of Citizen Perceptions." *Social Forces* 83 (2005): 1009–30.

Wellman, David T. *Portraits of White Racism.* Cambridge: Cambridge University Press, 1977.

Williams, Terry, Eloise Dunlap, Bruce D. Johnson, and Ansley Hamid. "Safety in Dangerous Places." *Journal of Contemporary Ethnography* 21 (1992): 343–74.

Wilson, William Julius, and Richard P. Taub. *There Goes the Neighborhood: Racial, Ethnic, and Class Tensions in Four Chicago Neighborhoods and Their Meaning for America.* New York: Knopf, 2006.

Winders, Jamie. "Nashville's New 'Sonido': Latino Migration and the Changing Politics of Race." In *New Faces in New Places*, edited by Douglas S. Massey, 249–73. New York: Russell Sage Foundation, 2008.

———. "Placing Latino Migration and Migrant Experiences in the U.S. South: The Complexities of Regional and Local Trends." In *Global Connections and Local Receptions: New Latino Immigration to the Southeastern U.S.*, edited by Jon Shefner and Fran Ansley, 223–44. Knoxville: University of Tennessee Press, 2009.

Zinn, Howard. *A People's History of the United States: 1492-Present.* New York: Perennial Classics, 2003.

Zukin, Sharon. "Gentrification: Culture and Capital in the Urban Core." *Annual Review of Sociology* 13 (1987): 129–47.

Index

Adams, Rebecca, 110–11
Affordability, 24–27, 49, 56, 100
Allan, Graham, 110–11, 178 (n. 18)
Anderson, Jean Bradley, 8
Anderson, Leon, 160, 180 (n. 3)
Attitudes: political and racial, 10–11, 42, 48, 50, 97–100, 121, 149

Black, Dan, 49
Black codes, 177 (n. 1)
Bonilla-Silva, Eduardo, 152
Bourdieu, Pierre, 17–18, 22–23, 54
Butler, Tim, 79

Cary, N.C., 27, 43–45
Chapel Hill, N.C., 28, 95–96
Charles, Camille Zubrinsky, 97, 123
Commodification, 45–48, 51, 151.
    See also Diversity
Creekridge Park, 152, 173 (n. 1); businesses in, 15–17, 124–26, 141–42; demographics of, 9–11, 16–17, 34, 40; descriptors of, 27–36, 102–4, 110; history of, 11–15; location of, 15–17, 152
Creekridge Park Elementary, 14–16, 50
Creekridge Park Neighborhood Association (CPNA), 1–4, 20, 34, 48–49, 60–63, 66–69, 71–73, 85–86, 142–46, 177 (n. 2); advertisements of, 3, 67–68, 70; events of, 1–4, 16, 69–70, 82, 87–88, 142–43; listserv of, 67, 76, 80, 83, 85, 89, 143, 155; meetings of, 16, 42, 63, 69, 82–83, 85, 142, 144, 153, 178 (n. 15); neighborhood development man-

dates of, 32, 51, 58, 75–76; newsletter of, 67–69, 142–43, 163; political influence of, 32, 57–58, 60, 76, 92, 144, 149; representation of neighborhood by, 4, 48–49, 60–63, 142–43

Denton, Nancy, 176 (n. 16)
Diversity, 23–24, 34–56, 148, 153–54; as code word, 94, 126–27; history of 23, 40; as ideology, 23–24, 39–40, 43–49, 51, 55–58, 149–53, 176 (n. 4); limitations of, 126–27; and safe spaces, 41, 95–97; and sexual orientation, 23, 35–36, 40–41, 95; synonyms of 34–35, 40
Du Bois, W. E. B., 7–8
Durham, N.C.: demographics of, 6–9; history of, 7–9, 87–88; and Latino/a migration, 8–9, 69–70, 104–5, 118, 134; politics of, 10, 42, 58; resident descriptions of, 34–35, 43, 92, 95–100, 104

Equity, 6, 23–24, 47–48, 69, 148, 151–54, 173 (n. 10)
El Centro Hispano, 9
Embrick, David G., 40, 176 (n. 4)

Feagin, Joe, 128
Fischer, Eric, 97, 179 (n. 2)

Gates, Gary, 49
Gayborhood, 99–100
Gentrification, 11, 53, 79, 148, 151
Giddens, Anthony, 17, 100

Glenn, Evelyn Nakano, 20, 66
Good intentions, limits of, 45, 50–52, 71–74, 149, 150, 152–53
"Greening" efforts, 60, 71–76, 144
Groveland Estates, 13–14, 78, 98, 121

Hall, Stuart, 23, 39
Habitus: definition of, 17, 22–24, 54; of white urban middle class, 17–19, 23–24, 36–56, 59–60, 85–86, 146–47, 149, 151, 176 (n. 3)
Herda, Daniel, 178 (n. 16)
Historic preservation, 13–14, 32–33, 176 (n. 15)
Hooks, bell, 51
HOPE VI, 86, 150, 178 (n. 24)
Housing stock, 11–15, 31–33, 54
Housing tenure, 11–15, 63–66, 88–89; attitudes toward renters 64–65; dominance of homeowners, 1–4, 66–69, 80–83, 85, 153; exclusion of renters, 92, 144–45, 150, 153
Hummon, David, 29

Ideology, 23–24, 55; color-blind racism, 23, 152; contradictions of, 34, 39, 132, 164. See also Diversity
Imani, Nikitah, 128
Integration, statistical, 4–7, 36–40, 92, 148, 150–51, 153
Interracial interactions. See Social interactions

Jackman, Mary, 86
Jones-Correa, Michael, 105

Landlords, 25, 84, 88
Latino/as: assimilation of, 109–10, 135–36; attitudes amongst, 11, 129–31, 132–34; attitudes toward, 11, 120–21, 129–31, 150, 179 (n. 27); incorporation of, 69–71, 134, 151; in the new South 8–9, 19, 97–99; and language barrier, 120, 134, 138, 145; meaning of, 173 (n. 4); migration of, 8–9, 97, 151, 174 (n. 19); networks of, 105, 134; political involvement of, 145–46; vulnerabilities of (documentation), 110, 119–20, 134, 140–41, 158, 174 (n. 24)
Lofland, John, 160, 180 (n. 3)
Lofland, Lyn, 160, 180 (n. 3)

Massey, Douglas, 176 (n. 16)
Merry, Sally Engle, 81
Methodology: mixed methods, 6–7, 151, 161–64; and positionality, 19–20, 110, 118–19, 155–61, 175 (n. 51), 175 (n. 54)
Mills, Charles, 18
Mobility, social: downward, 92; upward, 101–2, 135–36, 150
Moving to Opportunity, 86, 148, 150, 178 (n. 24)
Multiethnic, definition of, 6

Neighborhood Improvement Services, 41, 43–44, 60, 85, 89, 137–38
Neighborhood watch, 143–45

Omi, Michael, 94

Park, Robert, 174 (n. 11)
Paternalism, 73, 86–89, 92, 138–39, 151
Pets, role of in social interactions, 73–74, 77–78, 80, 85–86, 116, 125
Pine Grove Apartments, 14–16, 37–38, 48, 67–69, 71–73, 89–92, 140, 163
Police involvement, 117–18, 126; CPNA and 48, 60, 82, 149, 180 (n. 28); lack of, 116–17, 144, 147; and opportunity reduction, 83, 110; and reporting neighbors, 60, 83–85, 87, 89, 110–11, 118–20

Made in the USA
San Bernardino, CA
19 January 2017